ANNA
DUCHESS OF CLEVES

ANNA
DUCHESS OF CLEVES

THE KING'S 'BELOVED SISTER'

Heather R. Darsie

AMBERLEY

Half-title page: 'Wilhelm V of Cleves'. Engraving after Cornelis Anthonisz. (Courtesy of the Rijksmuseum)

Title page: 'Anna of Cleves'. Engraving by Wenceslaus Hollar after Hans Holbein the Younger. 1646. (Courtesy of the Rijksmuseum)

First published 2019

Amberley Publishing
The Hill, Stroud
Gloucestershire, GL5 4EP

www.amberley-books.com

ISBN 978 1 4456 7710 1 (hardback)
ISBN 978 1 4456 7711 8 (ebook)

British Library Cataloguing in Publication Data. A catalogue record for this book is available from the British Library.

Typesetting and Origination by Amberley Publishing.
Printed in the UK.

CONTENTS

FAMILY TREES

Anna's relation to Edward I of England

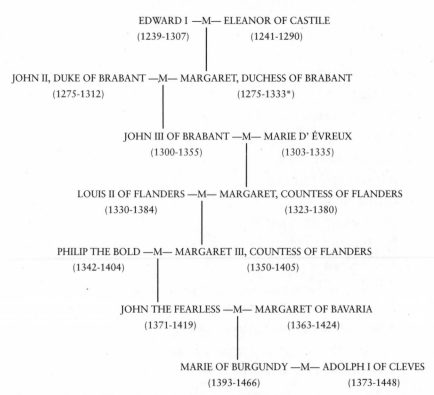

EDWARD I —M— ELEANOR OF CASTILE
(1239-1307)   (1241-1290)

JOHN II, DUKE OF BRABANT —M— MARGARET, DUCHESS OF BRABANT
(1275-1312)   (1275-1333*)

JOHN III OF BRABANT —M— MARIE D' ÉVREUX
(1300-1355)   (1303-1335)

LOUIS II OF FLANDERS —M— MARGARET, COUNTESS OF FLANDERS
(1330-1384)   (1323-1380)

PHILIP THE BOLD —M— MARGARET III, COUNTESS OF FLANDERS
(1342-1404)   (1350-1405)

JOHN THE FEARLESS —M— MARGARET OF BAVARIA
(1371-1419)   (1363-1424)

MARIE OF BURGUNDY —M— ADOLPH I OF CLEVES
(1393-1466)   (1373-1448)

Please see other chart illustrating Anna's relation to Adolph I of Cleves

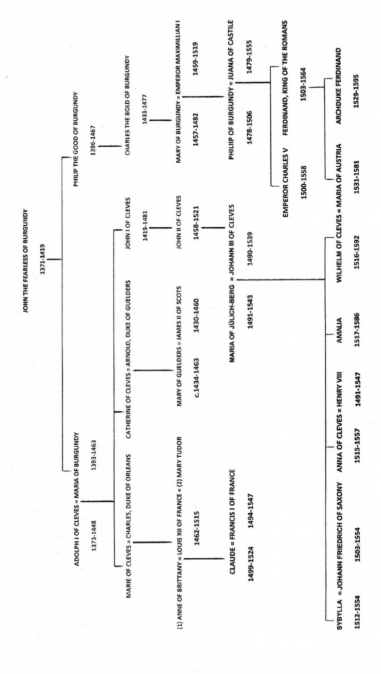

The Relationship Between the House of Cleves and the House of Burgundy

INTRODUCTION

Back in 2012, my interest in Henry VIII and his six wives was awakened, so I began reading any book I could get my hands on about these women. Whenever I read anything about Anna of Cleves, I always felt that her story was somehow incomplete. In summer 2015, I decided to start researching her life and thought I should write a biography about her if I found anything interesting. Needless to say, I think I did.

While completing my BA in German Languages and Literature, I took several courses on German history. These courses familiarised me with the Holy Roman Empire during the reign of Charles V, when Anna was alive. I thought more about how in every English-language book, she was called 'Anne of Cleves'. I suspected her given name was Anna, and began plotting the course which my research would take into German sources.

Having developed research skills while pursuing my Juris Doctorate, I knew I had to go straight to the original sources. I wrote a letter to the Mayor of Cleves in August 2015. He very kindly forwarded my letter to the Swan Castle in Cleves, who sent me a great deal of information and referred me to the proper archives. By Jove, this woman was indeed named Anna, and there was a lot more to her life than what has been believed for hundreds of years.

Anna's life and experiences from the German perspective are very different in some ways than what has been described in

English-language books. That is not to say that any English biographies about Anna are wrong, but rather that looking at the German sources helps to make more sense of Anna's life and short marriage. The German sources show what a valuable bride Anna was to any suitor, and why she stayed on in England after moving there in December 1539.

It is my sincere hope that this biography augments the generally accepted view of Anna, her family, and the political entanglements in which she was enmeshed. I also hope it brings more knowledge about German history to English speakers.

Throughout, I refer to Germany, Germans, and the German language. My use of 'Germany' refers to German-speaking Central Europe under the Holy Roman Empire. By 'Germans', I mean those living in the area that constitutes present-day Germany. I use the term 'German language' to describe the various Germanic dialects that were spoken in that area.

To frame Anna's life as a German woman, I chose to use the German, non-Anglicised, non-Gallicised names for Anna and her immediate family. I have used the umlaut in German place names as a gentle reminder of the Germanic perspective of the book.

ACKNOWLEDGEMENTS

I am fortunate enough to have an army of people who supported me during this project. Sadly, I know I will not be able to name them all. First and foremost, I thank my parents and brother, Burns III, Linda, and Burns IV, for their patience and love. My utmost gratitude to Melanie V. Taylor and Sara Bryson, who have shown me the way and never hesitated to play devil's advocate. I thank B. J. Maley, my dear friend and travelling companion, without whom I would not have been able to locate several details related to my research into Anna's life. I am grateful for the continuing interest in my life shown by Prof. B. Shelton, Prof. L. Schmall, and Prof. G. Anderson. Beth Wolden and Eli Vasilopoulos were excellent listeners every step of the way, and always willing to share my excitement. Thank you to Kris Piereth, who provided his unwavering support throughout the writing process, and encouraged me when I confronted obstacles. Finally, if they should one day read this introduction, I want to remind Sydney and Ellie to learn at least one foreign language, to ask, to try, and to always seek more knowledge.

Dieses Buch konnte ich nur mit Hilfe von vielen deutschen Menschen und Sprachlehrer schreiben. Ich muss Frau G. Vaughan, Frau Doktorin Djukic-Cocks, Frau Doktorin K. Barbe und Herr Doktor Brain danken, die mir die Deutsche Sprache und

Geschichte lehrten. Auch muss ich unter anderem das Staatsarchiv Nordrhein-Westfalen, Stadtarchiv Kleve, Stadtarchiv Solingen, Schloss Burg, Schloss Schwanenburg, Schloss Burgau, Stadt Kleve, Stadt Düsseldorf, und dem Stadtarchiv Duisburg danken, für ihre Geduld, Anleitung, und Hilfe. Ich wäre nachlässig, wenn ich der Familie Klimmek aus Duisburg nicht danken würde, im besonderen Tanja Klimmek. Ihre Freundlichkeit, Hilfsbereitschaft, und Freundschaft sind unbezahlbar.

I

ANNA, BORN DUCHESS
OF CLEVES

The year is 1515. The lands belonging to Jülich-Cleves-Berg ranged from the City of Cleves along the Rhine River to the west, then down to the Wupper Valley by Solingen to the southeast. The imposing Schwanenburg,[1] or Swan Castle, in Cleves, was perched upon a cliff overlooking the city and a tributary of the Rhine. Cleves likely derived its name from the archaic German word for cliff, or from the German word for clover. To this day, the city arms of Cleves are a red field with a small silver shield in the middle and three golden clovers. Anna's paternal grandfather, John II, kept his ducal seat in Cleves at Swan Castle.

From the Swan Tower of the castle, Anna's grandfather could scan a substantial amount of his domain. At the base of the Swan Tower from the ducal apartments, John II could have viewed the tributary and the comings and goings at two water gates at the base

---

[1] Swan Castle and the City of Cleves were utterly destroyed in the Second World War. The castle was rebuilt in parts, including the Swan Tower, but the ducal apartments do not survive. Were Anna to walk through Cleves today, she would mostly recognise the layout of the city streets and the rebuilt Swan Tower, but not much else. The destruction of the Swan Castle may be one reason why there are no extant – or discovered – portraits of Anna's sister Amalia or her parents, or any of Anna's siblings in their youth. If such portraits existed and were displayed at the Swan Castle, then they were destroyed with the building in the war.

of the cliff. He could also see the ancient city of Xanten, boasting Roman ruins and its mythological hero, Siegfried the Dragon Slayer.

Cleves had its own hero: the Swan Knight. The Swan Knight came to save the Duchess-Princess Beatrix, who was the sole heir of the Cleves territories. He arrived in Cleves sailing down the Rhine in his boat pulled by a white swan. The swan had a collar and chain of gold or silver about its neck, depending upon which version of the tale is told. The Swan Knight was willing to engage in combat to defend Beatrix, if necessary. Upon his shield he bore the escarbuncle of Cleves. Beatrix and the Swan Knight fell in love and had two sons. The only condition on their relationship was that Beatrix never asked after the Swan Knight's origin. One day, Beatrix asked her sons to inquire. With that, the Swan Knight completely disappeared. Broken-hearted, Beatrix died a few months later. The tower and castle are named for the knight.

The real Beatrix, who lived during the 8th century, was the daughter of a woman also named Beatrix and her husband, the last Steward of Cleves and Nijmegen. After her father died, Beatrix ruled over the areas of Cleves and Nijmegen. At first, she lived at a castle in Nijmegen in modern-day Netherlands. Later on, Beatrix rebuilt the ancient castle in Cleves. She married a man named Elias Gral, upon whom the Swan Knight myth is based. They had three sons. It is from Elias that Cleves received the gold escarbuncle upon a red field. And thus, the County of Cleves was created. It later became Cleves-Teisterbant.

The Dukedom of Cleves developed into an amalgamation of several minor territories, to include Jülich, Berg, Mark, and Ravensberg, and Guelders at times, with Cleves as its core. Cleves evolved through time by various marriages. At Anna's birth, Cleves was a large, powerful, wealthy entity occupying a strategically important location. Consequently, it was caught up in the maelstrom of European dynastic struggles among Spain, the Hapsburg Empire, and the emerging superpowers France and England.

Cleves-Mark is Created; The Powerful Women of Jülich-Berg

Anna's name was Anna von der Mark, as Henry VIII was Henry Tudor. The Von der Mark family of the territory of Mark, also known by the

Gallicised name of La Marck, has a long history. The Von der Marks claimed their family origin from the Orsini of Rome. Two brothers, members of the Roman nobility, followed the Holy Roman Emperor Otto III to Germany around the year 1000. One brother founded the House of Berg, and the other the House of Altena. Altena lies to the east of Düsseldorf. The *Grafen*, or Counts, of Altena-Mark are first mentioned in the 12th century. The first person named as Count of Mark was Adolf I, who died in the mid-13th century. He formally changed the family name from Altena to Mark.

Adolf I of Altena-Mark is considered the founder of the Von der Mark dynasty. Adolf moved the ruling seat from Altena Castle to Hamm in the County of Mark. The legend goes that Adolf founded the city of Hamm on Ash Wednesday of 1226. He reunited the Berg-Altena territories after 1226. The County of Altena was absorbed by Mark in 1262 after the death of the last Count of Altena.

A joined Cleves-Mark first emerged in the 14th century with Otto the Peaceful of Cleves. His first wife was the heiress of Mark. For the next fifty years or so, a series of battles, deaths, and childless marriages led to fluctuations of the Cleves-Mark territories. The territories were firmly united under Count Adolf III von der Mark in the late 14th century. He was the 28th Count of Cleves, and recognised as Adolf I of Cleves. Adolf III von der Mark's descendants held the territory of Cleves-Mark from 1368 until the death of Anna's nephew in 1609.

Women were important to the history of Anna's family, especially on her mother Maria of Jülich-Berg's side. It was common for women to act as regents in Jülich-Berg. In the early 14th century, Margarethe von Hochstaden held the regency for her son Adolf V of Berg after her husband died in 1259. Margarethe was regent for three years, ruling from *Schloss Burg*, or Burg Castle. She retired to Hückeswagen Castle for her widowhood. Margarethe lived to be over 100 years old. She was born before 1214 and did not die until January of 1314. Her daughter Irmgard married a Count of Mark.

In the late 14th century, Margarethe von Ravensberg-Berg was co-regent with her son, William II. Margarethe von Ravensberg-Berg married a Count of Jülich in 1338. Margarethe's husband Gerhard von Jülich established a branch of the combined territories of Jülich-Berg through his marriage to Margarethe. Marriage also enabled Anna's father Johann III of Cleves-Mark to lay claim to Jülich-Berg through his union with Anna's mother, Maria. Gerhard died in 1360 when his and Margarethe's only son was about twelve years old. Margarethe was co-regent of Jülich-Berg-Ravensberg with William II until he reached majority. She died in 1389, around the age of sixty-nine.

Next came Sophia of Saxony-Lauenburg in the late 15th century, who ruled for her husband Gerhard VIII of Jülich-Berg. Gerhard was the great-grandson of Margarethe von Ravensberg-Berg. Gerhard suffered from mental illness and had fallen into an irretrievable decline by 1456, roughly twelve years into their marriage. Sophia acted as regent for their son William VIII of Jülich-Berg – Anna's maternal grandfather – until Sophia was overthrown in 1470 by a robber-baron who held Tomburg Castle. William VIII and his brother defeated the baron and destroyed the castle in 1473.

Though she was very important to the history of Jülich-Berg, there are not many extant details about Anna's mother Maria. Maria was an only child who spent a considerable amount of her youth moving between the ducal palace in Düsseldorf and *Schloss Burg*, Burg Castle, in Solingen, as well as Burgau Castle in Düren. Burg Castle held special meaning for Anna's family. It was here, in this fortress dating back to at least the 12th century, that Anna's parents were betrothed. Anna was likely born in Düsseldorf, as well as her elder sister Sybylla. Though the ducal palace was badly damaged by a fire a few years before, the main rooms in which the ducal family lived remained largely intact. The main staircase was not repaired until around 1522. If Anna was indeed born in Düsseldorf, then she was likely baptized at the St Lambertus Basilica, which still stands. Within the basilica is a 15th-century baptismal font which could have been used for Anna's baptism. Unfortunately, records of Anna's birth and early life do not exist in any detail. It is generally accepted that Anna was born in or around Düsseldorf, which was part of the Jülich-Berg lands.

From Henry VIII's ambassadors it is known that Maria of Jülich-Berg shared a close relationship with Anna. From reviewing the *Landtagsakten*, or parliamentary acts, of Jülich-Berg around 1515 to 1520, it is apparent that Maria had a place at the meetings of parliament, and may have also been present at imperial diets. Maria may have been present at parliaments before and after this period, too;

the record of parliamentary acts over Maria's lifetime are voluminous. In the Landtagsakten, Maria is also referred to as the Regent of Jülich-Berg, and an early 20th-century mural of her in Burg Castle shows her holding a sceptre and standing to the right of Johann III, in the position typically reserved for a male ruler. Furthermore, Maria's input was considered at the aforementioned diets. Though women could not inherit territories, they could rule them.

Anna's maternal grandmother, Sybille of Brandenburg, was appointed governess of Jülich-Berg after the death of her husband and Anna's maternal grandfather William III of Jülich-Berg in 1511. Maria became Regent of Jülich-Berg and Johann of Cleves became Duke of Jülich-Berg thereafter, but Sybille of Brandenburg was appointed governess of Jülich-Berg and remained in that capacity until her death in 1524. Maria became the Regent of Jülich-Berg and Johann became Duke of Jülich-Berg thereafter, but Sybille of Brandenburg was appointed governess of Jülich-Berg and remained in that capacity until her death. Presumably, this allowed Anna's father to continue assisting Anna's paternal grandfather with the administration of the Cleves-Mark territories. Maria remained Regent of Jülich-Berg until 1521, when the duchies finally became the United Duchies of Jülich-Cleves-Berg. The parliaments of Jülich-Berg and Cleves-Mark functioned mostly independently of each other during this time.

Women in the Von der Mark family were strong-willed, as exemplified by Anna's paternal aunt, Anna. In the 16th century, Anna's father Johann III and grandfather John II, both raised at a Burgundian-influenced court, had an interesting relationship with Anna's headstrong aunt. This is the woman after whom Anna of Cleves was named, and was her only legitimate paternal aunt. At some point in or before 1517, Aunt Anna decided to marry the widowed Count Philip III of Waldeck, a petty German lord. This unpopular romance was frowned upon by John II. Given that this was the early 16th century and Aunt Anna was a noblewoman, she was not free to marry. She needed the approval not just of her brother Johann III and father John II, but also the Holy Roman Emperor Maximilian I. Aunt Anna was taken into custody by her family with threat of imprisonment in an attempt to thwart her plans to marry Philip. This did not settle the matter for Holy Roman Emperor Maximilian I or his successor, the young Charles V.

In 1519, it was determined that Aunt Anna must give up her inheritance rights and the rights of her children in exchange for a settlement of 10,000 guilders.[2] She went on to have four children with Philip, whom she had indeed married. She outlived him by about twenty-eight years, living from approximately 1495 until 1567. It is not known what impression this situation made on little Anna, the future Queen Consort of England. Anna was about four years old when her aunt settled things with her father.

Anna's paternal grandfather, John II, was known as 'John the Childmaker'. John II fought at the Battle of Nancy in 1477. From that adventure, John II gained a reputation as being both brave and peace-loving. He chose to distract himself from the stresses of battle and court life with women. He had no fewer than sixty-three illegitimate children, whom he maintained in various houses and castles in his Cleves-Mark territories. He supported the continued use of the Burgundian-style court.

Anna Is Born

> This year [of 1515], on [28 June,] the day before St. Peter and Paul, a second daughter was born to the eldest son of Duke John II of Cleves, Duke Johann III from Jülich and Berg. The godfathers were John von Waldeck, the abbess of Neuss, Petrissa von Oberstein, and Anna of Cleves, a sister of the Duke [Johann III]. The child was baptized in the name of Anna.

Anna von der Mark, Born Duchess of Jülich-Cleves-Berg, was the second child and second daughter of Johann III of Jülich-Cleves-Berg and his wife Maria of Jülich-Berg. As a Born Duchess and not a Duchess Consort, Anna held a place in the succession, as her mother Maria did for the Duchies of Jülich-Berg. Anna spent her early years at Burg Castle. This area was part of the Duchy of Berg, and its capital

---

2   10,000 carolus guilders in 1519 is equivalent to approximately €788,000, £697,000, or $920,000 today.

was Düsseldorf. Anna's older sister Sybylla was born 17 January 1512. Anna's brother Wilhelm followed on 28 July 1516. Finally, her younger sister Amalia was born on 17 October 1517.

There is debate as to Anna of Cleves' true date of birth. As far back as 1844 in English sources, Anna's date of birth has been given as 21 or 22 September in either 1515 or 1516. Agnes Strickland gave Anna's date of birth as 22 September 1516 in Volume II of her *Lives of the Queens of England*, published in the mid-1800s, citing Part I of *Royal Genealogies* by James Anderson, D. D., and published in 1732. Anderson simply gives Anna's date of birth as being in 1516, with no citation. Anderson also incorrectly states that Sybylla was born in 1510, when she was born in 1512. Wilhelm's exact date of birth is correctly stated, but Amalia is not listed at all. Thus, it seems that there is no reliable primary source cited by either Anderson or Strickland to show Anna's true date of birth. Strickland also relies on Maur-François Dantine's *L'Art de Vérifier les Dates*, published in Paris in the early 18th century. It gives the correct year of birth for Sybylla, and gives Anna's birth as 22 September 1515 with no citation to any source. Neither Wilhelm's nor Amalia's dates of birth are given, but the correct years of Anna's, Wilhelm's, and Amalia's deaths are given, although Wilhelm died on 5 January 1592 and *L'Art* gives Wilhelm's date of death as 25 June

The archives in Germany do not possess any documentation about the birth of Anna. It is possible that documents showing it have been lost. When looking at whether Anna was born in June or September, the June date is more likely for several reasons. First, the one primary source that does exist, *Die Chronik des Johann Wassenberch*, or Chronicle of Johann Wassenberch, is recognised as a contemporary source for events in the Lower Rhine area between 1492 and 1517, when Wassenberch suddenly stops writing. It is thought that Wassenberch died of plague in October 1517, as there was an outbreak around this time. A review of other dates pertinent to Anna's family, such as the marriage of her parents, and births of her older sister Sybylla and brother Wilhelm, correctly correspond with other known dates in the Chronicle of Johann Wassenberch. Here are Wassenberch's entries for 21 September 1515 and 22 September 1515:

In the same year [of 1515] on St. Matthew's Day [21 September], a farm was rented to Arnt Endrick Averlanck and his wife Druythen. They were to transfer their slaughter of 1½ gold guldens annually to the Knights Hospitaller in Duisburg...

In the same year there were many acorns everywhere. Already on Mauritius' Day [22 September] they began to mark the pigs with brands. More than 3,000 pigs in the Duisburger received a brand. Many of them came back during the breeding season.

Such were the events of note for Anna's parents in September 1515.

Second, there is the timing of Anna's birth and her brother Wilhelm's birth. In the 16th century, a Catholic mother went through a sort of purification process after the birth of a child. The mother was not reintroduced to society until approximately a month after the birth. The mother could not lie with her husband during that period. If Anna was born in late September 1515, her mother would not have become pregnant until around November 1515. For Wilhelm to be born in late July 1516, Anna's mother had to conceive immediately in November 1515. It also means that Wilhelm was born at least a month or so premature. This is certainly all possible, though a late June 1515 date of birth for Anna means that her mother could start conceiving as early as September 1515, resulting in Wilhelm being a full-term birth. This seems a more probable timeline for the birth of Anna and subsequent birth of Wilhelm.

Another example of conception times for Johann and Maria would be would be the time between the birth of Wilhelm in July 1516 and Amalia in October 1517. This time frame allows for the birth of Wilhelm, and for their mother to be reintegrated afterwards. For Amalia to be a full-term baby, she had to be conceived in roughly late January to early February 1517. Using the example of Wilhelm and Amalia, plus what is known about Catholic rites after the birth of a child, it is plausible that Anna was born in June 1515 and not September.

Finally, there is at least one 19th-century German secondary source that gives an earlier birth month for Anna. Specifically, Part IV of the *Zeitschrift des Bergischen Geschichtsverein* published at Bonn in 1867 gives Anna's date of birth as 1 July 1515. When taking into consideration the primary source, births of Anna's siblings, Catholic tradition, and German secondary sources, there is ample support for Anna's true date of birth being earlier than September 1515, on 28 June 1515 at the earliest and 1 July 1515 at the latest.

Early History of Anna's Immediate Family and Jülich-Cleves-Berg

Before investigating the young Anna and her siblings, it is important to know something of the United Duchies of Jülich-Cleves-Berg and local events that shaped how Anna and her family viewed the world. Anna's father Johann was born on 10 November 1490. Anna's mother Maria was born at some point in 1491. By 1496, Anna's father Johann of Cleves-Mark was engaged to her mother Maria of Jülich-Berg. Their marriage would not take place for another fourteen years, until 1510. The engagement between Johann and Maria was part of the agreement unifying the territories of Jülich, Berg, Ravensberg, Mark, and Cleves.

When the wedding festivities came, Johann rode out from Cleves southeasterly toward Düsseldorf to meet his bride on 12 March 1510. He brought with him a train of seventy horses and riders. Johann was honoured by the City of Duisburg, which lies between Cleves and Düsseldorf on the Rhine River. Duisburg honoured Johann with a gift of wine and fish, including carp, salmon, and pike. On 13 March, Johann and his court went to Düsseldorf. The roughly 20-year-old Johann enjoyed another reception and met his bride Maria. Maria was about 19. The marriage ceremony between the future Duke of Cleves, Count of Mark and the future Duchess Regent of Jülich-Berg was officiated by the Abbot of Kornelimüster[3] before Maria's parents and the courts of Cleves-Mark and Jülich-Berg. Maria was her father's heir, as she was his only child. Maria's parents were married for ten years before Maria was born.

The public bedding celebration for Johann and Maria took place on 6 October 1510, seven months after their private religious ceremony. It was a festive occasion, with Johann making the trek to Düsseldorf accompanied by an unmissable train of three

---

3 Kornelimünster, Aachen, North Rhine-Westphalia, Germany.

hundred horses and his armoured knights from both Cleves and Mark. The knights' armour was elaborate, polished and glinting.

Most armour in the early 16th century was made by smiths in either Germany or Italy. The Holy Roman Emperor Maximilian I elevated the sport of jousting to the kind of chivalric tournament enjoyed by Henry VIII. Maximilian's son Philip had married Juana of Castile, older sister to Henry's first wife, Katherine of Aragon. Eager to gain Henry's support against the French, Maximilian gave Henry a fine suit of armour. Henry was so enamoured of it that his subsequent armour was designed in a more Germanic fashion.

The 1510 festivities for Anna's parents were grandiose. The wedding feast took place in the old palace of Düsseldorf over three days. The best food and drink were given to the couple's guests, who enjoyed gentle entertainments. No debauched or violent games were on display for the wedding feast. Notable guests included canons from the Cathedral of Cologne and other cathedrals, the Elector of Saxony, the Count of Waldeck, and many, many other nobles, knights, counts, barons, servants, and members of the clergy. There were no fewer than seventy-two notable ladies at the celebration. Johann gave each of the young maidens who were present a gold ring, spending a total of 700 Guilders on them. The idea of giving a gift to the witnesses of a royal bedding charmed Anna's future husband Henry VIII, who also gave small gifts to those present for Anna and Henry's public bedding.

On 10 October 1510, Johann returned to Cleves with his court, where he hosted another extravagant feast that night, and one more the following morning. After making plain his affection for and loyalty to his friends at the feast, Johann went back to Düsseldorf in the territories of Jülich-Berg to retrieve Maria, his, 'dear, honorable, newly-wedded wife'. The knights and nobles who accompanied Johann to the feast returned to their respective areas in Cleves and the Mark.

Tragedy struck the old ducal palace of Düsseldorf a couple months after Johann and Maria's three-day celebrations. On 23 December, the entire palace burnt to the ground. The cause? The palace's cooks were trying to smoke bacon using juniper wood, and the fire got out of hand in the middle of the night. The loss of money, beds, clothing, and silverware was huge. Nothing was spared by the fire. Some of the palace's inhabitants escaped, but many were burned to death. It is not recorded if Maria and Johann were at the old palace in Düsseldorf for Christmastide. It would take a decade for a new palace to be built.

Maria's father, the Duke of Jülich-Berg, died on 6 September 1511 in Düsseldorf. This left Maria as the Duchess Regent of Jülich-Berg, and Johann thereafter became a Duke *jure uxoris*, or by the right of his wife. On the same day as the well-attended burial of Maria's father, 8 September 1511, Johann travelled through the lands newly under his dominion, where he was paid homage.

Things brightened up for the couple when Maria fell pregnant in late 1511. Maria and Johann welcomed their first child, Anna's older sister, on 17 July 1512 at around 7 o'clock in the morning. The infant was named Sybylla[4] after her maternal grandmother. Sybylla would grow up to be an important figure in the German Reformation.

Johann III enjoyed another consolidation of power in 1512 when the lands of Cleves and Mark formally joined. Cleves and Mark agreed to provide military and economic support to one another. This further melding of Johann's territories was crucial to centralising his power in the Lower Rhine region. Strategic control over the Lower Rhine had a huge influence on the flow of goods through the various tributaries of the Rhine River. Controlling a stretch of the river itself meant not only some dominion over commerce, but also control over how quickly troops could be mobilised or blocked.

Another castle caught fire in late 1512, Hambach Castle. The *Schneiderzimmer*, or Tailor's or Cutter's room, in the castle in Jülich had a defect in its chimney. The room in which firewood for the castle was stored was located directly below the *Schneiderzimmer*. When the chimney plate in the *Schneiderzimmer* failed, the sparks fell down into the room below and directly onto the firewood. The fire found its way to some gunpowder. The rooms of the castle were not laid out very well in terms of escape routes. Eighteen people died as a result of the fire and explosion, and much damage was done to the castle. It would take more than twenty-five years to fully rebuild Hambach Castle. Maria periodically lived in the castle after Anna moved to England.

---

4 Sybylla's name is commonly given the spelling of Sibylle or Sybille, but she signed her personal letters as Sybylla or Sybyla.

Returning to the exploits of Aunt Anna, a dynastic match was planned for House Von der Mark in 1514. Anna's paternal Aunt Anna was to marry Karl of Guelders. Negotiations began on 29 June 1514 at Angerort House[5] in Duisburg for the marriage and set the stage for a 'grand, magnificent, and festive parliament, such that had not been seen for over one hundred years'. Aunt Anna's and Duke Karl's children would inherit Guelders, a fractured, unstable duchy in the middle of the Jülich-Berg territory. By 24 September, it was clear that neither Johann III, who was then only Duke of Jülich-Berg by right of marriage, nor John II, the current Duke of Cleves, were supportive of the match. Guelders was a very important piece of territory owing to the rivers flowing through it. Leaders from Cleves, Jülich, Berg and Mark were present at the parliament, which lasted for three days. The details of who would inherit the Guelders lands after Aunt Anna of Cleves and Karl of Guelders died would affect the entire area. In the event, Aunt Anna was not in favour of the match, and never married Karl.

Anna's great-grand-aunt Marie of Cleves had married the Duke of Orléans. Their only son was Louis XII of France, Anna's third cousin. Mary Tudor, sister of Henry VIII, was briefly married to Louis XII. On the night of 31 December 1514, Louis XII received the last rites and passed away the next day.

The beginning of 1515 saw a transfer of power from the Holy Roman Emperor Maximilian I to his grandson, Charles V. The fifteen-year-old Charles, who would later challenge Anna's brother and older sister over territory and religion, received the Duchy of Flanders and Brabant. By this time, Anna's mother was pregnant with Anna.

As noted, Anna was probably born on 28 June 1515, possibly in the City of Düsseldorf. Anna's mother, Maria of Jülich-Berg, likely went to stay with her mother, Sybille, in Düsseldorf for the

---

5   Sadly, this building no longer exists. If one visits southern Duisburg, the ruins of Angerort House's foundation can be seen jutting from the bluff where the Anger Creek meets the Rhine River. A house is perched at the top of the bluff, showing the top two floors of what was left of Angerort House. Most of the original buildings and features which Anna knew were destroyed or renovated beyond recognition by the 1960s.

births of Sybylla of Cleves and Anna of Cleves. Twenty-four years younger than her future husband Henry VIII, Anna enjoyed a conventional childhood and upbringing for a German princess. In 1515, Anna's father became Duke Johann III of Cleves:

> Duke John II of Cleves, in the presence of his chancery and the representative of the cities, passed his dominion over the whole country and its inhabitants to his son, Duke Johann III of Jülich and Berg. In so doing, [Anna's grandfather John II] freed all those who had sworn their oath to him. Then everyone pledged and swore to serve the young duke [Anna's father], as their rightful master, and continue to be faithful and devoted to Cleves. From then on, the young gentleman held the title of Duke Johann III of Cleves, Jülich, and Berg.

Anna and her elder sister Sybylla were joined by their brother on 28 July 1516. Born in Cleves, the baby boy was not named for several more weeks. The family then moved to Cleves itself after the death of Anna's paternal grandfather, John II. On 1 September 1516, the little boy was baptised with the name of Wilhelm, possibly after his maternal grandfather William VIII of Jülich-Berg.

Anna's younger sister Amalia was born on or about 17 October 1517, probably in Cleves as Anna's parents were residing there by this time. Little did Anna's family know that two weeks later, the world would be rocked by a disgruntled lawyer-turned-monk and his ideas on reforming the Catholic Church.

Later Life of Anna's Siblings

Anna's older sister Sybylla proved to be bold, and seems to have had a typically rivalrous but affectionate sisterly relationship with Anna. Though there is scant information for Anna's and Sybylla's childhoods, there are a couple of tales that are found in the letters Sybylla wrote as an adult. In one instance, an angry Sybylla hurt little Anna's forehead by throwing a pair of shears at her head. It is unknown if any sort of scar was left, though no contemporary

English sources commented on any sort of obvious mark. (One assumes they were pinking shears, not the type used on sheep.)

Sybylla became Duchess and later Electress of Saxony upon her marriage in 1527 to Johann Friedrich of Saxony. She had four sons, of whom three lived to see adulthood. Sybylla was regarded as a great beauty, something captured by the engagement portrait of her painted by Lucas Cranach the Elder in 1526. Sybylla had golden-brown hair, not so different to Anna's blonder hair. Sybylla was a favourite subject of Lucas Cranach the Elder's workshop and numerous portraits of Sybylla were produced over her lifetime.

The Saxon court had a huge library, perhaps the largest in Germany at the time. A committed proponent of Lutheranism and church reform, Sybylla whole-heartedly supported her husband's military actions and was held in high regard by other reformers. Justus Menius wrote a dedication to Sybylla in his *Oeconomia Christiana*, which read, 'To the highborn Electress, Mistress Sybylla, Duchess of Saxony, *Oeconomia Christiana* concerns the proper keeping of a Christian household.' At least one letter showing Sybylla's correspondence with Martin Luther has been identified.

Sybylla's husband held a position of great power in the Holy Roman Empire. The post of elector, first created in the 13th century, gave the eleven holders the responsibility of electing the King of the Romans, also known as the King of the Germans. Upon being crowned by the pope, the King of the Romans or Germans became the Holy Roman Emperor. Electors would be summoned within one month after the death of the last Emperor and meet within three months of the summons to determine the candidates and cast ballots for the next. The Electors of Saxony acted as vicars with the Electors of Palatine during the interregnum.

Sybylla's husband Johann-Friedrich led the Schmalkaldic League, a defensive alliance formed amongst the Lutheran princes. The purpose of the League was to provide protection to the protestant states from the Holy Roman Emperor Charles V. Anna exchanged letters with Sybylla until the latter's death in 1554. The sisters were known to have a strong bond.

Anna's brother Wilhelm was thirteen months her junior, born in July 1516. Wilhelm would prove to be an ambitious duke and a devious, though perhaps not adept, politician. He became known as Wilhelm the Rich. He was raised predominantly at court and received an education in statecraft, along with reading, writing, religion of course, and other basic studies to ensure that a young nobleman would be prepared to rule his territory.

Anna's younger sister Amalia is a mystery to history. In the 1540s, Wilhelm, who was then Duke of Jülich-Cleves-Berg, sought an alliance with the Margrave of Baden. The Margrave's son and Amalia would marry to seal the alliance. The Margrave's two sons were Bernhard, who was rejected by his family due to his raucous and immoral behavior, and Karl, born in 1529 and twelve years younger than Amalia. Bernhard was a prodigal son and later returned to the Margrave's family. Karl and Bernhard would both become Margraves of Baden.

Wilhelm refused to marry Amalia to a debauchee, like Bernhard, or a mere child, like Karl. Amalia remained a spinster at Wilhelm's court until she died in 1586. Amalia helped raise Wilhelm's four daughters. As a staunch Lutheran, Amalia insisted upon her nieces being raised in that faith. Wilhelm raised his two sons to be Catholic. The disagreement between Amalia and Wilhelm over religion culminated in Wilhelm going after Amalia with his sword drawn. Amalia was saved by a servant, who slammed the door in his face.

A songbook now held in Berlin containing songs dedicated to the Virgin Mary, a selection of rhymes and short poems, and twenty-seven love songs, belonged to a Katharina von Hatzfeld. The book contains a poem by Amalia, written in her own hand, which describes someone pining for her beloved. Amalia was close to Katharina von Hatzfeld, despite Katharina being roughly twenty years younger. The object of Amalia's affection is unknown, if the person existed at all. Amalia may have contributed to the contents of the book beyond the poem by writing in the margin.

As a final stab at Wilhelm over religion, Amalia refused to go to her-sister-in law's Catholic funeral. Wilhelm outlived Amalia and had her buried in the Catholic St Lambertus Church in Düsseldorf. Wilhelm joined Amalia six years later, in 1592.

Anna Learns to be a Noblewoman; The Burgundian Influence

Anna and her sisters were given what could be considered a conservative education by their mother, with an emphasis on domestic skills. Most importantly, the young duchesses Sybylla, Anna and Amalia learned how to run and maintain a ducal household. The early 15th-century writer Christine de Pizan gives an idea of the important things a young noblewoman needed to learn to be successful:

> It is proper for such a [noble] lady or woman to be thoroughly knowledgeable about the laws relating to [properties of the lordship][6] ... taxes for various causes, and all those sorts of things that are within the jurisdiction of the lordship, according to the customs of the region so that no one can deceive her about them... There is nothing dishonourable about making herself familiar with the accounts... In addition [she] will do well to be a very good manager of the estate and to know all about the work on the land and at what time and in which season one ought to perform what operations... And likewise she should know all about the work of the vineyard if it is a wine-growing area.

A noblewoman's recommended education included checking the sheep and other livestock on a more or less daily basis, and occupying herself and her ladies-in-waiting with making clothes. Anna learned to embroider and mend:

> [A noblewoman] and her girls and young women will occupy themselves in making clothing. They will select the wool, putting the best quality to one side to make fine garments for her and her husband or to sell if she needs to do so. She uses the coarse wool for little children and for her women and household... This practice of running the household wisely sometimes renders more profit than the entire income from the land.

---

6   Christine de Pizan states specifically, '...laws relating to fiefs, sub-fiefs, quit rents, *champarts*'.

The lifestyle of a person living at court during the German Renaissance was different in detail from that of an English courtier. Counselors began working between six and seven in the morning, with the rest of the workers arriving to start the day sometime later. A duke in the Holy Roman Empire expected court officials to attend a minimum of one religious service each morning. Next came *Morgensuppe*, 'Morning Soup', which was a drink of either beer or wine, depending on a person's station at court. The first meal of the day came at ten o'clock in the morning, and lasted for around two hours. Work was usually completed by midday. However, high-ranking officials had to attend meetings on occasion in the afternoon.

The court would come alive in the afternoon, with gentlemen calling on the well-supervised and chaperoned ladies. Anna and her sisters came out of the *Frauenzimmer*, or Ladies' Room, to socialise at this time of day. Around two o'clock, snacks and refreshments were served. Four or five hours later, supper would begin. Supper was at times a lengthy affair, ending as late as nine o'clock when the cellars and kitchens were closed. Those who did not live at court would leave then. It was typical for a courtier to maintain some kind of residence in the city and close to court. A courtier would be bound to that apartment and could only give it up with the permission of the Lord Chamberlain.

Three or four hundred people could enjoy as many as nine courses of an evening at a German prince's table. At a supper that large, one can be sure that everyone from minstrels for entertainment to high-ranking nobles would be present. The feast itself could occupy several rooms. Dishes of venison and fish were accompanied by wines made from the grapes of the Neckar or Rhine river valleys. It was not uncommon for poor folk to be at such feasts, hoping to receive leftover food. The German princes were ostensibly concerned for poor and sick people, and were willing to give out food to those in need.

Some German courts enjoyed the hunt just as much as Henry VIII's court, and the sport was a great passion of the age. Burg Castle, where Anna's sisters and maternal family spent a lot of time, was originally a hunting lodge that developed into a castle. These events were often lavish. Unfortunately, a hunting party could wreak havoc on the labour of the peasants: it was not uncommon for crops to be destroyed. Hunting was a favourite pastime for the Jülich-Berg court. Several hunting lodges around Düsseldorf were built from 1373 to about 1400, including one such outpost being built into Düsseldorf's gate. Tournaments were another favourite, and injuries therefrom were the cause of death for two of Anna's forebears on her maternal side, Adolf IV and Gerhard I.

Anna, Sybylla and their little sister Amalia were raised almost exclusively by their mother and female attendants. Young German noblewomen were taught how to maintain the finances of a household, to sew and embroider, and how to cook. Anna did learn how to read and write, though the extent of any education she may have received beyond the practicalities of running a noble household and an education in the Christian faith is unknown. Anna's mother and father were Catholic at the time of their marriage and Anna's birth; but Anna's father was a friend of Desiderius Erasmus, and through his humanist teachings, Johann adopted a stance of religious tolerance toward both the Catholic and Lutheran religions. Lutheranism and the Protestant Reformation began in 1517 with Martin Luther's momentous Ninety-Five Theses, but were not formally articulated until the presentation of the Augsburg Confession at the Diet of Augsburg in 1530.

Anna led a fairly inconspicuous life at court. She and her sisters spent most of the day in the *Frauenzimmer*. There, Anna learnt how to run a household, including how to provide for and supervise her ladies and how to manage the kitchen. She surely learned how to cook, repair and refurbish clothing, and how to procure the day-to-day necessities for a household. Aside from the quotidian practicalities, the German princesses would send elaborate presents to one another, including exotic birds, horses, jewelry, and beadwork.

A German princess was educated by her governess, meaning that educations could vary greatly from household to household. A governess controlled how often a princess could interact with men.

There was an age limit for pages serving noblewomen. The standard was that a page had to be under twelve years old. There were formal visiting hours for the *Frauenzimmer*, and the court physician was the only man who could go to the *Frauenzimmer* after hours.

The Jülich-Berg court really began to expand its diversions and amusements under Anna's maternal great-grandparents in the mid-15th century. The court was known for its love of music, and first adopted a permanent set of court musicians at the behest of Sophia of Saxe-Lauenburg, Anna's maternal great-grandmother. Anna's maternal grandfather, Wilhelm VIII of Jülich-Berg, delighted in jesters and had four at court at the time of his death. Delicious foods were valued at court, including delicate pastries. A cook was sent as far away as Brabant to learn the art of pastry-making.

Court life in Cleves-Mark, Anna's paternal side, had a heavy Burgundian influence stemming from the marriage of Duke Adolf I of Cleves-Mark and Marie of Burgundy in 1406. Marie (1393?–1463) was the daughter of John the Good of Burgundy and Margaret of Bavaria. It is through this union that Anna is related to Louis XII of France, and Mary, Queen of Scots. Marie brought with her the tradition of having a female court to counter-balance the masculine, public court. This naturally led to the *Frauenzimmer*, or all-female rooms in which Anna and her sisters received their education.

The primary residences for the Dukes of Cleves were located in Dinslaken, Monterberg, Kranenburg, Schembeck and Winnenthal. In Cleves culture, widows of the dukes were given their own separate residences. The widows' residences included Monterberg, where Marie of Burgundy died in 1466, Dinslaken, and Linn. A Dowager Duchess of Cleves would be able to enjoy a court life in miniature at such domiciles.

From 1521, after the formal unification of Jülich-Cleves-Berg, Anna's family rotated residences. Anna would spend the winter in Castle Bensberg in Bergisch Gladbach, not far from Cologne, or occasionally in Düsseldorf. For the spring, the men in her family would usually take residence in Cleves together with some of the women, and then spend the summer at Hambach Castle in Jülich. Duke Johann III's counselors did not travel with the court at first. The counselors for Jülich-Berg would remain in and around Düsseldorf throughout the year, and the counselors to the northwest for Cleves-Mark did likewise in and around Cleves. In 1534, the counselors from Cleves-Mark finally went to Düsseldorf. An archive was established in Düsseldorf at some point in the early 1500s, so it made more sense to centralise the unified government there.

At court, Anna could expect to see four main officials who kept things in order: the *Hofmeister* or Controller, *Schenk* or butler, *Kämmerer* or Chamberlain, and the *Marschall* or Marshal. Literally translated, *Hofmeister* means 'Court Master'. The word also describes individuals who operated as the Master of Ceremonies or as Court Tutor; it has been translated as 'Comptroller', as well. The meaning depended on the needs of the court and the period in which the person held the position. Court Tutors were more common earlier on. Honorary service titles were given to members of the Cleves-Mark court beginning in 1417, after Anna's family was elevated from the level of count to duke. One important duty of the Controller up until 1515 was to judge and settle disputes between nobles in Cleves-Mark. This system faded away after the unification of Cleves-Mark and Jülich-Berg.

The influence of the Burgundian court contributed to the addition of other positions at the Cleves court, including a goldsmith. This is mostly because of Anna's great-grandfather, Duke John I of Cleves, whose mother was Marie of Burgundy. John I became Duke of Cleves in 1448. Court life was all-consuming not only for the courtiers and other important persons about Cleves, but also for the artisans and workers employed by the court. The Cleves court was larger than it had ever been previously. John I maintained connections with the Burgundian court throughout his lifetime. His changes and additions to the Cleves court led to a cultural highpoint, with the activities centred on Swan Castle in Cleves. Ambassadors of Burgundy and servants hailing from Burgundy were maintained at the Cleves court throughout the reign of John I, further facilitating the influx of Burgundian ideas about court life.

Court musicians and dwarves were first recorded at the Cleves court in 1411. Duke John I established a chapel choir consisting of around seventeen singers and musicians. During John I's reign, the court ballooned to 246 members. After a series of battles involving Guelders in 1497, the Cleves treasury was quite empty. There are no records of the installation of new musicians after that time. It is reasonable to assume that Anna's father, Johann III, enjoyed some of the musical developments while a young boy in Cleves. Another Burgundian element that followed Marie to the court of Cleves was the use of embossed wall decorations. In Cleves, these were covered in gold. The candle and firelight reflecting off the golden walls in Cleves must have been a sight to behold.

In this opulent, Burgundian-style court, the future first German Queen Consort of England grew up. She had examples of several strong, capable female relatives and received a practical education in how to manage her estates or those of her husband. However, no amount of education or supply of role models could have prepared Anna for what life had in store for her.

2

PEASANTS, LEAGUES, AND REFORMS

Before 1515, Anna's parents faced a series of setbacks, including bad weather, more fires, and civil unrest that threatened to spread throughout Jülich-Cleves-Berg. The winter of November 1510 to February 1511 in Jülich-Cleves-Berg was very cold. The Rhine River was frozen between Düsseldorf and Cologne, while parts of the south experienced a massive snowfall. When the rivers thawed and snow melted in February 1511, dykes broke, reportedly in the middle of the night. This put parts of Jülich-Cleves-Berg underwater. The cold, wet weather continued through March, April, and May, but fortunately, the grain crops actually benefitted from the extra snow and rain.

At about the time of Anna's birth, the Holy Roman Empire faced several threats: the run-up to and early part of the German Reformation, plus various revolts not strictly aligned with the German religious upheaval. Some of the revolts happened close to where Anna's family lived, causing alarm in the Jülich-Cleves-Berg territories. The German Reformation had taken hold by 1520, championed principally by the Elector of Saxony and Martin Luther. These events would influence the fate of Anna, her sisters and her brother.

The year 1513 saw the start of the Duisburg Revolution, which was an offshoot of the riots and revolt in nearby Cologne.

Duisburg is between Cleves and Düsseldorf. Anna's parents, the young Duke and Duchess and recently delivered of the infant Sybylla, faced the most dangerous political conflict in the history of Duisburg. The Duisburg Revolution was caused by frustrations over mismanagement of the city and social injustices. The issues came to a head on 13 February 1513. Informed that several masters of the city council had died, the citizens of Duisburg gathered to discuss their next steps. The powerful guilds met and decided to present two resolutions to what was left of the city council. It was an effort to reconcile the enormous number of privileges members of the council enjoyed with the restrictions placed on the citizenry. The revolution was fuelled by the lack of influence the people of Duisburg had over local politics. Only half of the city council could be elected by the citizenry, and the outgoing council could appoint the other half. The twelve judges were appointed exclusively by the sitting city council.

Twenty-four representatives went to the city gate early on 14 February 1513 and demanded the keys. The party then went to the mayor's house and demanded that the citizenry be notified to gather at the Minorite convent or be forced to pay a serious fine. The rebels presented their two resolutions to the gathered citizens of Duisburg. Both were written the night before, with one drafted at the Marien Guild and the other at the Antonius Guild. Any dissenting voices were threatened with decapitation. The rebels delivered the resolutions to the council, who were given time to read the documents, so long as the council promised to return them. Backed into a corner, the council agreed. The documents were copied out by the council's secretary and posted in the Marien Guild, not the city hall.

Anna's grandfather, John II of Cleves, caught wind of what was happening from his capital city. In late June 1513, Duke John II sent two letters to the council and *Burgerschaft* of Duisburg. He wanted to hear what happened from both sides and to understand the cause of the dissent. Four members of the council and eight members of the *Burgerschaft* travelled to Cleves to meet him and discuss their differences. The City of Duisburg paid the cost of the ship that transported the representatives up the Rhine to Cleves.

The parties met at the city hall in Cleves. The representatives of Duisburg were asked why they caused such an uproar, considering that no similar event had ever occurred in recorded history since the founding of Duisburg. The full extent of the discussion between Anna's grandfather and the representatives is unknown. The final decision was that all disputes between local authorities and the citizenry would be heard by the Duke in Cleves. John did not dismiss the charter drafted in Duisburg outright, but did defer any action under the pretence that his counselors were unavailable and that therefore could not make any decisions on the demands from Duisburg. In March 1514 Duke John II finally issued a decision regarding the Duisburg Revolt: a massive fine imposed on the city and the closure of the guild houses. The fine was reduced by two-thirds after several pleas from Duisburg, but the guild houses were shut down.

Later on, in 1514, a universal peace was established between Anna's grandfather, father, the Duke of Saxony-Lauenburg,[7] the Archbishop of Cologne, Franz von Waldeck, the Bishop of Münster, and others. It was hoped that this would settle the current unrest and keep the peace.

Luther, Saxony, and the German Reformation

The German Reformation, *reductio ad absurdam*, was a complex movement that began in the early 16th century with an upstart monk. Martin Luther was born on 10 November 1483 in Eisleben, Thüringen. In 1501 Luther went to the University of Erfurt to study law. He received a Master of Arts degree in 1505. After a dramatic turn of events, Luther chose to abandon his study of the law for theology at Wittenberg, and in 1511 Luther became a professor there. On the evening of 2 July 1505, the 31-year-old Luther was on his way home on horseback when a vicious thunderstorm overtook him. A lightning bolt struck a tree not far from him and his mount, terrifying man

---

7   Today this area occupies the Federal States of Lower Saxony and Schleswig-Holstein.

and presumably beast. Reminded of his inevitable demise and the judgment to come, Luther prayed aloud: 'Help, Saint Anna! I will become a monk!' Luther survived the rest of the journey home and on 17 July 1505 entered St Augustine's Monastery in Erfurt.

In 1517, indulgences were sold in Saxony, with the usual promise that those who purchased them would reduce their time in purgatory. The sale of indulgences was the last straw for Luther. He wrote a letter on 31 October 1517 to Bishop Albrecht of Mainz, declaiming on good Christian behaviour and flaws he found in the local church and in Rome. This document became known as the Ninety-Five Theses, though it was not originally meant to be doctrinal in nature. Luther was the vicar of Saxony and Thuringia at this point, and possibly knew Anna's future brother-in-law, Johann Friedrich.

Luther was excommunicated in 1521 and ordered to appear before the Diet of Worms. Fearing for Luther's life, Johann Friedrich's great-uncle, Elector Frederick III of Saxony, known as Frederick the Wise, ordered Luther 'kidnapped'. Luther hid in Wartburg Castle under the protection of Frederick III. He posed as *Junker Jörg*, or Squire George. It was here, under the advice of Philippus Melanchthon, that Luther translated the New Testament into vernacular German. Luther purportedly used Erasmus's Greek translation of the Bible as a template. Luther published the translation in 1522. Modern German finds its foundation in Luther's translations of the Old and New Testament. Anna's future brother-in-law, Johann Friedrich, was about eighteen years old when Luther was hiding in Wartburg. It is not unreasonable to assume that Johann Friedrich was at least introduced to Luther's teachings by people about court, if not by Luther himself.

Martin Luther posed a serious threat to the Holy Roman Empire. In short, fracturing the Germanic territories and pulling funds away from the Holy Roman Empire destabilised the areas in charge of electing the next Holy Roman Emperor after Maximilian I. Maximilian's grandson became Charles V in 1519 after defeating Frederick the Wise of Saxony. The other contenders for Holy Roman Emperor contemporary with Charles V and Frederick the Wise of Saxony were Francis I of France and Henry VIII of England. This illustrates the power of Saxony in 1519 on an international level. Having caught wind of Luther's suggestions to the Church, Pope Leo X called Luther to Rome. Refusing to send his own subject out of his jurisdiction, Frederick was able to negotiate with Leo X to keep Luther within Frederick's territory.

Leading up to the marriage alliance forged between Cleves and Lorraine for Anna, and Cleves and Saxony for Sybylla, the Germanic territories faced a vicious series of (overlapping) wars from 1515 to 1523, from 1522 to 1523, and again from 1524 to 1525. The first was known as the Frisian Revolt, the second as the Knight's War, and the third was known as the Peasants' War. The different territories were ruled to varying degrees of authority by the Holy Roman Empire. Some were entirely under the control of the Empire. A few city-states were independent of the Empire to a degree, some being ecclesiastical states of the Empire. Still others were free cities. The cities had to pay taxes to the Church in Rome. To evade the payment, the city-states and other territories established their own churches so that German money was paid to local churches, and not to Rome.

Three Revolts

In 1515 the people of Friesland, to the north of Anna's territories, rebelled against the Emperor. Friesland as Anna knew it extended roughly from Lower Saxony and Schleswig-Holstein in Germany along the coast of the North Sea through North Holland in modern-day Netherlands. This area is also known as the German Bight. Friesland experienced varying degrees of unrest and civil war throughout the 15th century. The nobility had a troublesome, opportunistic faction within it. These were arrivistes, former commoners who took over properties when established noble families either died out or were killed. In addition, the Frieslanders in general were tired of the numerous foreign invaders, including from Holland, Denmark, and duchies surrounding Friesland.

The peasant army called themselves the *Arumer Zwarte Hoop*, which means Black Heap of Arum. Arum is a small city in Dutch Friesland. The army was led by the apparently large and semi-legendary Pier Gerlofs Donia, nicknamed *Grutte Pier* or 'Great Peter'. Great Peter chose to join the rebellion after his home and family were destroyed by the Emperor's out-of-control forces.

He was joined by a young man named Wijerd Jelckama, who took over after Great Peter's death in 1519 or 1520.

Once the uprising had started, Karl, Duke of Guelders, chose to join with the rebels against the Holy Roman Empire. This was the same Duke Karl of Guelders originally intended as Aunt Anna's husband. Guelders was immediately south of Friesland, with Jülich-Cleves-Berg wrapping around and to the south of it. In essence, if any party controlled Friesland, it controlled entry to several rivers that flow through the Netherlands and Germany, creating a chokehold on commerce. The same effect could be achieved through control of the Duchy of Guelders, which included the County of Zutphen. This was a serious threat to the Empire. Duke Karl hired mercenaries to fight alongside the Black Heap.

The pirate and rebel Great Peter died not in battle but disillusioned and in retirement in 1520, though not before he managed to take out almost thirty ships belonging to the Dutch and thus, the Holy Roman Empire.[8] Great Peter and Jelckama were briefly able to hold two castles in the Low Countries. As mentioned, Jelckama led the Black Heap of Arum after Great Peter's death, but Jelckama was not able to organise and motivate the Black Heap as well as Great Peter. Duke Karl recalled his troops in 1520, which seriously weakened the already ineffective Jelckama. He was eventually captured and beheaded in Friesland in 1523, along with what was left of the Black Heap.

While the Frisian revolt was petering out, the Knight's Revolt gained momentum. Begun in 1522, this series of battles was also called the Knight's War or the Poor Baron's Rebellion. Another struggle against the Holy Roman Empire, this war was about the status of the Imperial Knights. Feudalism was alive and well in Germany in 1522. The system was taking money away from the knights and putting it into the pockets of the Holy Roman Emperor and his imperial cities, plus various remaining feudal lords who

---

8 It is unclear whether Great Peter really existed. However, the fleet of ships were indeed seized, Karl of Guelders did help the rebels, and the Frisian Revolt was a serious event.

maintained the free cities. Advances in military technology made the Imperial Knights less formidable, meaning that the various cities could better defend themselves.

The revolt was led by the knights Franz von Sickingen and Ulrich von Hutten. There was a religious element to the war. The two knights envisioned a unified Germany under one government, free of the multitude of principalities and bishoprics. This idea required the support of the peasantry if it were to have any hope of succeeding. Operating out of von Sickingen's Castle Ebernburg, von Hutten and Sickingen distributed propaganda pamphlets promoting the ideas of Renaissance humanism and Lutheranism. Castle Ebernburg hosted Reformists including Johannes Oecolampadius, Johann Reuchlin, and Martin Bucer. Martin Luther was invited to take refuge there after the Diet of Worms, but went with the Elector of Saxony, instead.

Von Sickingen dedicated his energy to harrying towns up and down the Rhine, which flows past Cleves and Düsseldorf. Von Sickingen launched a campaign against the Imperial City of Trier, but was ill-prepared to make the siege effective and lost. Trier is about 320 kilometres or 200 miles from Cleves. He retreated to his castle of Landstuhl, where he himself was besieged in May 1522 and died of his wounds. Von Hutten, who fled to Switzerland, died a few months later of disease.

The final war that had an impact Anna's family was the Peasant's Revolt, 1524–1525. The rebel forces consisted mostly of farmers and peasants. The series of revolts swept from southwest to east, with well-regimented noble armies slaughtering the rebels. Early Anabaptists, who were radical Protestants, supported the rebels.

The first offensive began in 1524 in the City of Stühlingen, about 645 kilometres/400 miles southeast of Cleves. It continued east to what is now Bavaria. In March 1525 the rebels disseminated the Twelve Articles. They promoted Luther's idea of a plain reading of the Bible, from which the Twelve Articles were drawn. The purpose of the Articles was to do away with tithes, unlearned clergy, and other perceived wrongs. The Articles represented a significant break from the Catholic Church and the Holy Roman Empire. Martin

Luther did not support the revolt. He published a polemic 'Against the Murderous, Thieving Hordes of Peasants'. The peasants used Luther as a rallying cry nevertheless. Luther published the work to disassociate himself from the rebels' violent actions. His protest was against the Church – 'Render unto Caesar...'

The uprising became a revolt in Thuringia, threatening the Landgrave of Hesse and Saxon territory. The rebels were hunted down and massacred around 15 May 1525. Battles took place in Würzburg in May and June, and Freiburg, a Hapsburg-controlled city, was attacked. The Peasants' Revolt ended in September 1525.

By 1526, it was clear that portions of Germany were not in favour of rule by the Holy Roman Empire – nor were those parts of Germany happy to see German money going to the Pope. Disillusioned by poor treatment from the Empire and Imperial forces, peoples up and down the Rhine were trying to break the Imperial and Catholic stranglehold.

Sybylla and Anna: Marriage Negotiations with Saxony and Lorraine

Anna turned eleven in 1526 and her older sister Sybylla turned fourteen. The two older Von der Mark girls were now in the marriage market and sold, at least on paper. Sybylla was betrothed to Johann Friedrich of Saxony, future Elector of Saxony, on 8 September 1526. A marriage treaty involving the succession of both Anna and Sybylla was ratified on 13 June 1527, just before Anna's twelfth birthday. Anna was betrothed to Francis, the son of Duke Anton of Lorraine.

Francis was the grandson of Philippa of Guelders and great-great grandson of Catherine of Cleves. This further bolstered the hold which Jülich-Cleves-Berg hoped to have on Guelders because Francis was the only legitimate male heir of Duke Karl of Guelders. Anna would continue as Duchess of Lorraine, and her male issue would inherit Guelders.

Sybylla's groom, Johann Friedrich, was more prestigious and powerful than Anna's when looked at through the lens of the

Holy Roman Empire and not just the alliances of the duchies. Johann Friedrich would become a Prince-Elector of Saxony, which was much more exalted than a mere duke. A marriage between Sybylla of Cleves and Johann Friedrich of Saxony was first proposed by the Holy Roman Emperor Maximilian I in 1518. Johann Friedrich married fourteen-year-old Sybylla of Cleves on 9 February 1527. He became Elector of Saxony on 16 August 1532. Johann Friedrich's uncle, as mentioned above, harboured Martin Luther in 1521 after the Diet of Worms. Luther was tucked away at Wartburg Castle under the protection of Friedrich.

In comparison with the English structure, the nobility was set up differently in Germany. The English monarchy was usually hereditary, though sometimes the kingdom had been taken through force of arms. German nobles, on the other hand, had the job of electing the next Holy Roman Emperor whenever the position became available. By the time Charles V became Emperor, the position was quasi-hereditary in that it was expected that a relative of the previous emperor would succeed. The Emperor still had to be formally elected. The King of the Romans was the emperor-elect. The King of the Romans or Germans was next in rank to the Emperor. The terms 'King of the Romans' and 'King of the Germans' were used interchangeably. Archdukes, relatives of the Holy Roman Emperor, existed in Austria. In Germany, there were prince-electors. The eleven electors chose the King of the Romans. Below the electors and archdukes were dukes, landgraves, margraves, and counts, put in its simplest form.

Territories of the Germanic part of the Holy Roman Empire were in favour of so remaining, but a growing portion did not wish to remain within the Empire. Religion was used as a lever to break away. The Schmalkaldic League grew out of the desire to unite against the Empire and observe Lutheran reformist ideas.

Augsburg, Saxony, and Schmalkalden
Religious tensions following Martin Luther's Ninety-Five Theses of 1517 were exacerbated by the Diet of Worms in 1521,

and publication in 1522 of Luther's translation of the New Testament. These culminated in the Diet of Augsburg. The Diet took place in 1530. The Holy Roman Emperor Charles V wanted to negotiate over the schism caused by Luther's ideas. A document called the Confession of Augsburg was submitted to the Emperor, laying out the Lutheran articles of doctrine. The Confession was submitted by the Lutheran princes, which included Sybylla's father-in-law, John, then-Elector of Saxony. Two other documents were submitted by some southern German cities, but the Confession became the major doctrinal statement for Lutheranism.

After a time of review and debate between the Emperor's theologians and the Lutheran princes, the parties were at an impasse. On 19 November 1530, the Emperor granted a Recess. The Recess gave the various attendees at the Diet of Augsburg until 15 April 1531, just over five months from the beginning of the Recess, to come back to the Catholic fold and receive forgiveness. Four of the Recess's sixty-four paragraphs are aimed directly at the Elector of Saxony:

§ 3. Neither the Elector of Saxony … nor [his] subjects shall force their sect … on Our subjects or those of the Holy Empire, or the other electors, princes, and estates. And if some subjects of the Elector of Saxony… whatever status they may have, adhere to, or wish to adhere to, the old Christian faith, they shall not be disturbed in their churches and chapels or in their ceremonies and Masses, nor shall any further innovation be introduced in them. Nor shall the regular clergy, men, or women, be in any way hindered from hearing the Mass, confessing their sins, or administering or receiving the Blessed Sacrament.

§ 4. Furthermore, the aforementioned Elector of Saxony the five princes, and six cities join Us and the other electors, princes, and estates against those who deny the Blessed Sacrament. Further, rather than splitting away from Us … they should advise, promote, and aid our actions against those people, just as, as mentioned above, all of Our electors, princes, and estates have, to the extent that they are involved, given us their approval and affirmation...

§ 6. Furthermore, through the laws of God and of man, also the Gospel, We command that no one shall be deprived by force of what is his .... We are daily approached with complaints and pleas from expelled abbots and abbesses who seek help in recovering their properties... It is therefore Our strict command that the Elector of Saxony and his allies immediately, and without delay, allow these expropriated monks and other clergy to reoccupy the monasteries and properties in their territories, from which the occupants have been expelled.

§ 7. The aforementioned Elector of Saxony and his allies have not wished to accept Our gracious Recess and have even rejected it in part...

Thus the Recess enumerates the various offences committed against the Catholic faith, and it closes with:

We ... command that this, Our Recess, shall be fully obeyed and enforced in all of its stipulations, provisions, and conceptions regardless of earlier Recesses enacted by our previous Imperial Diets, insofar as these Recesses and ordinances may be detrimental to the faith. And We command it despite any objections, opposition, and appeals that have been or may be directed to a General Council, to Us, or to anyone else.

Rather than obeying the Emperor, the Lutheran estates chose to form an alliance at the town of Schmalkalden. The adherents to the new Lutheran religion rejected the articles enumerated in the Recess of the Diet of Augsburg. On a presumably cold day in February 1531, three months away from the Emperor's deadline, the Elector of Saxony met with Landgrave Philip of Hesse in the town hall. The town hall complex in which John of Saxony co-founded the Schmalkaldic League was built in 1419. It remains standing in Schmalkalden. The League started as a defensive coalition against

Charles V. It eventually developed into more of a diplomatic organisation. Francis I of France, himself a Catholic who was prosecuting the Protestants in his own territory, supported the Schmalkaldic League because it was inimical to Charles V.

Members of the League agreed to contribute infantry and cavalry for the mutual protection of each. The League never took serious military action against Emperor Charles V. Instead, members of the League reclaimed property from the Catholic Church and removed religious leaders. It is fair to compare this type of activity to England's dissolution of the monasteries. In 1537, the League drew up the Schmalkald Articles (*Schmalkaldische Artikel*). The articles were another proclamation of Protestant faith. Martin Luther was involved in drafting these new articles but could not fully participate due to illness, suffering from kidney stones. The League did meet at Luther's private home when drafting the articles to facilitate his input. They were to be incorporated into the Lutheran Book of Concord in 1580.

The Schmalkaldic League is frequently cited as a reason why Thomas Cromwell thought Henry VIII should marry Anna. Erroneously, it has been stated that Anna's brother Wilhelm was a member of the League. It was Anna's brother-in-law, Johann Friedrich, the Elector of Saxony, who was a member of the League by the time Henry VIII came calling in 1539.

Philippus Melanchthon and More Imperial Diets

Another important figure in Reformation Germany was the Saxon intellectual Philippus Melanchthon. Melanchthon was fourteen years younger than Luther, born on 16 February 1497. Melanchthon lost his father when he was only eleven years old. The boy went to live with a relative, who subsequently enrolled him in schooling that led to university. Melanchthon started studying theology around 1516, just before Luther posted his Ninety-Five Theses. Melanchthon was well-educated by this time, having received his Master's Degree. He became a professor of Greek at the University of Wittenberg in 1518. By then, Melanchthon was familiar with the ideas of Erasmus.

Once at Wittenberg, Melanchthon was exposed to Luther's influence. It was Luther, at the behest of Melanchthon's great-uncle, who asked Melanchthon to accept the position at Wittenberg. Melanchthon began publishing his Lutheran-leaning arguments in 1521. By 1529, he attracted the attention of the Saxon Elector John. Elector John was patron and protector of Luther, after Frederick the Wise harboured the monk at Wartburg castle.

In March 1529 Melanchthon attended the Diet of Speyer with Elector John. The 1529 Diet followed on from the 1521 Diet of Worms and the 1526 Diet of Speyer. The 1526 Diet was attended by the Archduke Ferdinand, the brother of Charles V, who later became King of the Romans in 1531. The Emperor could not attend the Diet, so delegated Ferdinand to introduce instructions at the opening on 25 June 1526. Ferdinand demanded that the German princes stop rebelling. The princes demurred. The 1526 Diet of Speyer resulted in a sort of armistice, wherein the German princes governed their respective territories as they saw fit until a general council was called to resolve religious matters. This opened the door for Elector John of Saxony and Landgrave Philip of Hesse to do as they pleased concerning their Protestant leanings.

On 15 March 1529 the Diet again met at Speyer. Once more, Charles V could not attend. Charles was intent on placating or winning over the rebelling German Protestants. Unfortunately, his instructions were not received in time by his brother, the Archduke Ferdinand. Ferdinand ordered that the Protestants abandon their religious reforms and that all German states resume the observation of Catholicism. The princes protested this order via the drafting of an appeal. At that moment, Protestantism as a political force was born.

Melanchthon Reports on the United Duchies

Melanchthon published *Instructions for the Visitors of Parish Pastors in Electoral Saxony* in March 1528, a reaction to the poor knowledge of local clergy. Luther provided the preface. He argued that secular intervention was necessitated by a lack of properly trained bishops in Saxony. Luther travelled around the districts of Saxony in 1527 and discovered the clergy's shortcomings. On a subsequent visit in 1528, he was shocked by the fact that the clergy were doctrinally sound but could not do something as basic as recite the Lord's Prayer. Luther then drafted and published the Large and Small Catechisms in April and May respectively of the following year. Melanchthon went on to draft the main text of the Augsburg Confession of 1530.

Continuing throughout the 1530s as an integral part of the Saxon Protestant movement, Melanchthon was asked to determine the state of religion in Cleves in 1539 and report to Johann Friedrich. It was known that Anna's mother Maria was devoutly Catholic. It was also known that Johann III was in favour of Erasmus's teachings, and that he had forbidden the circulation of Luther's writings. Johann III, Anna's father, died in early February 1539 leaving the United Duchies to her brother, Wilhelm. In March of that year, Melanchthon wrote his findings about the state of religion in Jülich-Cleves-Berg while he was in Frankfurt am Main.

He found there were three religious groups in the United Duchies, none of which could really be considered Lutheran. First, a large number of the nobility, including the Duchess Maria, were openly and devoutly Catholic. In Melanchthon's opinion, this portion of the population 'clung [to the] crude and unlearned papists, monks, and priests'. The nobles had their children enter into the ecclesiastical life in hopes of becoming bishops.

Second, a slightly smaller part of the population, though powerful, was more inclined toward reform. But overall, a lot of the traditional Catholic ceremonies were preserved in typical religious observances. Melanchthon compared it to the situation springing up in Cologne, wherein about a tenth of the population became Protestant against the ruling family's wishes. In Cleves, Melanchthon found that this middle group was quite Catholic but glossed over with a kind of Protestant sheen.

The third group consisted of 'vermin and Anabaptists'. Anabaptist teachings had certainly permeated. Johannes Oecolampadius was in the Low Countries, just across the Rhine from the United Duchies. Oecolampadius viewed the Eucharist differently from Melanchthon and Luther. Rather than believing that the bread and wine truly were the body and blood of Christ, Oecolampadius believed that observing the Eucharist was a plea for spiritual union with Christ and not the literal consumption of Christ's body.

Overall, Melanchthon opined, one had to be careful. There were factions equipped to severely delay or prevent the effectuation of Protestantism. Melanchthon believed the nobles to be a deeply irrational and conservative lot, not easily willing to part with what he saw as Catholic superstitions. Because of this, priests in the Duchy of Cleves were very powerful.

Specifically pertaining to Wilhelm, Melanchthon believed that he was not afraid of the Emperor or his demands that all Protestant German lands return to Catholicism. Wilhelm was certainly interested in Protestant teachings at the very least. Melanchthon told Johann Friedrich that he believed encouraging and supporting the young Wilhelm could help further the Protestant cause. He expressed his fear that if Wilhelm did not take up the Reformation, he would 'persecute like the Burgundians', meaning the Hapsburgs, with much shedding of Christian blood. That would naturally lead to unrest amongst the citizens of Cleves. The Anabaptists were restless, and Melanchthon was concerned about what baleful influence they might have on the Reformist churches.

Melanchthon believed that the Burgundian Persecution, as he called actions by the Hapsburg Holy Roman Empire, would not long be suffered by the citizens of Cleves if they had a powerful prince to protect them. Melanchthon thought that Wilhelm needed to be guided toward the cause of the Reformation, otherwise he could find himself bound to the papists. Melanchthon was worried that if Elector Johann Friedrich or his Protestant representatives did not act quickly, the papists would get to Wilhelm and turn his mind against the Reformation.

Thankfully, Melanchthon believed, Wilhelm was blessed with a certain sensibility. Melanchthon assured Elector Johann Friedrich that his young brother-in-law would easily identify any slippery approaches made by the papists. Wilhelm seemed to have his thinking aligned with the Reformist movement. Another postive: a lot of people from the Duchy of Jülich studied at the University of Wittenberg. The University was where both Luther and Melanchthon were professors. These students were ordered by the nobles to visit the local cloisters and parishes to preach the correct doctrine. It was hoped that they would find persons to further the Lutheran cause. Monks and others were forbidden from preaching in Jülich. Wilhelm seemed open to a 'visitation', like the one Melanchthon and Luther made in Saxony in the late 1520s.

Melanchthon recommended having children in Cleves and other Reform-minded duchies instructed in the religious reformed manner as prescribed in the Small Catechism. This would influence the rest of the community. He also recommended that monks should not be discouraged from returning to private life. After the reforms had been in place for a year, Melanchthon thought a general meeting amongst the German states should be held to determine matters of religion. Melanchthon acknowledged that even if a meeting were held, the Reformist movement might not win through because of the 'rough-blooded papists'.

Desiderius Erasmus

Part of Melanchthon's optimism regarding Wilhelm was probably based on knowing that both Wilhelm and Johann III corresponded with Desiderius Erasmus. Erasmus was a Catholic but enjoyed a relationship with Luther. Both men translated the Bible and were largely in agreement as to their respective translations. Erasmus died in 1536, Luther lived another ten years. Erasmus and Luther had different missions. Luther looked to reform the Church completely, whereas Erasmus wished to expand the thinking of the Church.

Erasmus wrote to Anna's brother Wilhelm on several occasions. He sent Wilhelm the preface to *Declamatio de pueris statim ac liberaliter instituendis*, on education for children, in a letter from Freiburg dated 1 July 1529. The book itself was published in September of that year. To thank him, thirteen-year-old Wilhelm sent Erasmus a silver cup in October 1529. In a second letter bearing the same date and written from the same location, Erasmus wrote to Wilhelm, 'We are both habitual hunters, distinguished prince, you in the dark woods and I in old libraries.' The letter talks of the biblical figures David and Job, Erasmus closing the letter with, 'I trust that Christ will guide your excellent nature that you will suffer neither the tears of David nor the misfortunes of Job. Yet the wise man should fortify and equip his mind for all the chances that may befall a human being.'

Erasmus sent at least one long letter to Wilhelm in 1531. Dated 26 February 1531 and written at Freiburg, it contained the introduction to *Apophthegmata*. The book was published in March 1531. Erasmus wrote to Wilhelm, then not quite fifteen years old, 'Since you accepted so amiably, most illustrious young Prince Wilhelm, and not only you, but both of your renowned parents, the two little books I sent you previously as a pledge of my loyalty to you, it seemed proper to add to them something worthy of your noble rank and more useful...' *Apophthegmata* was a collection of Greek wisdom, which Erasmus hoped would teach Wilhelm about war, peace, and morality. Erasmus told Wilhelm that the book was written 'for a young prince, and through you for all boys and young men who are pursuing liberal studies'.

Erasmian counselors helped Johann III establish a policy wherein Anabaptists were dealt with harshly and Lutherans were not threatened. Johann III's policy allowed for a moderate reform of the Catholic Church. Johann, himself a Catholic, repeatedly invited Erasmus to settle in Cleves when the Reformation was taking too strong a hold in Basel. Johann's ordinance of 1532 to 1533 put constraints on some Catholic ceremonies, called for more training and supervision for parishes, and set out that all preaching should be based on scripture. Though softening his stance toward reform, Johann still banned Lutheran writings.

It is reasonable to assume that Anna's parents sanctioned Wilhelm's reading of Erasmus's works. They would know what letters and packages were sent to their only son, the future Duke of Jülich-Cleves-Berg. By Erasmus sending his works and writing letters to the teenage Wilhelm, he was hoping to keep Wilhelm aligned with the Catholic school of thought. In light of Duke Johann of Cleves' church ordinances and Erasmian leanings,

Johann Friedrich of Saxony needed Melanchthon's report to determine whether Wilhelm viewed Lutheran teachings favourably and would make a good addition to the Schmalkaldic League. What Melanchthon reported was that the Reformation had found purchase in the United Duchies by way of Jülich to the southeast of Düsseldorf, but not to the far northwest in Cleves. Though Wilhelm had Lutheran sympathies, he ultimately chose to keep Johann III's ordinances concerning the Catholic Church and church reform as they were.

Cromwell, knowing that Wilhelm had two unmarried sisters and of his Lutheran sympathies, thought that either Anna or her younger sister Amalia would make a suitable bride for Henry VIII. During a period of distraction for the Holy Roman Emperor, Cromwell began approaching Cleves in 1538 for one of its daughters.

3

1538

Anna and, arguably, Amalia, first came to Thomas Cromwell's attention via a letter from John Hutton dated 4 December 1537. Hutton was at court in Brussels, tasked with finding matches for Henry VIII. Henry's third wife, Jane Seymour, died not two months before, on 24 October 1537. She died from complications following the birth of Henry's only legitimate son, Edward. Hutton mentioned a few ladies at court in Brussels, including Christina of Denmark, Duchess of Milan, and that Johann III had 'a daughter, but there is no great praise either of her personage or her beauty'. It is not known how Hutton came by his information, or rather, impression, nor if he was telling Cromwell about Anna or Amalia.

Antagonism between the Holy Roman Emperor Charles V and Francis I of France was simmering just below the surface in early 1538. And to the vexation of Charles V, the heirless Duke Karl of Guelders had not ordered the duchy to be handed over to Charles when Karl died. Charles determined to assert his right to Guelders, though he was tied up with other issues in his vast empire and had to leave the matter for a while.

In January 1538, it was thought that Anna's brother Wilhelm would marry Duke Anton of Lorraine's daughter, niece of Duke Karl of Guelders. Before this, Christina of Denmark was a potential match for Wilhelm. Duke Karl, who was in decline by this time, offered to give the Duchy of Guelders as dote for Anton of

Lorraine's daughter. Wilhelm was interested in gaining control over Guelders, so he no longer needed to wed Christina of Denmark if Duke Karl's niece brought Guelders into a marriage with Wilhelm. Henry instructed Sir Thomas Wyatt, English ambassador to the Imperial court, poet and alleged former lover of Anne Boleyn (probably in love with – but not a lover of) to communicate that: 'As the PROPOSED marriage of the duchess of Milan and the duke of [Cleves] and Juliers is stayed, the King might honour the said duchess by marriage, considering the reports of her.'

Christina of Denmark was part of Charles V's extended family. Charles V had four sisters and two brothers, all of whom married well. Charles's eldest sibling, Eleanor, became Queen of France. Charles himself became the Holy Roman Emperor and King of Spain. His younger sister Isabella married Christian II of Denmark, and later died in exile near Ghent at the age of twenty-four following her husband's deposition. Interestingly, she received both Protestant and Catholic communion before her death. Christina of Denmark was one of Isabella's daughters. Charles V's brother was Ferdinand, who went on to become the King of the Romans and after Charles, Holy Roman Emperor. Charles's second-youngest sister was Maria of Austria, who married Louis II of Hungary. Maria was widowed young and never remarried, and Charles appointed her his Regent of the Low Countries. Charles' youngest sister was Catherine, who became Queen of Portugal. The size of Charles's family and its grand marital alliances helped keep his position stable and free from threats.

Around 25 January 1538, Cromwell learned that 'Many of the subjects of the duke of [Guelders] have done homage to the duke of Cleves, which is here evil taken.' Duke Karl was still alive, and praising Wilhelm or Johann III as the future Duke of Guelders was out of turn. This behaviour upset the Emperor, whose representatives were 'sent to the duke of Cleves to stop this and to clear all promises made concerning the duchess of Milan'. The settlement of what would happen to Guelders once Duke Karl died was already under dispute, with Wilhelm becoming the heir apparent. Cromwell was told '[there] is a marriage concluded between the son of the duke of Lorraine and the daughter of the duke of Cleves.' It was not specified whether the daughter was Amalia or Anna, but Cromwell knew as early as January 1538 that there may have been some sort of impediment to a Cleves match for Henry.

Johann III sent ambassadors to the Imperial Court at Brussels in late April and early May 1538 to try and cement a match between Wilhelm and Christina. Duke Karl of Guelders was continuing to show poor health, and so it was looking more and more likely that Wilhelm would become the next Duke of Guelders. Johann III also sent the ambassadors to resolve the Guelders matter. Anna's family were distant relatives of Duke Karl of Guelders. The people of Guelders preferred a hereditary duke, even if he was a distant relation, to being directly under the Holy Roman Emperor.

The Hapsburg-Valois Wars

Put briefly, Francis I of France and Holy Roman Emperor Charles V engaged in bitter feuds over who had the lawful claim to the Duchy of Milan. These feuds were part of the Italian Wars, also called the Hapsburg-Valois wars. The first war between Francis I and Charles V took place from 1521 to 1526, resulting in Francis's capture. Francis signed the Treaty of Madrid on 14 January 1526 to secure his release. In it, Francis gave up his claims to Italy and Burgundy, amongst other territories. Francis's sons – the Dauphin Francis III of Brittany and the future Henry II of France – were held as security by the Emperor for several years, deeply affecting the youths. Francis, a widower, agreed to marry Charles V's sister, Eleanor.

Within about six months, there was an uprising in Milan and Francis sent his French troops to try and reclaim the duchy. A new chapter in the Italian Wars, the War of the League of Cognac, was named after a military league that Pope Clement VII tried to create to diminish the growing power of the Holy Roman Empire. The War of the League of Cognac took place from summer 1526 until 1530. During it, Charles V's uncontrollable army sacked Rome in May 1527 and held Pope Clement VII hostage.

Critically for Henry VIII, the Pope's capture thwarted his attempts to annul his marriage to Charles V's aunt, Katherine of Aragon. Henry eventually effected his annulment in 1533 after breaking with the Catholic Church, allowing him to marry Anne

Boleyn in 1533. Anne Boleyn gave Henry his second surviving daughter, Elizabeth, born 7 September 1533. Anne Boleyn was beheaded in May 1536 as the result of manufactured criminal charges against her, and her marriage to Henry annulled. Elizabeth joined her half-sister Mary, who was born on 18 February 1516, in being illegitimate. After Anne Boleyn's downfall in May 1536, Henry married Jane Seymour. Jane Seymour gave birth to the future Edward VI on 12 October 1537, only to die from post-birth complications on 24 October 1537, leaving Henry a widower with a single legitimate male heir and two illegitimate daughters.

Turning back to the War of the League of Cognac, Francis's mother Louise of Savoy and Charles's aunt Margaret of Austria negotiated the Treaty of Cambrai. Louise of Savoy and Margaret of Austria were sisters-in-law through Margaret's marriage to Louise's brother Philibert II, Duke of Savoy. Philibert died in 1504. Margaret was a widow twice over by the time she was twenty-four; she chose not to remarry and instead remained installed as Regent of the Low Countries, a position later assumed by her niece Maria of Austria. The Treaty of Cambrai, signed on 5 August 1529, is sometimes referred to as the Peace of the Ladies. Terms included Francis surrendering additional territories to Charles V and paying a hefty ransom of 2 million écus to secure the release of his sons.

Things remained relatively peaceful between Francis and the Emperor until 1536. The Emperor's niece, Christina of Denmark, married Francesco Maria Sforza on 4 May 1534, making Christina the Duchess Consort of Milan. Sforza died on 2 November 1535, leaving Christina a widow at the age of roughly fourteen. Sforza's death reignited the dispute between Charles and Francis, causing a third war.

Charles V and Francis I both attempted to keep the peace in Milan by suggesting suitors for the widowed Christina. Charles V naturally wished to reinforce the Imperial claim to Milan, and initially favoured the marriage of Christina to Prince Ludovico of Piedmont. Prince Ludovico was a cousin of Christina's. Both Christina of Denmark and Prince Ludovico could claim the Catholic monarchs Isabella and Ferdinand as their great-grandparents.

Ludovico was descended from Maria of Aragon, and Christina was descended from Isabella, who became Queen of Denmark.

All this came to naught when Ludovico died in late November 1536. In December 1536, Christina was first moved to Pavia where she remained until coming under the care of Maria, Regent of the Low Countries. Christina was suggested as a match for Henry VIII. Hans Holbein was sent in March 1538 to make a portrait of the sixteen-year-old widow. Christina and the Regent Maria considered a match with Henry rather coolly.

While the matter of Christina's widowhood and future marriage negotiations was being attended, the Emperor and Francis I were wrestling over the heirless Duchy of Milan. A French army entered Piedmont in March 1536 before capturing the City of Turin in April. The Emperor launched a counter-attack in the French territory of Provence later that summer. In the meantime, Francis's forces had gained considerable Italian support and were on the move toward Genoa. Francis had allied himself with the Ottoman Empire, who were renowned for their naval power. The Ottoman force planned an attack on the port city of Genoa. Though Genoa remained unharmed by the Ottomans and the French, the Emperor realised that trying to battle both forces would stretch his resources dangerously thin. In 1537, an Ottoman fleet harried the Italian coast, unsettling Charles.

The Truce of Nice

Charles V set out from Spain to Nice in April 1538. Along the way, his galleys encountered a few French ships, which they chased, capturing at least one. The ship was later released. Sailing on to Nice, the Spaniards were not immediately allowed entry into the town or castle, with the exception of a few Spanish officials, because the Duke of Savoy feared that Nice would be captured for the Emperor. The Pope finally landed in the area and retired to a Franciscan monastery in the French territory just beyond Nice. Charles met with the Pope there. Charles did not initially appreciate the danger in which he placed himself by going into French territory, and thereafter demanded that the Pope come to Nice. The town and castle were closed to the Emperor at this point.

Francis arrived a few days later, bringing Queen Eleanor, Charles's sister, with him. For a time, French envoys went to the Imperial court, Imperial envoys went to the French court, and both went to the Papal court. The displays of wealth and grandeur shown by these envoys and their hosts are reminiscent of the gorgeous festivities at the Field of Cloth of Gold, the meeting between Francis I and Henry VIII in 1520. Francis finally went to speak with the Pope on 2 June 1538. To be safe, Francis was accompanied by 4,000 of the Swiss Guard, half of the total force he had brought with him.

On 3 June, Charles V and a company of 2,000 Spaniards travelled to meet with Pope Paul III at the Franciscan monastery. On 4 June, Charles sent his officials to continue the conversation with the Pope. In the meantime, French officials met with Charles. On 5 June, those same French officials met with the Pope. This back-and-forth continued for the next couple of days. Queen Eleanor herself went to visit the Pope on 7 June. Charles returned to the Pope on 8 June. In the meantime, the people of Nice 'were doing great injury to all those who entered their town, and chiefly to the Spaniards'. The residents of Nice were so bold as to 'slay servants of noblemen and officials of the Emperor's court'. Exasperated, Charles threatened to set Nice on fire if the inhabitants did not cease their violent behaviour.

Queen Eleanor went to visit her brother Charles on 10 June. She was received in as grand a fashion as the Emperor could muster. Linen awnings were set up outside the palace to protect his sister and her court from the late-spring Nice sunlight. Eleanor was arriving by ship, with both the French and Spanish-Imperial ships saluting each other and discharging celebratory rounds from their guns.

Once Eleanor and her court landed, Charles 'advanced a few steps, stretched his hand to his sister, and when on the pier embraced and kissed her most affectionately, his countenance beaming with joy'. Charles and Eleanor spent such a long while there that a great crowd gathered on the pier, which 'suddenly gave way and all were precipitated into the sea, though in very shallow water, so that no one received any injury'. Charles himself fell into the water, grabbing his sister's hand and causing her to fall in. The sea carried away Charles's cap. Charles and Eleanor recovered themselves and laughed about their dip, and how ridiculous the ladies looked in their wet gowns.

Once at the palace, Charles ordered that a new gown be provided for Eleanor, but some of her ladies were faced with the prospect of wearing breeches, as that was the only dry clothing available.

In June 1538, Charles V, Francis I, and Pope Paul III met at the castle in Nice[9] to discuss a truce. Francis and Charles more or less refused to speak directly to each other, so the Pope was seen scurrying between the two monarchs to settle terms. The Truce of Nice was signed on 18 June 1538. A letter to Charles's wife, the Empress Isabella of Portugal, stated that the only good thing to come out of the Truce of Nice was that Emperor Charles would be home soon.

Brides from the Continent

By June 1538, Henry was beginning to consider a match with Anna or Amalia. It was rumoured that Henry sent Hans Holbein the Younger to produce portraits of the sisters. This was untrue, as Holbein was on his way to the Imperial Court in Brussels to create a likeness of Christina for Henry.

Karl of Egmond, Duke of Guelders, died on 30 June 1538. Upon his death, Wilhelm was created Duke of Guelders. Regent Maria was informed that 'The young duke of Cleves is sworn throughout the towns [of Guelders].' Henry now favoured a marriage between the new Duke of Guelders and the Lady Mary. There was talk of marrying a daughter of Johann's to Francis of Lorraine, nephew of Karl of Guelders. Duke Anton of Lorraine petitioned the Emperor around this time to assert his right *jure uxoris* to Guelders because he was married to Karl's twin sister Philippa. The claim came to naught.

Cromwell was told in late July 1538 that the Emperor sent 'ambassadors to the duke of Cleves, but there is small hope that they will obtain the dukedom [of Guelders]'. This was another early signal to Cromwell that things did not sit well between Charles V and Anna's father Johann, or her brother Wilhelm.

---

9   This fortress was destroyed in 1706 on the orders of Louis XIV. It is rumoured that many of the stones from this large fortress, which included a cathedral, the original site of the medieval village of Nice, and a chateau converted into a military strongpoint, now pave parts of the Promenade des Anglais.

Henry VIII was warned in August 1538 of the dispute between Charles V and Wilhelm over Guelders. He was told that, 'the duke of Cleves holdeth [Guelders] as this day, yet it's their chief head and lord and [so] all the Guelders doth take him...' The Regent Maria sent ambassadors to convince Wilhelm to turn Guelders over to the Emperor. Henry learned that at the time Wilhelm was

> ...22 years of age, very wise and hardy and much beloved. It is said that the Emperor bought of the old duke of Guelders all Gelderland, but there was no writing scaled and he has broken his covenants, so he must make a new appointment with this young duke of Cleves.

Now both Henry and Cromwell were aware of the tension between the United Duchies and the Holy Roman Empire, though neither one of them may have understood how dangerous the entanglement would become. Wilhelm's position as Duke of Guelders became the subject of dispute between the Emperor Charles V and Wilhelm for over nine years.

Wilhelm, along with Henry and the young Duke of Lorraine, was vying for the hand of Christina of Denmark in August 1538. In a letter to Charles V, Eustace Chapuys, Imperial Ambassador, addresses Cromwell's consternation at a marriage between Wilhelm and Christina.

> Two or three times, during this conversation, the King [Henry VII] said he was already too much advanced in years to wait much longer and he must press the matter of the marriages as much as he could; which assurance we can hardly reconcile with his coolness in the affair.

Henry appeared not to be dealing even-handedly with the Emperor because of his desire to find a husband for the Lady Mary. Chapuys continues:

He had formerly sought only to conclude his own and postpone the other; now he is seeking to negotiate that of the Princess [Mary] only, his object being, we think, to draw from your Majesty some declaration about Milan which would sow discord between you and Francis.

While Charles V was trying to arrange a good marriage for his niece, Christina of Denmark, other matters demanded his attention.

Cromwell was very interested in marriage negotiations concerning Christina of Denmark and Anna's brother Wilhelm. It was rumoured as early as July 1537 that Christina would marry Wilhelm. The Emperor hoped that through such a marriage, the United Duchies would remain calm and that Saxony would come into greater compliance.

Cromwell considered that the Emperor's actions in supporting the marriage of Wilhelm at a time when Henry was pursuing Christina was 'injurious' to Charles V's reputation. Chapuys responded that he did not believe it to be so, 'but that, considering the manner in which [Henry's] negotiation had been conducted, he thought the Emperor would be justified in doing so...' Chapuys wished to 'proceed to business' with Cromwell about a marriage between Henry and Christina.

Christina and her older sister Dorothea were daughters of the overthrown King of Denmark. A usurper sat on the Danish throne, and Dorothea wanted to regain it. However, any marriage between Henry and Christina required that Dorothea hand over to Christina her right to claim the throne. Chapuys believed that 'the matter should be referred to the Emperor's arbitration ... for the Emperor is far more partial towards the King than towards any other of the parties.' Cromwell persisted in his rudeness to Chapuys, saying 'that it was the Emperor, not the English, who were cold; if there were any difficulty his master would give 20,000 crowns out of his own purse.' This shows a certain desperation on the part of Henry, in apparently being willing to pay a hefty sum toward a potential bride's dowry.

Francis I was inevitably not supportive of a marriage between Wilhelm and Christina of Denmark, which would draw Wilhelm nearer to the Emperor. It was reported in September 1538 that 'neither the English nor any other would alter Francis' affection for the Emperor. Francis will not help the duke of Cleves to the proposed marriage.' Francis wanted to uphold the three-month-old Truce of Nice, but could not agree to Wilhelm's to marriage to Christina. The might of Guelders and the United Duchies posed too serious a threat to Francis.

At some point in the autmn of 1538, portraits of Anna, Wilhelm, and Amalia were made. They were likely painted by Barthel Bruyn the Elder, who was frequently employed by Johann III. It seemed that Wilhelm and Anna would find marriage matches soon, and that the twenty-one-year-old Amalia would follow shortly after. Having updated portraits of the unmarried Von der Mark siblings would be useful during negotiations.

On 6 October 1538, the young Christina of Denmark was described to Henry as, 'a goodly personage of stature higher than either of us, and competently fair, but very well favoured, a little brown'. The same letter confirms that Christina's hand was sought not only by Henry and Duke Wilhelm but also by gentlemen in France. Henry's chances of wedding the young widow were diminishing. He would have to seek another Imperial bride.

Though the marriage of Wilhelm to Christina would form a familial tie to the Emperor, it was not necessarily something which the Emperor sought, because Wilhelm was showing signs of keeping Guelders for himself. Maria of Austria, Regent of the Low Countries, said as much in a letter to her brother the Emperor in November 1538. She was unsure of the Emperor's direction when it came to any further negotiation between Wilhelm and Christina. Maria was protective over Christina, only wanting the best for her and Charles' niece.

Sir Thomas Wyatt was now an ambassador to the Imperial court. Henry sent Wyatt a letter from Hampton Court Palace on 28 November 1538, declaring that Henry believed Charles V was friendly toward him, and yet, 'how coldly he proceeds in the marriage of the lady Mary and the Infant Don [Louis].' The Emperor offered 'to give Milan to Don [Louis] and after the truce and his meeting with the French King...repeated to Wyatt that he was still willing and at liberty to fulfill his overtures'. Charles V appeared to take steps after that to settle Milan on Don Louis, but then later told Wyatt that the opportunity had passed.

Henry was unsettled by the Emperor's ongoing disposition toward the Lady Mary, his cousin. Mary's mother Katherine of Aragon was Charles V's maternal aunt through his mother Juana of Castile. The Emperor's counselors, gathered at the Regent's court, 'expressed surprise at the request that the lady Mary should be taken in that degree in which she stands by the laws of the realm, to succeed only in default of lawful issue, and thought the Emperor would refuse it, if only for the honour of Don [Louis]'. Additionally, Henry required that Don Louis swear an oath, 'that in the event of his succeeding to the throne [of England] he would observe inviolate the laws of this realm'. This was considered a peculiar request by the Imperial counselors – 'such an oath beforehand was not customary.' Henry wished for the Lady Mary to wed Don Louis and gain Milan, but would not allow Don Louis to break or presumably change any laws of England if he succeeded to the throne. The counselors thought that the Emperor would never accept a match within that framework; and especially as the Lady Mary had been declared illegitimate when Henry had his marriage to Katherine of Aragon annulled.

Henry believed that the Emperor objected to a marriage between the Lady Mary and Don Louis because they were too closely related. Henry's next move was to have Wyatt suggest Mary as a potential bride for Wilhelm. That would leave Christina free to marry Henry. If Charles V did not wish to match Mary with Wilhelm, then Wyatt was supposed to suggest the Duke of Urbino. Wyatt was supposed to discourage any of the Emperor's aspirations surrounding a large estate for Mary, should she marry Don Ludovico.

On 1 December 1538, Wyatt reported that Duke Johann III was sending an ambassador from Cleves to England. It was thought that the ambassador could give better information to Henry about the Emperor's intentions surrounding Mary's and

Christina's suitors. Charles V wrote to his sister Maria of Austria, Regent of the Netherlands, a few days later, saying that should they not make any headway with England or Cleves they should see what could be arranged with Lorraine. He was likely talking about Christina's future.

By New Year's Eve 1538, the French ambassador to the English court, Castillon, believed that something had gone wrong for Francis I over the match with Cleves. It seemed that around this time, Henry was beginning to prefer the friendship, or at least political alliance with, Emperor Charles V. That meant that Henry would ideally seek to marry either Christina of Denmark, or another woman from the Holy Roman Empire. Anna became that woman.

4

JANUARY–JUNE 1539

The year 1539 began with suspicion in the Holy Roman Empire over Henry purportedly building preliminary alliances with Cleves, Denmark, the Elector of Saxony, and the Landgrave of Hesse, thus effectively, the Schmalkaldic League. In England, Cromwell was sorting out marriage treaties for Henry's eldest daughter and for Henry.

Maria of Austria, Queen of Hungary and Regent of the Low Countries, was not interested in seeing her niece, Christina of Denmark, married off too quickly. Maria hosted Christina at her court and Maria's permission was needed for any marriage proposals. Thomas Wriothesley, the English ambassador to the Imperial court, praised the wisdom of Christina. Wriothesley believed that Christina was more inclined to a marriage with Henry VIII because he was King of England, rather than with Francis of Lorraine or Wilhelm of Cleves. Neither Francis of Lorraine nor Wilhelm were yet Dukes Regnant of their respective territories, as the fathers of both young men were alive in January 1539. Maria prevaricated on the question of Henry by saying she had to wait for guidance from her brother, the Holy Roman Emperor Charles V.

On receipt of the King's letters we spoke with [Maria], but could not induce her to further treaty till she hear again out of Spain... I know some of them labour to avert the Duchess's mind from the King and rest herself upon [Francis of] Lorraine[10] or [Wilhelm of] Cleves. But [Christina] seems wiser than they, and would rather remain a widow than from the likelihood of being a queen to fall so low and be an underling, as she must be if she marry either of them, their parents being alive... If the King is determined this way, he must give days of payment for the 100,000 *crs.* of her dote; for money is here and in Spain so 'dainty' that the Emperor would leave both his cousins (sic) [Christina of Denmark, Duchess of Milan and Princess Mary Tudor] unmarried rather than part with that sum.

If Henry hoped to marry Christina, he had to be both patient and willing to expend a large sum of money.

On 9 January 1539 Eustace Chapuys, the Imperial Ambassador to England, reported a conversation with Thomas Cromwell earlier in the month whilst the two were at mass. Cromwell, who assisted Henry's suit for Christina of Denmark's hand, said to Chapuys that he

...wondered at [the Emperor's] coolness about the marriage of the King with the duchess of Milan, and that he saw clearly that [the Emperor] wished to bestow her on the son of Cleves and of Lorraine. I said it would be a fine thing if he could give her to both and make of one daughter two sons-in-law; but, joking apart, he ought to presume [that the Emperor] knew the difference between the said lord (Henry) and the said matches (*partys*), provided the conditions offered were equal.

Chapuys believed at the time that Henry sought an alliance between England and Cleves by wedding Lady Mary to Anna's brother Wilhelm. Furthermore, Chapuys believed that Henry would give Wilhelm a large amount of money for the purpose of warring with

10 To whom Anna was previously betrothed.

Charles V. Henry was despairing of his suit to gain Christina's hand, and hoped that marrying Lady Mary to Wilhelm would give Henry the strength to face the Emperor, should the need arise. Even worse in Chapuys' eyes, Henry sent his various masters of artillery to Guisnes, Calais and the Scottish frontier, amongst other places, to examine and prepare those areas for battle.

Anna Becomes a Candidate

Henry sent instructions on 20 January 1539 to Christopher Mount, then in Germany, ordering Mount to visit the Duke of Saxony, regardless of where that duke was. It seems that Henry was talking about Johann Friedrich, who held the dual titles of Elector and Duke of Saxony.

If meeting Johann Friedrich proved difficult, Mount was then to seek out Burckhardt, the Vice-Chancellor of Saxony, to arrange a meeting with the Duke of Saxony. Next, Mount was to

> ...present the King's letters credential, and say the King thanks the Duke and ...[that] His Majesty marvels that since the Duke's orators went from hence with favourable weather and were soon home, he has had no answer upon the communications had with them here. Moreover, it is said that the Duke intends to alter certain leagues and that the Emperor has said he trusts the princes of Germany will be conformable to the rest of Christendom; the King wishes to know the Duke's mind upon the matters reported by his orators and also upon this.

Here, Henry is worried that Johann Friedrich would revert to the old Catholicism. Mount was 'to find out the inclination which both dukes of Cleves, [Johann III and Wilhelm], bear to the bishop of Rome; he shall also enquire, in case they are still of the old popish fashion, whether they will be inclinable to alter their opinions.'

In early 1539, it was not clear to Henry whether Anna's family was Catholic or whether, perhaps through the marriage of Sybylla of Cleves and Johann-Friedrich, Elector of Saxony, the Von der Marks were inclined toward Protestantism. It would not be meet for Henry to wed Lady Mary to another Catholic, especially considering that Mary was the granddaughter of the proud and formidable Catholic Monarchs, Ferdinand and Isabella.

Cromwell sent his own instructions to Mount on the same day, again directing Mount to speak with Vice-Chancellor Burckhardt. Burckhardt previously represented the Duke of Saxony in England, and apparently he had discussed with Cromwell the prospect of a marriage between Anna's brother Wilhelm and the Lady Mary. Cromwell assumed by Henry's facial expression that Henry approved of the idea. Cromwell added that, although Henry was willing to go to great lengths for the Duke of Saxony, he would not give any approval of the marriage until the Duke of Saxony was ready to make a formal proposal. Cromwell directed Mount to

> ...diligently enquire of the beauty and qualities of the eldest of the two [unmarried] daughters of the duke of Cleves, her shape, stature, and complexion, and, if he hear she is such 'as might be likened unto his Majesty,' he shall tell [Burckhardt] that Cromwell, tendering the King's alliance in Germany, would be glad to induce the King to join with them, specially for the duke of Saxony's sake, who is allied there [with the Von der Mark family], and to make a cross marriage between the young duke of Cleves and lady Mary, and the King and the elder daughter of Cleves.

Typical of Henry's wishes, Cromwell instructs Mount, 'First it is expedient that they should send [Anna's] picture hither.' Henry wanted to see if his potential future queen was attractive.

A little more than a week later, on 28 January 1539, Mount arrived in Antwerp. Mount learned that a Diet would be held in Frankfurt during Lent, with the Emperor and the Evangelic (Schmalkaldic) League. Mount set off to see the Duke of Saxony as quickly as he could. He tells Cromwell about the Cleves and Guelders situation:

Nothing is said about the duchy of Guelders, and it is thought that the duke of Cleves will take peaceful possession of it. The Emperor has certainly written to all the Electors to obtain the duchy, and on the other hand the duke of Cleves has referred his claim to the Electors. Perhaps the case will be committed to twelve men.

An account given to Michael Mercator in Brussels on 3 February 1539 gives an idea of the citizens of Guelders' feelings towards Anna's brother: 'I hear that Guelders is tired of its lord, and, moreover, that he does not come into the country.' The citizens of Guelders began paying homage to Wilhelm a year before. They had seen little of him since then and had had no meaningful actions taken on their behalf.

On 6 February 1539, Anna's father, Johann III, through whose marriage with Maria the united the Duchies of Jülich-Cleves-Berg were created, passed away. This left the twenty-three-year-old Wilhelm as Duke of the United Duchies, and of Guelders. The land and river sections controlled by Duke Wilhelm now allowed him to block the flow of commerce or movement of troops, if he so wished.

The possibility of Charles V using military force to claim Guelders was very serious by March 1539. In the Low Countries around this time it was heard that, 'the [Diet in Frankfurt] have sent for the [Duke of Cleves]... Some say they are to go against England, others against the [Duke of Cleves] and Guelders.' The purpose of calling Wilhelm to Frankfurt seemed clear: Wilhelm could either peacefully surrender Guelders, or suffer the consequences. Charles V

...must have of the land of Brabant and Holland 15,000 guldens and of Flanders 28,000 to be paid in two years, professedly for an expedition against [Guelders]. The towns are content to pay the money but will not deliver it to the Emperor, preferring it to be placed in four men's hands of their own choosing ... for they will not have war against England.

This correspondence indicates that in early 1539 the Emperor was considering going to war with England, too. The mutual threat to England and Cleves pushed the marital alliance along; but the way in which King Henry would address a threat from the Emperor was very different from how the new Duke Wilhelm would behave.

Cromwell was encouraged by the Elector of Saxony's support of an alliance between England and Cleves. Cromwell informed Henry on 18 March that he

...this morning received letters from Chr. Mount and Thos. Paynel, written at Frankfort on the 5th, reporting an interview of Mount ... with the duke of Saxony. He promised for the love he bore to the King to do his best to advance 'this honest affair' ... when he met with the other Princes.

Johann Friedrich found a marriage between one of the Von der Mark daughters and Henry to be good politically, religiously, and militarily. Johann Friedrich 'agreed that the matter required speed'.

Mount made an effort to obtain a portrait of the elder daughter, Anna. Johann Friedrich promised to send send one, but said his painter Lucas Cranach, Court Painter to Saxony, 'was sick at home'. Mount passed along that: 'Everyone praises the lady's beauty, both of face and body. One said she excelled the Duchess [Christina of Denmark] as the golden sun did the silver moon.' This report of Anna, if true, was certainly positive, and it shows that she was regarded by her own people as attractive. Cromwell was hoping Lucas Cranach the Elder, court painter to Anna's sister Sybylla's court, would be able to make a new portrait of Anna and send it to Henry. Cranach and his workshop executed numerous portraits of Sybylla during her time as Duchess of Saxony, including Sybylla's engagement portrait from 1526.

Cromwell received disturbing news from around 24 March from Antwerp. War was predicted. The Empire would attack Denmark, England, or Guelders – though the threat to England was not considered realistic. The report stated:

The duke of Cleves shall have the duchess of [Milan], and ambassadors are expected from Cleves this day at the court of Burgundy, but the [Emperor] is certainly determined to have Guelders for the House of Burgundy whether the duke of Cleves have this lady or not.

Charles V was actively doing something about it.

Artillery is made daily in Antwerp and all the spiritualty in the Emperor's lands are assessed to an enormous sum of money to maintain the war; yet they pay much more to the Pope; still they would be content to pay it all to avenge the Pope's quarrel against the king of England.

There was a real fear in spring 1539 that Charles V was willing to attack England over the break with the Catholic Church. Henry was excommunicated by the Pope on 17 December 1538, potentially exposing England to Catholic military threats. With this and the Guelders controversy, Cromwell saw an ally in the United Duchies who could help England contain the Empire's might.

The political intrigues of Cromwell's agents Paynell and Mount in Frankfurt had not made much headway by early April. The negotiations between Cleves and England were put in front of Johann Friedrich, Elector of Saxony, but Payne and Mount did not receive any sort of response. Members of the Schmalkaldic League were the only ones allowed in to speak with the Elector of Saxony. The peace upon which the Emperor and the Elector of Saxony, amongst others, agreed in Nuremberg would be of benefit to no one outside the Schmalkaldic League. Payne and Mount interpreted this as a move by Johann Friedrich and the Schmalkaldic League to purposefully exclude England from the Peace of Nuremberg. One of the terms included that no new members could be added to the Schmalkaldic League until at least 1540.

Better news, Duke Wilhelm's ambassadors seemed supportive of Henry's suit to marry Anna. Wilhelm sent representatives to Saxony to receive Johann Friedrich's input. Charles V was trying to appease the powerful Elector of Saxony, who was willing to uphold the terms of the Peace of Nuremberg. This meant that Henry might have to wait if he wanted to join the Schmalkaldic League, even if he married Anna within the next year.

The Emperor on the Move; and his Great Loss

Cromwell learned that war with the Holy Roman Empire was a viable threat to Cleves and possibly England in mid-April. Henry learned, 'The Bishop of Lunde[11] ... has advised the Emperor not to make war against England till he has broken the power of [England's] friends in Denmark, Cleves, and Almayn.'[12] Worse yet, the Emperor Charles V was moving his army and it appeared to be headed for Germany.

Stephen Vaughan, a merchant and English diplomat in the Low Countries, was a servant of Cromwell's. Vaughan relayed to Cromwell intelligence about the Emperor moving his troops into Germany. The troops were to be provisioned with plenty of pikes and gunpowder. The Imperial Admiral from Genoa, Andria Doria, was also on the move with the Venetian fleet.

At this time, the Holy League created by Pope Paul III in 1538 consisting of the Holy Roman Empire, the Republic of Venice, the Papacy, Spain, and the Maltese Knights, was warring with the Ottoman Empire. The Ottomans were encroaching on Hungary and the eastern coast of Italy. Though the Imperial forces being present in Germany certainly seemed threatening, the fact that they were meeting up in the Archbishopric of Lühnde was significant. At that point, the Imperial Army could head north to Denmark and make good on the Emperor's threat, or head southeast to defend against the Turks.

Cromwell was further informed of rumours circulating around Brussels. It was thought that the Emperor would wed Christina to Duke Wilhelm and provide an additional sum for her dowry, quite a lot more, if only Duke Wilhelm would give up Guelders. Overall, the feeling in Brussels at the time was that Duke Wilhelm would wed the Lady Mary. The people of Brussels were quite impressed with the celerity shown by Henry in assembling provisions, should England be attacked by Charles V; it was believed that neither the Emperor nor

---

11 Lühnde, Lower Saxony, Germany; in the northern middle part of Germany, between the United Duchies where Anna lived and the Saxon territories where her sister Sybylla lived.

12 Germany

Francis I of France could gather together so much might in such a small amount of time. And Henry was indeed bracing himself for war.

Charles had no real desire to go against Henry. The Imperial ships amassing at that time were not destined for the English coast. Charles V was hopeful of peacefully settling matters with Cleves. A six-month peace between the Germans and the Emperor was agreed upon by late April 1539. The Emperor was tied up with the intrigues of Francis I, who had just made peace with the Turks. The Venetians abandoned the Holy League, too, wiping out a substantial part of the Holy League's skilled naval force. Francis I was not terribly interested in a six-month peace, and wished to challenge Charles V in his pursuit of the Duchy of Milan.

Burckhardt, Vice Chancellor of Saxony, arrived in England with other German dignitaries on 28 April 1539. It was thought that Henry wished to discuss a marriage between the Lady Mary and Anna's oldest nephew by her sister, Sybylla, Johann Friedrich II. On May Day 1539, Marillac wrote to Francis I's agent, Anne de Montmorency, that Henry was well pleased with Francis's disposition toward him. Henry took great comfort in knowing that Francis had no desire to move against England anytime soon.

The relief of the English court was palpable. To show Henry's amity with the French, Henry invited Francis's ambassador Charles de Marillac to his chambers. Henry and Marillac conversed for two hours. Henry felt assured of the Germans. The Emperor, however, was aboard a ship from Spain bound for Flanders. It was generally agreed at the time that the Emperor's attention would be concentrated on the various disputes over territory and religion in Germany. As a failsafe, Henry prepared England's defences.

Tragedy struck the formidable, thirty-nine-year old Holy Roman Emperor Charles V on 1 May 1539: his beloved wife, the thirty-five-year old Empress Isabella of Portugal, passed away. She gave birth prematurely to a stillborn boy around 21 April 1539 and never recovered. Empress Isabella was much adored and respected by her husband, and she frequently acted as Regent of Spain when

Charles V was out of the country. A reputedly very beautiful, intelligent woman, she gave Charles V three surviving legitimate children: Philip II of Spain, the Holy Roman Empress Maria, and Joanna, Princess of Portugal.

Charles V was so grief-stricken by the loss of Isabella that he locked himself away in a monastery for the summer of 1539. When he re-emerged, Charles refused for the rest of his life to wear anything but black, or to remarry. Posthumous paintings and statues of Isabella were commissioned by Charles.[13] For Anna, the Emperor's grief and seclusion meant a temporary cessation of aggression against her brother, allowing for progress in negotiations for Anna's marriage.

On 2 May 1539, it was not yet known that the Emperor had suffered such a monumental loss. The various cardinals serving Charles V had yet to hear any guidance from him about the situation with England. Cardinal Reginald Pole, an enemy of Henry's, was informed by Charles that the time was not yet ripe to attack England. The Emperor was tied up with matters in the Low Countries, and was concerned over how the Lutherans would behave if England was attacked or even defeated by the Holy Roman Empire. Ultimately, the Emperor gave Cardinal Pole the impression that he deferred to Francis I's opinion on the matter.

Charles's sister, Maria, Regent of the Low Countries, was preoccupied with news coming out of Germany. The Diet of Frankfurt settled that the German princes would bar any new members to the Schmalkaldic League or any 'Confederation of Religion' until the autumn of 1540. It was thought that by then a new confederation could be created that would better advance the German princes' religious aspirations. This meant that Henry was not guaranteed a partnership with the Elector of Saxony, amongst others, even if he married Anna.

Maria, Regent of the Low Countries, summoned Duke Wilhelm to Brussels in late April, wishing to settle the Guelders matter. Wilhelm

---

13 Charles V died in 1558, likely of malaria. Isabella and her husband were finally reunited in death and laid to rest at the Basilica in El Escorial in 1574. They were later removed to the Royal Pantheon of Kings at El Escorial in 1654, though the gorgeous tomb in the Basilica remains.

demurred and instead sent Chancellor Johann Hograve. Chancellor Olisleger and the Marshal of Cleves later departed for Brussels to join Hograve. After the Brussels meeting, Chancellor Olisleger returned to Cleves and was supposed to meet with Cromwell's men Nicholas Wotton and Richard Berde. Olisleger never showed. Wotton and Berde did not receive any communication from Olisleger until late in the evening, when they were asked to stay an additional day. The men complied, and around 1 May, they were delivered a message from Duke Wilhelm through Chancellor Olisleger.

The response given to Wotton and Berde, full of the usual euphuistic diplomatic language, was ultimately no answer at all. Olisleger informed the gentlemen why Duke Wilhelm could not come to meet with them himself, then told the men that Wilhelm was concerned as to how big a dowry would be required by Henry VIII, should either Anna or Amalia marry him. Wilhelm wanted to know what security his sister would enjoy in England as a Dowager Queen, and under what terms Henry would agree to an alliance with Wilhelm.

The question of what provisions would be made for either Anna or Amalia should they outlive Henry shows the care and concern Wilhelm had for his sisters. Henry was born in 1491, Anna in 1515, and Amalia in 1517. It was probable that, barring any issues with childbirth complications or some other catastrophe, Henry's chosen Duchess of Cleves would outlive him. Without answers to these questions, Wilhelm could not begin to consider offering one of them as a bride to Henry.

To show his goodwill, or his seriousness in entering an Anglo-Cleves alliance, Wilhelm sent portraits of Anna and Amalia to England. These were the portraits painted by Barthel Bruyn in late 1538. The painting of Anna is now in the possession of the Rosenbach Museum in Philadelphia, Pennsylvania, and has a blue background. Trinity College Cambridge possesses a portrait of an Unknown Woman with a yellow-orange background, who could be Amalia. The unknown woman is wearing a forehead cloth that says, 'A Bon Fine', which is identical to the cloth which Anna is wearing in the famous Holbein Portrait that hangs in the Louvre. This same forehead cloth is a feature in the Anna of Cleves portrait held by St John's College Oxford, though that portrait was made in the late 16th century, after Anna's death. The St John's portrait combines features of the Rosenbach and Louvre portraits, and there exist other portraits very similar to the one at St John's. The portrait of Wilhelm has a blue background like Anna's, making it more difficult to decide whether the Trinity portrait is indeed Amalia.

Olisleger gave Wotton and Berde the excuse that Wilhelm did not have an opportunity, try as he might, to meet with his powerful brother-in-law, Johann Friedrich. As per the 1526 alliance between Cleves and Saxony, the Elector's input was required for any proposed marital arrangements for Anna or Amalia. Wotton and Berde scoffed at this, reasoning that men such as Wilhelm and Johann Friedrich were too busy to meet with each other in person. After all, Vice Chancellor Burckhardt of Saxony had already met with Johann Friedrich. When he was in Frankfurt, Burckhardt spoke to the English Ambassador and the Cleves Ambassador about Johann Friedrich's consent to the Anglo-Cleves alliance.

Wotton and Berde became even more exasperated because they knew that Burckhardt already gave Johann Friedrich's advice to Wilhelm. Moreover, Wotton and Berde reasoned, no lengthy deliberation was needed because wedding either Anna or Amalia to Henry would be a great honour to the United Duchies and Von der Mark family. It was unnecessary for Henry to make a full declaration of his intent to marry Anna or Amalia before the details of the Anglo-Cleves alliance were agreed, as Wilhelm had so much to gain by the marriage.

After this unpleasantness, the men turned the discussion back to the portraits of Anna and Amalia. They said Henry was more interested in Anna, though the king was content to receive the portraits of both women. However, neither Wotton nor Berde had seen either Anna or Amalia, so they could not confirm the accuracy of the portraits. Olisleger, after doing his best to reassure Wotton and Berde of Wilhelm's sincere intent, attested to the accuracy of the portraits. As is famously known, Wotton and Berde whined that they had only seen Anna and Amalia in heavy garments such that only a minuscule part of the sisters' faces could be seen, to which Olisleger wryly inquired whether the men should be allowed to see the Duchesses of Cleves in the nude. Olisleger warned that Wilhelm would be most displeased to learn of Wotton and Berde's reaction to Wilhelm's message.

The conversation next touched upon the suggestion that representatives of Wilhelm, given full power to negotiate and enter into agreements, should go to England to formally offer Anna to Henry VIII. The matter should not require much consideration by Wilhelm, who could then reasonably demand a declaration of Henry's intent to marry Anna. It would only take five or six days for Henry's declaration to reach Wilhelm, and another five or six days for Henry to receive Wilhelm's affirmation. Wotton and Berde were reasoning that the matter of Anna's marriage should not take more than a fortnight for Henry and Wilhelm to decide.

Though certainly interested in a marriage between Anna and Henry, Wilhelm just could not spare the representatives to go to England. He needed some delegates to stay in the United Duchies, with a couple specifically in Guelders, a delegation to the Diet of Worms, and his highest-ranking officials to Brussels, including Olisleger. It would be another couple of weeks before Wilhelm could send anyone to England.

Henry's ambassadors then inquired as to whether Anna was truly free to marry their master. They were aware of the old agreement between Anna's father Johann III and Anton of Lorraine, father of Francis of Lorraine. As far as the English ambassadors knew, a sum of money was given to Karl of Guelders to support the alliance. Other payments were made to Anton too. Johann did everything required of him except have Anna actually marry Francis of Lorraine. To that end, it could be assumed that Anna was as good as married. But Olisleger knew the details of the original arrangement and its termination, and explained that the agreement was only between Johann and Anton, and that Anna had not agreed to the marriage. In other words, because Anna had not consented to wed Francis of Lorraine, the betrothal was never finalised. Anna was free to marry. Liking this response, Wotton and Berde suggested that Anna should then be offered in marriage to Henry, seeing as how Anton of Lorraine had not kept faith with Johann. It had, after all, been about twelve years. Wotton and Berde reasoned that they heard that Francis of Lorraine was married to a French princess. If Francis was free to marry, then so was Anna. However, Olisleger had not yet heard any news of the marriage of Francis of Lorraine, musing that it must have happened rather recently, if at all.

The Elector of Saxony was already determined that he would resolve any outstanding issue of Anna's incomplete betrothal with Francis of Lorraine, along with trying to end the Guelders controversy. Unfortunately, it proved difficult to assemble Elector Johann-Friedrich of Saxony, Duke Anton of Loraine, and Duke Wilhelm of Cleves. Johann-Friedrich endeavoured to meet with Anton immediately to formally end the incomplete engagement of Anna. These attempts at progress for Anna's hand in marriage, designed to help Henry, were met with scorn by Berde and Wotton. They again accused Wilhelm of causing delays. Olisleger, who was becoming exasperated with these English ambassadors, reminded them that it would be foolish for Duke Wilhelm to negotiate Anna's marriage with Henry at a time when she had any kind of previous entanglement. This cut no ice with Berde and Wotton, believing as they did that Francis of Lorraine had already married a French princess. Hoping to appease the ambassadors, Olisleger offered to take a moment so he could meet with other Cleves officials who had returned with him from Brussels.

The members of Wilhelm's council came up with two options for Wotton and Berde: first, they could stay in the United Duchies until Wilhelm himself returned from Brussels and have the portraits of Anna and Amalia sent ahead to England, after which ambassadors of Cleves would be sent to Henry; or second, Berde and Wotton could leave for England with the portraits in their possession, and Henry could expect an answer from Wilhelm as soon as he returned from Brussels. The ambassadors chose the first option since Henry had not recalled them yet. The answer given, Chancellor Olisleger recommended that the men bide their time in Cologne, which was closer to Düsseldorf and the ducal seat.[14]

After some discussion as to whether Wilhelm would swiftly send ambassadors to England, Olisleger assured them that Wilhelm

---

14 Cleves is about 95 kilometres from Düsseldorf, whereas Cologne is only about 45.

would so do as soon as he could. Olisleger himself was working toward the goal of sending ambassadors to England in the very near future. Wilhelm would give his answer to Henry as soon as he could. Shortly after the conversation between Wotton, Berde, and Olisleger concluded, Olisleger and other Cleves court officials departed for Brussels.

By early May, Wotton and Berde had formed some opinions about the situation with Emperor Charles V. They believed that Charles would be willing to accept a very large sum of money from Wilhelm in exchange for the Emperor renouncing his claim to Guelders, assuming that Charles would not try to take Guelders by force. This would mean peace between Wilhelm and Charles V – in which case there would be no reason for Anna to marry Henry and create the Anglo-Cleves alliance. Another possibility was that Wilhelm would marry Christina of Denmark and Wilhelm would give any dowry received from Christina to Charles V, along with additional monies. This would have the same result: Charles V would give up his claim to Guelders.

But, there was a third possibility, about which Berde and Wotton warned Cromwell: it seemed it was not yet too late for Duke Anton of Lorraine to fulfil his end of the marriage contract between Anna and Francis of Lorraine. Duke Anton, whose son Francis claimed a right to Guelders through his mother Philippa, could request that Wilhelm pay additional monies to Anton. Anton and Francis would then relinquish their rights to Guelders, and seal the agreement with the marriage of Anna and Francis. Anna's heirs would hold a claim to Guelders thereafter. However, this would require Johann Friedrich's blessing. Up to this point, the Elector of Saxony appeared to be in favour of the Anglo-Cleves alliance. But Wilhelm could choose to honour his father's agreement with Duke Anton.

Wotton and Berde then told Cromwell, significantly, 'as for my [Lady Anna] he knows well enough that her beauty will [get her] a good husband, though she have not the Duke of [Lorraine's] son at all.' Anna's beauty would get her a good husband. Anna's elder sister Sybylla was reported to be a great beauty, and Anna had that reputation as well. Wotton and Berde acknowledged that one or none of these situations could occur, but that it was important to consider all the possibilities. Berde and Wotton left Cleves around 10 May 1539 for Cologne. They stopped in Düsseldorf hoping to meet with Duke Wilhelm. The men looked forward to receiving the portraits of Anna and Amalia, which they promised Cromwell would be delivered to England with speed.

The Six Articles

At Westminster, Parliament was sitting by the end of April 1539, the first time in three years. In attendance, other than King Henry and his many lords, were representatives from Saxony and other German territories. The relationship between Henry and his former nephew Charles V was beginning to warm, with the renewed cordiality influencing one of the most important outcomes of that parliament, the Statute of Six Articles, an 'Act Abolishing Diversity of Opinions'.

In late April to early May, Anna's brother made his first formal moves against Charles V by sending letters to the people of Ghent, who of late had asked Francis I to be their sovereign instead of Charles V. Wilhelm explained to the people of Ghent why it was he, and not the Emperor, who lawfully inherited Guelders. Wilhelm went so far as to ask Ghent to refuse any help to the Emperor in the event of war between him and Duke Wilhelm. Francis I turned down the offer to be the sovereign of Ghent and informed Charles of Ghent's request, and Ghent dutifully forwarded Wilhelm's letters to Charles V. Francis I and Charles V were at this time peaceful with one another, unwilling to act without each other's consent. This, in turn, gave some hope to the Pope that France and the Holy Roman Empire might move together against England. This was another piece of logical support for the Anglo-Cleves match.

By the middle of May 1539, the dukes of Saxony were requesting aid from Henry VIII. Wilhelm had entered the German City of Münster. To the east of Cleves territories, Münster was controlled by Anna's paternal Aunt Anna, her family, and Aunt Anna's brother-in-law, Franz von Waldeck, Bishop-Prince of Münster, Osnabrück and Minden. If rumours were true, then this action by Wilhelm was in open rebellion against Charles V. Guns were seen being taken toward Münster. Come the end of May 1539, negotiations for Wilhelm's marriage to Christina of Denmark clearly stalled. Charles V was still in mourning over the death of Empress Isabella, and keeping himself secluded.

It was widely known by this point that Charles would do everything in his power to wrest Guelders from Anna's brother. The Empire's soldiers were without direction and after roughing up a couple of cities in Germany, ultimately disbanded and went home. Wilhelm was holding a parliament during the week of 11 June 1539 to sort out how best to move forward for the safety and prosperity of the United Duchies.

In the first half of 1539, the German princes enjoyed amity with Francis. It did not last. Francis double-crossed the German princes at the Diet of Frankfurt when it became known that he would support the Emperor. As a reaction, the German princes dispatched their ambassadors to Henry VIII's court.

In early June, the Statute of the Six Articles was made law in England. Introduced by Thomas Howard, Duke of Norfolk, the Statute of the Six Articles was a blow to Thomas Cromwell.

First, that in the most blessed Sacrament of the Altar, by the strength and efficacy of Christ's mighty word, it being spoken by the priest, is present really, under the form of bread and wine, the natural body and blood of Our Saviour Jesu Christ, conceived of the Virgin Mary, and that after the consecration there remaineth no substance of bread and wine, nor any other substance but the substance of Christ, God and man;

Secondly, that communion in both kinds is not necessary ad salutem, by the law of God, to all persons; and that it is to be believed, and not doubted of, but that in the flesh, under the form of the bread, is the very blood; and with the blood, under the form of the wine, is the very flesh; as well apart, as though they were both together.

Thirdly, that priests after the order of priesthood received, as afore, may not marry, by the law of God.

Fourthly, that vows of chastity or widowhood, by man or woman made to God advisedly, ought to be observed by the law of God; and that it exempts them from other liberties of Christian people, which without that they might enjoy.

Fifthly, that it is meet and necessary that private masses be continued and admitted in this the King's English Church and Congregation, as whereby good Christian people, ordering themselves accordingly, do receive both godly and goodly consolations and benefits; and it is agreeable also to God's law.

Sixthly, that auricular confession is expedient and necessary to be retained and continued, used and frequented in the Church of God...

It is therefore ordained and enacted ... And be it further enacted ... that if any person or persons ... contemn or contemptuously refuse, deny, or abstain to be confessed at the time commonly accustomed within this realm and Church of England, or contemn or contemptuously refuse, deny, or abstain to receive the holy and blessed sacrament above said at the time commonly used and accustomed for the same, that then every such offender shall suffer such, imprisonment and make such fine and ransom to the King our Sovereign Lord and his heirs as by his Highness or by his or their Council shall be ordered and adjudged in that behalf; And if any such offender ... do eftsoons ... refuse ... to be confessed or to be communicate ... that then every such offence shall be deemed and adjudged felony, and the offender ... shall suffer pains of death and lose and forfeit all his ... goods, lands, and tenements, as in cases of felony.

Of most offence to the Ambassadors of Saxony was the prohibition on marriage for priests. This realigned religion in England with the Catholic Church, situating religious concerns more in line with Catholic France and the Catholic Empire, and much less so with Protestant Germany. And on 8 June 1539, in a gesture of respect to Charles V, Henry had a service performed for the deceased Empress Isabella and he wore mourning clothes. Despite these outward signs, Henry had over one hundred of his ships prepared for war and was continuing work on fortifications.

Desperately, after the passing of the Six Articles, Cromwell sent instructions to Wotton in Cleves to press the matter of Anna. Wotton was directed to meet with Anna's mother Maria first, then Duke Wilhelm. Cromwell determined it preferable that Wotton should meet with Maria and Wilhelm at the same time. Specifically, Wotton was to tell Maria and Wilhelm

> ...that the King not only esteeming the honour of the house of Cleves and [especially] of the Duchess, and the Duke now being of the [same head] but also conceiving from Wotton's advertisements upon the last discourses between him and the [Chancellor Olisleger that] the said Duchess and Duke do bear [very hearty] and entire love and affection towards the [King's] Majesty and would be glad to make demonstration of their [good] wills and inclinations by some conjunction and knot of marriage ... thanks them for their gentle disposition, which shall prove well employed.

Cromwell desired Wotton to do everything in his power to learn from Maria what the decision was regarding Anna marrying Henry. Concerning the matter of the outstanding marriage pact made by Anna's father and Anton of Lorraine, Henry was willing to overlook this if proof could be given that Cleves had otherwise legally withdrawn. Wotton was to encourage speedy resolution of the outstanding pact. Henry wanted twenty-three-year-old Anna, and not the twenty-one-year-old Amalia. Once Wotton had an opportunity to review the relevant legal documents, Henry would send others with the power to conclude the marriage negotiation.

Cromwell wanted Wotton to use flattery when speaking to Maria, to tell her that 'the King has heard of her virtue and wisdom, and other things to her praise, as shall seem to the purpose.' Cromwell told Wotton that he must see the documents cancelling Anna's Lorraine entanglement. If Maria and Wilhelm stated that Anna was bound to Lorraine, then Wotton must protest by stating that Olisleger did not present the situation as such. Overall, Cromwell wanted Wotton to continue asking for proof that Anna was completely unavailable, and threaten delay by referring back to Henry if only Amalia was available. If Wotton discovered after extended inquiry that Anna was indeed still bound to Francis of Lorraine and only Amalia was offered after these attempts, then Wotton should give the impression that Henry would be just as pleased with Amalia as with Anna.

No matter what, the men should try their utmost to see Anna and Amalia, one of whom would be the future Queen Consort of England. If the portraits were not sent yet, then Wotton should demand a look at them and send reports as to their accuracy. Finally, concerning payment of Anna's dowry, 'the King prefers virtue and friendship to money.' That must have been music to Wilhelm's ears: he was already preparing for the ruinously expensive possibility of war against the Holy Roman Empire over Guelders. Now he could focus on funnelling his funds into that enterprise rather than paying money as a dowry to the King of England.

By the end of June 1539, Henry VIII seemed anxious over the plans Charles V and Francis I had for England. It was obvious in Henry's mind that something was afoot. It was at times difficult to discern whether Charles was interested in attacking England because of the impending Cleves-England-Saxony alliance, or if Charles was amassing his fleet betwixt Spain and Flanders because of the threatening Ottoman Empire, or the brief revolt of the City of Ghent.

Henry approved of the Six Articles, which could smooth over religious concerns with France and the Holy Roman Empire, but distanced England from Saxony. Anna's brother needed a powerful ally, badly. Cromwell was beginning to lose his grip on the English Reformation as well, and an alliance with the powerful United Duchies would hopefully give access to the Schmalkaldic League, even if no new members were being added at that time. It was hard to know what was happening on the Continent, as all the intrigues left England as something of a bystander – but in a position that could turn dangerous at any moment.

5

JULY–DECEMBER 1539

It remained unclear in early July 1539 whether Duke Wilhelm wanted to pursue a marriage to Christina of Denmark. Maria of Austria, Regent of the Low Countries, departed for the marches of Guelders to treat with Wilhelm about the duchy. The two planned to meet in 's-Hertogenbosch.[15] She was expected to stay in the area for at least eight days for this, and to bring the Brabant into conformity with the Emperor after the uprising in Ghent. Cromwell was informed of the difficulties in the Brabant and the on-going issue over the succession of Guelders. It was thought that the proceedings between the Regent Maria and Duke Wilhelm, or his representatives, were of a secretive nature. Hopefully, Wilhelm could reach some sort of agreement with the Emperor through Charles's sister, the Regent Maria.

Henry was as concerned as ever that the French were intending to invade. Marillac, Francis I's ambassador to England, reported that Henry had no intention himself of attacking France, and that Henry was more displeased by the Pope's attempts to lure the Emperor Charles V and Francis I away from their rapprochement with Henry. France and the Holy Roman Empire adhered to the Catholic faith and supported the Pope in Rome: England, despite

---

15 This city's name is a contraction from the Dutch language meaning, 'the duke's forest', and is known as Bolduque in French.

the passage of the Six Articles, was considered a nation of heretics. Though the Six Articles were largely in line with the Catholic faith, Henry would not restore the abbeys and he would not return to the Catholic fold and put England back under the purview of the Holy See. Henry did not go far enough in the schism for Johann Friedrich's ambassadors.

A rumour was afoot by mid-July that, as a show of support for Anna's family, Henry would assist with a German invasion of France. The rumour was taken at court with a large pinch of salt, as the behaviour of the Saxon ambassadors evinced no great friendship between Henry and Johann Friedrich, and by extension, Duke Wilhelm. It was generally understood that English resources were to be expended for German martial endeavours only when absolutely necessary.

In fact, Henry began disassembling his military forces at this time. There was no cogent threat from either Francis I or Charles V. A large English naval force at Portsmouth of approximately ninety ships was disbanded. Though upwards of 10,000 men were released from the ships' crews, they could be quickly called back to service.

In the first part of August 1539, Wotton reported to Henry that he met with Duke Wilhelm on 31 July at Düren, part of Jülich. Wotton gleaned from the meeting that Johann Friedrich was sending his representatives to Wilhelm to advise him about the proposed union of Anna and Henry. Once Johann Friedrich's men arrived, they along with Wilhelm's men would be sent to England in hopes of concluding the matter.

The men from Cleves included Chancellor Dr Heinrich Olisleger, with whom Wotton and Berde were treating, and Wernherus von Hoghestein, Prefect. As far as Wotton knew, 'they should have power to treat and conclude everything, as in the King's last instructions, especially to offer a decent sum as dowry.' Wotton was under the impression that a copy of the agreement between Johann III and the Duke of Lorraine would either be delivered to Henry by the ambassadors, or given to Wotton before he returned to England. Alternatively, the Cleves council was willing to, 'publish that lady Anne is not bound by any covenants made by the old duke of Cleves and the duke of Lorraine, but is free to marry as she pleases.' (Anna was not of course 'free to marry as she pleased'; hardly any noblewoman was.) Wotton quietly attempted to gain a copy of the marriage compact between Anna's sister Sybylla and her husband Johann Friedrich. Provisions of that compact also related to Anna's position as heir to the United Duchies.

Wotton reported that Hans Holbein arrived at Düren to make the portraits of Anna and Amalia, and that Holbein's work was accurate. Anna was of gentle disposition, and was brought up predominantly by her wise mother, the respected Duchess Maria of Jülich-Berg. Like her sisters Sybylla and Amalia, Anna stayed with her mother until she was ready to marry.

Anna delighted in embroidery, and may well have embroidered the pearls onto the smock which she wears in both the Louvre and Rosenbach portraits. She could have embroidered the pearls onto the cap she wears in the Rosenbach portrait as well. Anna could read and write in German, which realistically is all a German duchess needed to learn. It is unknown whether Anna had much exposure to other languages in her childhood, but she reportedly could not meaningfully communicate in anything other than German by August 1539. A bright woman, Wotton had no doubt that Anna would learn English quickly. Anna was not known for engaging in the less sober antics of court, having a more reserved nature. Her brother Wilhelm was similarly serious-minded.

There were significant cultural differences between the English and German courts, with the Germans regarding the English as debauched. It was believed that the English drank to excess too often, and that music sometimes indicated frivolity of mind. The tradition of love songs and singing was made popular at German courts by the *Minnesängern* during the Middle Ages, but that entertainment eventually went away and became a form of entertainment for common folk. *Meistersängern*, or Master Singers, created guilds in the late Medieval to Early Modern periods, bringing the art of poetry and courtly singing to the populace. The Master Singers would engage in contests in their various towns. Anna could not play any instruments or sing. Anna probably knew popular tunes from this time, though the performance of such at court was not considered refined.

The Danish Union is Abandoned; the Cleves Match Progresses
The end of Henry's pursuit of Christina of Denmark was marked by
the possibility of England aligning itself with Christina's paternal
great-uncle, Frederick, who usurped the throne of Denmark in
1523 after rebels forced Christina's father Christian II to abdicate.
He became Frederick I of Denmark. After Frederick's death in
1534, his son became Christian III of Denmark.

Around 17 August 1539, Henry received a letter from Christian
III of Denmark. Christina was a devout Catholic along with the rest
of the Hapsburg family. Her cousin Christian III was Protestant.
Now, Christian III was interested in working with Henry and
against the papists. The kings discussed forming a league against
the Emperor, and Henry wanted a meeting in England. Given that
Christian III's ambassadors would need to travel a long way and
through Imperial waters, Christian urged Henry to meet with him
in one of the German port cities on the North Sea, like Bremen or
Hamburg. To try to bring about this league, Christian took the
initiative and wrote to Anna's brother-in-law Johann Friedrich,
Elector of Saxony, and also wrote to the Landgrave of Hesse.
Ultimately, Christian III and Henry VIII never met.

On 1 September 1539 Hans Holbein returned to England
bearing the famous Louvre portrait of Anna of Cleves. Duke
Wilhelm's ambassadors were purportedly on their way to see
Henry to conclude the matter. Henry was under the impression
that Johann Friedrich was sending his own delegation, too.
Henry's standing with the Schmalkaldic League was volatile: the
temporary moratorium on adding new members to the League
was in effect and Henry had offended Johann Friedrich by
passing the Six Articles into law. In Henry's attempts to remain
friendly or at least neutral in his dealings with France and the
Holy Roman Empire, he was very close to alienating Anna's
powerful brother-in-law.

Henry, Cromwell, the Duke of Norfolk, and others were positing
the idea of a new alliance with France. When Henry was out
hunting with Marillac, the French Ambassador to the English
court, Henry addressed the worrying rumour concerning his aiding

a German force to invade France. It was not possible in the first place, according to Henry, on purely practical grounds. Henry did not have any intelligence from Germany. He had no way of coordinating such an invasion. Furthermore, Henry sought to put Marillac and his master at ease by saying that the warships and other preparations were for fear of Emperor Charles V invading England. Once it became clear that Charles was doing no such thing, Henry released his men and ceased preparation for war. Henry had no desire to invade anyone, and was happy to stay on his island. Even if the Emperor were paranoid about Henry marrying Anna, Henry would probably not intervene in the struggle for Guelders.

Duke Wilhelm's delegation arrived in England a few days later. Dr Olisleger and others arrived from Cleves, along with Johann Friedrich's vice-chancellor, Burckhardt. A capable ship captain was recommended to Cromwell as someone who could ferry Anna from Germanic territories to England, as the man was familiar with harbours in the major cities of Hamburg and Bremen, and with Friesland. Duke Wilhelm's territories of the United Duchies of Cleves and Guelders were right next to each other and below Friesland. Theoretically, it was simple enough for Anna to travel north through her brother's domains to one of the port cities or a location in Friesland, then board a ship across the North Sea to England. However, there was the inherent danger of a sea voyage in the autumn or winter, and the looming threat of the Holy Roman Empire. Anna's ship could easily be intercepted by the Emperor, exposing Anna to being taken hostage or worse.

Count Frederic, Elector of the Palatinate, husband of Dorothea of Denmark and Norway and brother-in-law to Christina of Denmark, chose to visit Henry in September 1539, most likely to continue negotiating for Henry's marriage to Christina. Before the death of Dorothea's aunt, the Holy Roman Empress Isabella, on 1 May, Dorothea and Frederic were pressing Dorothea's claim to the throne of Denmark and Norway. Their primary ally in ousting the usurper Christian III was Dorothea's uncle, the Holy Roman Emperor Charles V. Simply put, Charles V was not as exercised over Dorothea's claim as the Empress Isabella had been. If Count Frederic, Elector of the Palatinate, could broker the marriage between Henry and Christina, then Dorothea would gain a powerful ally who could pose a realistic threat to Christian III. This was not a sound strategy since Henry was friendly with Christian III by September 1539, so it is doubtful that Count Frederic's plan would work. Besides, the embassy from Cleves was already on its way. Having completed his summer progress, Henry retired to Windsor, where he awaited the arrival of Count Frederic, Elector of the Palatinate.

The passing of the Six Articles was still a thorn in the side of the Schmalkaldic League. Part of the reason given for the passing of the Six Articles is surmised in a letter of 16 September to Philip, Landgrave of Hesse and co-founder of the League:

> The crafty [Stephen Gardiner, Bishop] of Winchester bears rule, who has warned the King that if he proceed with the Reformation it will lead to commotion and the principal lords of England will be against him. Henry yields to his suggestions the more readily because the [Bishop], who has been some time his ambassador in France, holds out to him a hope that Francis will also depose the Pope and ally himself with him on the understanding that the Reformation go no further.

There was a serious concern that Henry would forsake his new German friends.

Charles V Loses Influence; and Final Considerations

In autumn 1539, opinions about the Holy Roman Emperor were worsening in England. This could be attributed to the Emperor's abandonment of his niece Dorothea's cause, who was now looking to Henry for help; and also to how the Emperor was managing the Guelders issue with Anna's brother. William Fitzwilliam, the Earl of Southampton, wrote to Cromwell in September: 'What dishonour it was to the Emperor to practise the stealing of the duke of Cleves' towns and the handling of the Count Palatine.'[16]

---

16 'Count Palatine' is an alternative title for the Elector of Palatine. In this instance, Count Frederic is the Elector of Palatine or Count Palatine of the Rhine.

The groundswell of feeling against the Emperor was influenced by Henry's pending match with Anna.

Wilhelm was not pleased with Count Frederic's presence at the English court, and interpreted it as an attempt by the Count to lure Henry away from marriage negotiations for Anna and pair him with Christina of Denmark instead. Wilhelm's concerns were unfounded. It was unlikely at this point that Henry would reconsider a marriage to Christina, as he had discussed forming a league with Christian III of Denmark, son of the usurper of the Danish and Norwegian thrones. Wilhelm was entertaining either a double marriage with England wherein he would wed the Lady Mary and Henry would wed Anna, or Wilhelm was interested in marrying Christina of Denmark if the Emperor would allow it. A match between Wilhelm and Christina was almost impossible to imagine by the end of September 1539, as it was rumoured that Anna's brother Wilhelm was gathering munitions in Guelders.

Elector Johann Friedrich was mightily displeased over the passing of the Six Articles. He could not get past this action by Henry. English envoys sent to Saxony were not believed when they attempted to show Johann Friedrich that the Six Articles were much less severe than the Elector believed. Anna's brother-in-law was having none of it. Elector Johann Friedrich thought the Six Articles were tyrannical, against the doctrine found in the Gospel, and worth publicly refuting.

In preparation for finalising negotiations, Anna's future husband Henry had to decide what would be required of and for her brother:

1. What dote [Wilhelm] will require?
2. What dower [Wilhelm] will appoint, with the qualification of the same?
3. What number of lords, ladies, &c., shall accompany [Anna]?
4. To appoint some noble personage to go over and make the espousals, and to remember his way thither and furniture.
5. Who shall be captains in the King's ships?

6. What number of gentlemen shall go in them, and what apparel the soldiers, mariners, and gunners shall have?
7. To remember the furniture of [Anna's] own ship.
8. To appoint the place where [Anna] shall land.
9. What great personage shall meet her at landing, and how accompanied?
10. To remember the furniture of the landing-place and of the lodgings she shall lie in by the way.
11. Who shall eftsoons meet her if the King shall be distant from the place of landing?
12. Where she shall repair to his Majesty?

Besides these practical queries, an analysis of the marriage treaty for Anna's sister Sybylla was desirable, perhaps necessary. That could assist Henry and Wilhelm in determining who should pay what for Anna's dote.[17]

When discussing Anna's dowry, it is important to remember that the idea of her marrying the King of England or king of anywhere always seemed unlikely. As a woman of the Holy Roman Empire, the highest rank she could marry – if not the Emperor himself or an archduke – would be an elector, as her sister Sybylla had, or a duke. The dowries associated with such marriages were lower than what would be reasonably required by the King of England. The extra expense was not something Anna's father could have prepared for before his death in 1539. The speed with which negotiations for Anna's marriage to Henry advanced did not allow Johann III or Wilhelm to accumulate the money or items necessary for Anna's kingly dote.

Extra monies available to Duke Wilhelm were in any case slowly and quietly being used to prepare for war with Emperor Charles V over Guelders. As mentioned earlier, Anna's brother was known to posterity as 'Wilhelm the Rich'. He certainly had money, though probably not enough to pay the increased dote for Anna to marry a king at the same time as funding a war. Concerning dotes and

---

17 A dote is the amount of money or assets provided by the bride's family, whereas the dowry in this context refers to the widow's dowry, should the bride outlive her husband.

dowers for Anna and Sybylla, the prior agreements with Saxony included the following:

> The duke of Saxe had in dote 25,000 florins, paid in three years, and gave 6,600 in dower, jewels, and municipals if she [Sybylla] over-live. The old duke of Cleves covenanted that if the Duke that now is died without issue male, his dukedoms of [Cleves, Jülich] and [Berg] and the marchionate of Ramesburgh (Ravensberg) should go to the duke of Saxe, who should pay 160,000 florins in four years towards the marriage of the other daughters, [Anna and Amalia,] whereof there be now two living.

These are not great sums. Even less was the original dote agreed to and dower required for the match with Francis of Lorraine. To wit: 'The dote with the lady Anne to have been 30,000 florins, the dower 5,000, with like conditions of inheritance after the duke of Saxe, in case he should die without heirs.'

Wilhelm was reliant upon Henry's beneficence and forbearance over the money, and he had other practical concerns for the marriage. As mentioned, Wilhelm did not have a large amount of money to give because of the brewing war over Guelders. Also, it was likely never contemplated that Anna would marry anything more than an Elector, and even that may not have been terribly likely. Wilhelm would have set aside an amount more closely in line with what was proposed for Anna's marriage to Francis of Lorraine. Regardless, Wilhelm trusted Henry would treat Anna just the same in terms of finance as he had treated his prior queens.

Wilhelm found the issue of who would inherit what – should Anna have children with Henry – of great import; a line of succession for both England and the United Duchies needed to be laid out. Should Anna outlive Henry, it was desired that she could leave England with all her household goods, her jewelry, and her dower properties and incomes as a widow.

Meanwhile, the intrigues of Guelders and Denmark were roiling in the background. Wilhelm could not come to an agreement yet with Emperor Charles V. Anna's mother Maria was helping

Wilhelm to govern the United Duchies at this point. Count Frederic of the Palatinate continued to appeal to Henry for help in regaining the throne of Denmark for Frederic's wife, Dorothea. Count Frederic even went so far as to suggest overthrowing Dorothea's uncle, the Emperor Charles V, so that a new Emperor could be installed. Henry was not going to take on that task.

Anxious to move forward with his marriage, Henry wished to conclude things before winter set in. On 26 September, Henry wrote to Wilhelm to thank him for his letter dated 4 September 1539, sent from Düsseldorf. Henry thanks Wilhelm

> ...for the goodwill he shows for concluding the alliance between them, of which his ambassadors and those of the duke of Saxony have spoken. Suggests speed in concluding the matter, as winter is approaching. Sends the bearer, a sea captain, to learn the best port to which to send ships for the conveyance of the lady.

Marillac kept Francis informed of Anna's marriage plans. Ambassadors of the Elector of Saxony and of Nuremberg arrived to further treat with Henry on behalf of their masters. Henry was in very high spirits in late September 1539, perhaps attributable to his impending wedding with Anna. Very friendly toward everyone, Henry made a point of inquiring after Francis's wellbeing and that of his family.

In early October 1539, Wilhelm confessed he really could not pay any significant sum for Anna's betrothal. He pointed out he had been Duke of Cleves for less than a year. He recognised that, as a consequence, Henry may not offer any dower for Anna at all if she outlived him Wilhelm appealed to Henry's vanity by suggesting that he trusted the king to provide for Anna in any case.

Now all that was left was to determine whether Anna would come over the water or overland. Wilhelm fretted for his sister's health and safety, as she was

> ...young and beautiful, and if she should be transported by the seas they[18] fear much how it might alter her complexion. They

---

18 The Duke Wilhelm and the Dowager Duchess their mother, Maria.

fear lest the time of the year being now cold and tempestuous she might there, though she were never so well ordered, take such cold or other disease, considering she was never before upon the seas, as should be to her great peril and the King's Majesty's great displeasure.

Though the fears of subjecting Anna to seasickness, disease, and a ruined complexion were real enough, the main reason to send the lovely bride-to-be overland was the threat from the Emperor. Anna and her retinue would make an attractive target for anyone wishing to support the Emperor, and it would be incredibly difficult to come to Anna's aid once news of her capture at sea reached either Henry, Wilhelm, or Johann Friedrich. A passport from the Emperor to allow Anna's safe conduct throughout his domains was highly desirable, though Anna's family did control several important trade routes via the rivers in each respective duchy under their power.

Henry had already begun preparations to ferry his German bride to England. Ten ships were suitably fitted to conduct the future Queen Consort across the North Sea, and Henry ordered that the apartments typically used by his queens be refurbished in preparation for Anna, though we don't know where: possibly Hampton Court Palace, Whitehall Palace or St James's Palace; Henry was expecting Anna as early as mid-November 1539. It was probably around this time that Cromwell sought out Holbein to embellish the ceiling of the Chapel Royal of St James's Palace in honour of Anna.

In early October 1539, it was recorded that the Archbishop of Canterbury and others promised that Anna's agreed-upon dote of 100,000 florins would be written off once Anna arrived in England. Henry himself would sign and seal the ceding of the debt. Finally, on 4 October 1539, Henry was ready to sign the marriage contract.

The Marriage Treaty

The treaty was consented to a month earlier on 4 September 1539 by Anna's mother Maria, her brother Wilhelm, and Anna herself. Two copies of this document exist in the State Archives of Nordrhein-Westfalen, one in Latin and one in German. Known as the Beer Pot Documents for the image of a beer stein at the bottom, within which are a clover leaf[19] and crown, both documents were signed by Anna: 'Anna, Born Duchess of Jülich, Cleves, and Berg ... signed in my own handwriting.' At the bottom of the Beer Pot Documents can be found the seals of Lord John a Doltzike, *eques auratus* (Knight of the Golden Spur); Friedrich Burckhardt, Vice-Chancellor to Johann Friedrich of Saxony; William ab Harff, Master of the Hall or *aulœ prœfecto*; and Heinrich Olisleger. These men signed on behalf of Anna's brother Duke Wilhelm.

The marriage treaty signed in London on 4 October 1539 can be found in the State Archives as well. The document itself, in Latin, is fascinating. It includes the signatures and seals[20] of Thomas, Archbishop of Canterbury; Thomas, Lord Audeley of Walden, Chancellor; Charles, Duke of Suffolk; Thomas, Lord Cromwell, Keeper of the Privy Seal; William, Earl of Southampton, Great Admiral; and Cuthbert, Bishop of Durham. The terms of the agreement:

1. That a marriage has been concluded, by commissioners, between Henry VIII., king of England, &c., and lady Anne, sister of William duke of Juliers,[21] &c., whose other sister, the lady Sibilla, John Frederic duke of Saxony, &c., has received in matrimony.

2. That the duke of Juliers shall within two months, if he can obtain safe conduct, convey, at his own expense, the lady Anne his sister honourably to Calais.

3. That there the King shall receive her, by his commissioners, and traduct her thence as soon as possible into his realm and there marry her publicly.

4. That if safe conduct cannot be obtained, which is very unlikely, the Duke shall send her, as soon as possible, to some sea-port and transport her thence to England with a suitable convoy of ships at his expense.

---

19 A reference to Cleves, which has three gold clovers on its coat of arms.
20 On the back of the wax seals one can see the fingerprints.
21 'Juliers' is the French equivalent for 'Jülich'.

5. That the Duke shall give with her a dote of 100,000 florins of gold, viz., 40,000 on the day of solemnisation of the marriage and the rest within a year after.

6. That the King shall give the lady Anne, under his seal, a dower in lands worth yearly 20,000 golden florins of the Rhine, equal to 5,000 mks. sterling money of England, as long as she remains in England. And if, after the King's death, she have no children surviving and would rather return to her own country, she shall have a pension of 15,000 florins, payable half-yearly, for life, and her own dress and jewels; and it shall be at the choice of the King's heirs to pay the pension or redeem it with 150,000 florins. The sealed grant of this dower to be delivered to the Duke's commissioner on the day of the marriage and a true copy of it to be sent to the Duke ten days before her traduction.

7. If the Duke die without lawful issue, and his duchy go therefore to the lady Sibilla, wife of John Frederic duke of Saxony, according to their marriage contract, and they in turn die without lawful issue, the succession shall go to the lady Anne. In the event of the succession going as aforesaid to the duke of Saxony a sum of 160,000 florins shall be paid within four years to the two sisters, the ladies Anne and Amelia, or their heirs; or if the succession come as aforesaid to the king of England he shall pay the 160,000 florins to the lady Amelia and her heirs.

8. If the succession go to Saxony as aforesaid, and either of the two other sisters die without children, her share shall accrue to the surviving sister or her children.

9. If the succession go to Saxony, then the lady Anne shall have, besides her dowry, the castles of Burdericum in Cleves with 2,000 florins a year, Casterium in Juliers with 2,000, and Benradum in Berg with 1,000, for life.

10. That the duke of Juliers shall keep the King informed by letter of his proceedings for the transportation of the lady Anne, so that the King may thereby time his preparations for her reception.

11. That the King and the said dukes of Saxony and Cleves shall confirm this treaty by letters patent under their hands and seals to be mutually delivered within six weeks from the date of this present, viz., by the King to the duke of Cleves and by the dukes to the King.

With that, Anna was set to become the first German Queen Consort of England.

The treaty was clearly important for the succession of the United Duchies of Jülich-Cleves-Berg. Wilhelm, in fact quite early in his rule, laid out a plan just as Anna was becoming Queen Consort. At the time, only Sybylla was married and there had been no meaningful discussions. Sybylla had three surviving sons, namely Johann Friedrich II, born in 1529,[22] Johann Wilhelm I, born in 1530; and Johann Friedrich III, born 1538. A fourth son, Johann Ernst, was born and died in 1535. So by October 1539, according to clause 7, it was unlikely that the United Duchies would ever come under the dominion of England.

Preparations for Anna's Safe Conduct; and The French Perspective

The next step was to secure safe conduct for Anna through Imperial territory. Anna had to pass by Ghent, which was not yet fully under the authority of the Emperor, and through the rest of the Low Countries before she could enter France and pass to English-held Calais. Given the fraught situation over Guelders, it was imperative that Anna be guaranteed safe passage to England. Arthur Plantagenet, Viscount of Lisle, Deputy of Calais, awaited confirmation of this from Maria of Austria, Regent of the Low Countries and Queen of Hungary.

---

22 There is a portrait in the Royal Collection recently identified as being a Cranach original. It was put on display in November 2017. It is possible that this portrait is of Sybylla and her eldest son, or of Johann Friedrich and his mother. The portrait was a gift of Prince Albert of Saxe-Coburg-Gotha to his new wife, Queen Victoria. Prince Albert and Victoria were descended from Sybylla of Cleves through Sybylla's second son, Johann Wilhelm I. One of Victoria's and Prince Albert's grandfathers was Franz, Duke of Saxe-Coburg Saale, who descended on his paternal side from Sybylla's son.

He wrote on 11 October 1539, 'the Queen [of Hungary] will send a gentleman to conduct the ambassador of the dukes of Saxony and Cleves through the Emperor's countries. I have no news yet from her Majesty.'

Count Frederic of the Palatinate assisted in procuring Anna's safe conduct, with hopes that Anna would arrive in England as early as November. Duke Fredric's helpfulness in this was surely inspired by his ongoing desire to secure assistance from Henry in reclaiming the throne of Denmark for his wife, Dorothea. Count Frederic was much too late; as we have seen, Henry's alliances with the German princes included the current King of Denmark, even if he was a usurper.

Lord Lisle was ordered to have Calais in pristine condition, and to pave the streets as necessary. The house known as the Exchequer was made ready for Anna. All this had to be accomplished by the middle of November. Maria, Regent of the Low Countries was quick to award the safe conduct for Anna despite the ongoing unrest in Ghent, and a passport dated around 27 October 1539 bearing Charles V's official seal was prepared.

Elector Johann Friedrich was perturbed, if not enraged, by the conclusion of Anna's marriage treaty because Henry was actively enforcing the Six Articles. A letter written in late October 1539 to Johann Friedrich by one of his advisers echoed his master's feelings on the matter. If men with a firmer grasp of the burgeoning Lutheran religion were sent to England, 'they might have withheld the King from his godless determination'. Johann Friedrich's primary adviser, Vice Chancellor Burckhardt, and another Saxon ambassador, were sent to England back in June 1539 to announce the coming of a great embassy from Saxony. They were not intended to debate the religious issues with Henry VIII or his parliament. Had the Elector been aware of what the English parliament was contemplating during late spring 1539, Elector Johann Friedrich would have sent men much better equipped to debate religious doctrine. The letter to Johann Friedrich goes on to say: 'It is clear the King of England cares little for God's word or truth.' Worst of all, it did not seem that England would give up the Six Articles.

As leader of the Schmalkaldic League, the Elector of Saxony could not offer support to Anna's new husband or country. For

Thomas Cromwell, this must have caused some alarm. After all, the German match was made upon the pretence of being connected to the Schmalkaldic League, and more importantly, the military might of Anna's brother-in-law. The Elector's utter condemnation of the Six Articles meant that Henry's chance to gain a powerful German ally was swiftly slipping away. Added to that was the simmering Guelders war. It is unclear how much of this was realised by Henry or Cromwell at the time Henry concluded his marriage treaty with Anna.

Martin Luther himself wrote a letter to Johann Friedrich, incredulous as to Henry VIII's solemnised stance on religion. Though Luther and Henry quarrelled in the past,[23] Henry seemed to understand the 'tyranny' of the papacy when he broke from the Pope in the early 1530s. But now, Luther opined at length to Elector Johann Friedrich:

> [t]hat Henry VIII. is acting against his conscience is clear; for he knows our doctrine and observances are at least not against God's word. Yet in his [Six Articles] he says some of them are against God's law, though he has read many writings addressed to him on the subject... We understand also that he has spoken much of this learning and condemned France for persecuting it, for he knew it was right... Moreover [Henry] has many pious preachers ... whom he heard and tolerated for a time. Yet now he denounces these doctrines worse than the Pope, and threatens with death those who do not accept these articles. A terrible persecution has begun, for many lie in prison expecting punishment. Yet he used this very teaching which he now persecutes for a time for his own advantage.

Here Luther is surely referring to Henry breaking with Rome so that he could abandon his first, aged and no longer fertile, wife. Far from a religious reformer, Luther saw Henry as merely an exploiter of the break with Rome for his own ends:

---

23 In the early 1520s, Henry VIII wrote a pamphlet condemning Martin Luther, resulting in Pope Leo X bestowing the title, *Fidei Defensor*, or Defender of the Faith, on him in 1521, which Henry's successors have borne to this day.

Seeing that the Papal power must fall, he urges great Kings to set up religions for their own convenience. That will lead to fearful blindness. Fears that Henry cares nothing for the honor of God. He told the Vice-chancellor [Burckhardt] that he meant to govern his kingdom himself; which showed that he cared little for this learning but meant to make a religion for himself. Think therefore it will be useless to give Henry another warning.

Johann Friedrich at the very least looked up to Luther, and Anna's sister, Sybylla, was known to correspond with him. The Schmalkaldic League formed because of Johann Friedrich's belief in and adherence to Luther's preaching. And now, this powerful religious figure was disgusted by how Anna's new husband treated the question of religion.

The French understanding of why Anna of Cleves was marrying Henry VIII was threefold. First, Henry's desire to be in league with Anna's brother-in-law and the other German princes, from whom Henry believed he could receive effective military aid if and when required; should the Holy Roman Empire or France besiege England, Cleves was able to come at the enemy from another front. Second, Henry had great hopes of influencing the German princes, such as the Elector of Saxony, in the realm of religion and swaying them away from what he viewed as extremism. Third, the ambassador Marillac tells Francis I, is Henry's 'desire of issue (as he has only one male child), which he could not better have than with the said lady, who is of convenient age, healthy temperament, elegant stature, and endowed with other graces, as the said King affirms'. Now all Henry had to do was bring Anna to England.

By 25 October 1539, it was decided that Anna would travel by land. The fleet Henry assembled would not sail. Though the journey from the United Duchies through Flanders posed its own threat, as the people were disappointed that Henry was marrying Anna and not their beloved Christina of Denmark. The people of Flanders simply did not like Cleves. There was a small possibility that Anna and her family could change their minds and send her via sea, but the season for a safe journey was receding as quickly as the daily tides. It was assumed that Anna would arrive in time for Christmas, after being feasted and fêted magnificently all the way from Cleves to Calais. Anna's new subjects could not wait for her safe arrival.

In a letter written on 25 October to Montmorency, the Constable of France, Marillac reported on the unrest in Flanders and the great discontentment of the people, which Henry's council found disconcerting:

> They are painting and arming some ships, apparently to bring the lady by sea, although, to deceive those who would hinder it, they still give out that she is coming by land. The fact is they are troubled either by that or by the rumour that the duke of Cleves has attempted something against the Emperor.

Henry, upon hearing the news that Anna was granted an Imperial passport, dashed off a quick letter to Maria of Austria. He thanked the Regent, asking that Maria augment the passport, if necessary, for Anna's safety. Henry wished for Anna to be comfortable and secure on her journey through the Imperial territories.

A letter written by Melanchthon from Saxony reached Henry in early November 1539. In it, he asks Henry 'after the [Six Articles] issued against the pious doctrine which the writer's party profess, to read and consider this their complaint, especially as it is written for the welfare of the Church at large'. Melanchthon places the blame for the enactment of the Six Articles squarely on the shoulders of Henry's bishops, using subtle and perhaps fallacious language to reason with Henry. Melanchthon admonishes him: although he may have second thoughts about the English Reformation, he should not take such a large step backwards toward orthodoxy. The danger of this regression is what compelled Melanchthon to write; it would be a great tragedy should Henry fall back into the clutches of Rome.

It was thought in Germany that Henry's leadership in pulling away from the Catholic Church would influence his neighbouring

Catholic Monarchs to follow suit. But now, it was feared by Elector Johann Friedrich, the Six Articles were having the exact opposite effect. Ultimately, Melanchthon – and thus Elector Johann Friedrich – was seeking an amendment of the Six Articles. A reply was sent off to the Germans, wherein it was expressed that the English could not understand the Elector's objections. Just because Henry made decisions concerning the Church of England, this did not mean he was returning to papal authority.

Anna was expected to arrive in England around 25 November 1539. In order for Henry and the country to prepare, Parliament prorogued until 14 January 1540. Henry originally planned to meet Anna in Canterbury. Aside from being along the route from Dover to London, Canterbury of course had the beautiful Cathedral. And on the Buttermarket, leading to the Cathedral, was a gate erected during the reign of Henry VII. The tall, detailed gate displayed the arms of Henry VII, Henry's older brother Arthur Tudor, Katherine of Aragon, and the Beaufort portcullis. If Henry met Anna in Canterbury, he could show Anna this cathedral and its impressive gate bearing the (admittedly somewhat brief) record of the Tudor dynasty.

Henry sent the Lord Admiral and a company of men to meet Anna at Calais. Duke Wilhelm would send roughly four hundred mounted men with his elder sister to conduct her safely. Once in Calais, Anna and some of her company would sail to Dover, where the rest of Henry's council would meet her. Then the council would escort Anna to Canterbury. Ideally, the marriage would be made and consummated in Canterbury, and Anna could be crowned Queen Consort in February 1540. In the meantime, Henry would wait for Anna at Hampton Court.

Honor Grenville, Lady Lisle sent gifts from Calais to her new queen through Olisleger in early November 1539. Lady Lisle could expect to meet Anna very soon, possibly by 7 or 8 December, and provide entertainment for the queen-in-waiting while she waited for favourable weather to cross the English Channel. One gift was a piece of embroidered cloth, likely a frontlet, worn across a woman's forehead and a very common piece of practical adornment in Germany, like Anna's frontlet bearing the words, 'A Bon Fine' in the Louvre portrait by Holbein.

Anna was praised as an intelligent woman by foreign visitors to her lands. Miguel Mercator in a letter to Cromwell dated 11 November from Grave, wrote of Anna that he '[gives] praise to God for the alliance with the most illustrious, beautiful, and noble lady Anna de Clefves,[24] who has a great gift from God, both of sense and wit. It would be difficult to describe her good manners and grace.' Mercator sent an image 'imitated to the life' to Henry, which could possibly be of Anna. Sadly, the letter is not specific regarding the subject of the image, though it is reasonable to assume that the image is of Anna, given the rest of the letter. And Mercator didn't just send one. He sends Cromwell 'three images of silver and three of lead, by which he will perceive that sent to the King is well imitated'. Again, it is reasonable to infer that these images are of Anna, though no such silver or lead images of her have yet been identified.

Sir Thomas Wyatt received instructions from Henry around 15 November 1539 to report to the French court. He was to relieve the current ambassador to the Holy Roman Empire, and learn what he could about the purpose of Charles V's visit to France. Wyatt's observations and intelligence from this appointment proved invaluable to Henry. They also had a serious impact on Anna's marriage.

Cromwell was growing rather impatient by 17 November, and sent what was likely a rude or condescending letter to Stephen Vaughan. Cromwell was irritated that it was taking so long for correspondence from Cleves to arrive in England. Vaughan explained that he was following normal procedure in sending letters along from Cleves, under instructions not to spend Henry's money without good cause. Cromwell claimed frustration because he did not know what was happening, at which Vaughan scoffed. Vaughan could tell Cromwell all sorts of things, if only he had Henry's permission to accompany Anna to England.

The Emperor Charles V was heading to Brussels to see his sister Maria of Austria, and hopefully to meet with Francis. Charles V, a

---

24 Another alternate spelling of Cleves.

widower, was interested in exploring a marriage to Francis' daughter Margaret. Charles 'greatly stomached' the Anglo-Cleves union: the broader alliance between England and some of the protestant princes was a real threat. Having secured a marital alliance with France,[25] he could regain control of the cities in open rebellion to him, then head on to Guelders to attack Duke Wilhelm and regain that territory. Guelders, with all its rivers running through it, was much easier to attack in the winter once the water was frozen.

The Emperor was expected in Brussels before New Year's Day 1540, though nothing was certain. The potential for Anna's train crossing paths with the Emperor's seemed like a dangerous prospect. However, Charles's sister Maria of Austria promised to send her own men to conduct Anna through Maria's domains to Gravelines. Anna had another threat to worry about: Cardinal Pole was instructed to convince Charles V and Francis I to refuse safe conduct for Anna.

It was known in Rome that Charles V was planning on meeting with Francis I, and that Anna had to go right through their territories to get to England. Henry's enemy Cardinal Pole lived in France to escape Henry's wrath. Cardinal Pole was directed to encourage the refusal of Anna's passage, 'if it is true that [Anna] is a Lutheran'. In the end, Anna was granted safe conduct and did not meet with any trouble along the way. Anna and Henry's marriage and the accompanying amity with the Germans was seen by the Pope as a development 'which is daily extending its poison in all directions'.

The plan for where and when Anna would meet her new husband had changed once more by the end of November 1539. Now, after arriving in Calais as early as 8 December, Anna would cross the Channel, head to Canterbury, then meet Henry at Greenwich instead of Canterbury, to celebrate the marriage and Christmas. Henry moved from Hampton Court to Westminster to await news of Anna's arrival. By 12 December 1539, Anna would already be in Calais, learning about her new kingdom.

---

25 This would create a double-alliance, as Charles' sister Eleanor married Francis I in 1530. Eleanor and Francis did not have children.

6

QUEEN ANNE

Anna first travelled from Düsseldorf to Berg, covering the duchies of Jülich and Berg. Anna next went to Cleves, and thence to Ravenstein. Before going across Imperial territory, Anna required the passport. At the request of Anna's brother Duke Wilhelm, the Emperor Charles V replied, 'he would nothing at his request, but for his most dear and loving cousin's sake, the King of England, she should pass.' He commanded all his subjects 'to away[t] of her grace as though she were the [empress]'.

After Ravenstein, Anna and her train crossed into the Low Countries. There they made stops at Tillburg and Hoogstraten before staying in Antwerp. The English merchants then living in Antwerp rode out to greet her, wearing great golden chains and velvet coats. Antwerp was so lit with torches that night became day. Anna spent the night in Antwerp and stayed all the next day. The cortège stayed in a great house belonging to the English. Anna was originally expected to arrive in Antwerp on 2 December, staying for just one day, and be in Calais by 8 December. She was already behind schedule. There were at least seven more stops planned before her arrival in Calais. Stephen Vaughn was praised by Wotton to Cromwell:

Mr. Vaughan and the merchants should be thanked for my lady's entertainment at the English house here. Lord Bure says he never saw so many people gathered in Antwerp at any entry, even the Emperor's. What with my lady's train, and Mr. Vaughan, and the merchants, it was a goodly sight.

They left the day after, but not before the merchants could give their new queen a gift. Anna moved on toward Stekyn. From Stekene to Polken, then on to Bruges. After Bruges, she went to Oudenburg, and finally entered French territory. Anna made stops at Newport and Dunkirk before arriving in Gravelines, where a gun salute in her honour was set off on the morning of 11 December. While Anna was in Dunkirk, she attended a church service where an apparently seditious sermon was preached. The exact contents of the sermon are unknown, but Wotton and the Earl of Southampton did not believe it was destructive or dangerous.

Arrival in Calais

Anna arrived in the Pale of Calais between seven and eight o'clock that evening, where she was received by the Lord Deputy of Calais, the Lieutenant of Calais castle, the Knight Porter of Calais, and the Marshall of Calais, amongst others. They were all wearing costly velvet and great, golden chains. A battalion of Henry's fine English archers, bedecked in the king's livery were present too, and the entire company escorted Anna and her party to a place about a mile outside Calais.

Just outside the city, another group of Henry's important nobles were present to receive their new queen. They included Sir Thomas Seymour,[26] the Earl of Southampton, Gregory Cromwell, and Sir Francis Bryan. They were wearing purple, blue, or red satin damask, and velvet of the same colours, and of course their chains.

As Anna and her entourage continued, Henry's ships fired a great volley of guns and Calais responded with its own ordinance. Finally, Anna came to the Lantern Gate of Calais and saw two of Henry's ships, the *Sweepstakes* and the *Lyon*.

---

26 Brother of Anna's predecessor, Queen Jane Seymour.

The ships were bedecked with a hundred golden banners and had two hundred gunners. Thirty-one trumpets were blaring, and a curious double-drum unfamiliar in England was being played as Anna passed by and entered Calais. She was finally in her new kingdom, even if still south of the Channel. To mark this, around one hundred and fifty guns went off. The smoke was so thick that Anna and the rest of the train could barely see each other.

The chronicler Edward Hall describes Anna's final stops and arrival in Calais:

> The 11th day of December at the Turnpike on this side of Gravelines was the Lady Anne of Cleves received by the Lord Lisle Deputy of the town of Calais and with the spears and arms of horsemen belonging to the retinue there … and so marching toward Calais a mile and more from the town met her Grace the Earl of Southampton great Admiral of England, appareled in a coat of purple velvet cut on cloth of gold and tied with great aglettes and trefoils of gold, to the number of 300 and baudrickwise he wore a chain, at the which did hang a whistle of gold set with riche stones of a great value.
>
> And in this company, 30 gentlemen of the King's household very richly appareled with great and many chains, and in especial Sir Francis Bryan and Sir Thomas Seymour's chains were of great value and strange fashion. Beside this, the Lorde Admiral had a great number of gentlemen in blue velvet and crimson satin and his yeomen in damask of the same colors, and the Mariners of his ship in satin of Bridges, both coats and slops of the same colors, which Lord Admiral with low obeisance welcomed her, and so brought her into Calais by the Lantern Gate, where the Ships lain the Haven[27] garnished with their banners, pencils and flags, pleasant to behold.
>
> And at her entry was shot such a peal of guns, that all the retinue much marveled at it. And at her entry into the

---

27 Harbour.

town, the Mayor of the town presented her with 100 marks in gold. And before the Staple hail stood the Merchants of the Staple well appareled, which likewise presented her with 100 sovereigns of gold in a riche purse, which heartily thanked them, and so she rode to the king's place called the [Exchequer].

During Anna's delay in Calais, 'goodly jousts and costly banquets were made to her for her solace and recreation'. It is reasonable to assume that she took advantage of this time to practise her English. Anna may have started to learn English while she was in the United Duchies, since she remained there for a couple months after it became clear that she would be the next Queen Consort of England. Unfortunately, there are no records of this. It is certain that she had interpreters during her time in Calais, though it is not specified how much she relied upon them. The interpreters were Wilhelm's officials who accompanied Anna during her journey and were to finish negotiating an alliance with Henry.

The planning for Anna's arrival was meticulous and closely followed. The Council of Calais and its Lord Deputy met Anna as soon as she entered the English Pale, after which they headed toward St Peter's for Anna to be met by the Lord Admiral and his company. Once assembled, Anna was to be brought to her lodgings at the Exchequer.

After a banquet on 12 December, Anna watched a joust. The weather was too poor for her to sail to England the next day. Anna's crossing was repeatedly delayed by bad weather. She stayed in Calais for about fifteen days, certainly longer than intended. Unfavourable tides were recorded on 12 December, and Anna and her party knew they probably had to remain in Calais until at least 21 December. There was a sliver of hope that Anna might arrive before Christmas. Part of Anna's entourage was left behind at Calais. Anna wished to bring with her

...Gylmyn, who is taken for first of her gentlewomen ... also the widow of the late lord of Wissem, sister to Willik, steward of Cleves, who is 'howmestrinne,'*i.e.*, governor to the other gentlewomen ... eight pages, one being son to the earl of Waldeck, my lady's cousin germain, ... my lady's steward, formerly the Duke's waltgrave, *i.e.* master of forests... There are also a secretary, a chaplain and others. Making in all 88 persons.

Saxon Vice-Chancellor Burckhardt, Overstein, Hoghestein, and Dr Olisleger of Cleves were to cross over to Dover with Anna, but would return home once she was secure in her new kingdom.

Henry wanted to please his new bride and took particular interest in a certain German custom. Wotton shared with Henry the traditions of the *Bruidstuckes* for the wife's party and the *Morgengabe*, wherein the king gives his wife a gift. The gift is of no specific amount, but presumably the greater the lord and his joy, the greater the gift. *Bruidstuckes* were given to the gentlewomen and gentlemen responsible for the wedding feast and celebrations. For the women, it was usually in the form of jewelry. The bride and groom's noblemen could expect to receive something like a handsome gown, cap, or jacket made of a fine material. Apparently, Johann Friedrich did this when he married Anna's sister Sybylla. It is not explicit whether the *Bruidstuckes* was observed in the United Duchies or was simply a Saxon custom, but it was kind of Henry to take an interest in his new bride's culture. The *Morgengabe* was a gift of money given to a new bride the morning after her wedding.

Anna wanted to learn a card game that Henry enjoyed. She asked, via Olisleger, if there was someone available to teach her. It is not clear if Anna asked through Olisleger because she did not yet have a grasp of English, or because a noblewoman at court would not ask to play cards with men, or converse directly with them. Given the customs in the United Duchies surrounding the *Frauenzimmer* and strict public chaperoning of ladies, either is possible.

Anna requested that the Earl of Southampton assemble some of her new English subjects to sit with her at supper. Initially, Anna's request was declined, but the Queen Consort renewed her request. Southampton gave in. At least seven nobles joined her: 'Lord William, Lord Hastings, Lord Grey, Lord Tailbois, Messrs. Bryan, Seymour, Knevet, and Gregory Cromwell'. Of Anna's demeanour at dinner it was reported, 'Her manner was like a princess.'

Homesick by 18 December 1539, Anna requested that Southampton open a packet of letters he recently received. The Duchess of Cleves was hoping there might be a letter for her. Unfortunately, there were only letters to Cromwell and none for Anna. Despite all this and the long journey to Calais, Anna was purportedly in good health. The seas around Calais were dreadfully rough, causing the wreck of a merchant ship from Holland. Anna and her train would stay in Calais a while longer.

On Christmas Eve 1539, Anna was still held over in Calais, and it was anticipated she would remain for at least another five days. Henry moved to Greenwich for the Christmas festivities and to await his bride. He was planning on meeting Anna a mile or two outside of Greenwich.

It was suspected by this time that the Lady Mary would wed Duke Philip the Contentious, Count Palatine of Neuburg, an area in lower Bavaria. Duke Philip was about thirteen years older than Mary, and at the time, a Protestant. He previously visited Mary at her father's court on 8 December 1539, where he gave Mary a gift and a kiss. Mary was taken with the Duke, despite their religious differences, but no marriage came about. Mary was turning twenty-four in 1540. Her stepmother, Anna, turned twenty-four in 1539.

Fateful First Meeting

Anna and her large train finally left Calais for England on 27 December 1539, arriving at Deal by around five o'clock in the evening. She and her entourage moved on to Dover, where Anna was met by Charles Brandon, Duke of Suffolk and his wife, Catherine Willoughby, amongst others. Catherine Willoughby and Anna would remain friends for the rest of Anna's life. Had things gone according to plan, Anna would have arrived directly in Dover and then moved on to Canterbury. Thomas Cranmer, the Archbishop of Canterbury, and several bishops were to meet Anna outside Canterbury. Along with other gentlemen, this party of church officials were to take Anna to her lodgings there. Due to the weather or the extreme delays, Anna did not go to Canterbury.

Anna's next stop on her way to her new husband was Rochester. The Duke of Norfolk with his company would meet Anna outside Rochester, and in similar fashion to the previous waypoints, bring Anna and her company to their lodgings. Anna had her first meeting with Henry in Rochester.

It is not known if Anna had ever seen Henry's portrait. It is more than possible that Anna conversed with Hans Holbein while he was painting her portrait in Düren at Burgau Castle, and Holbein described Henry to her. Perhaps Holbein told Anna more about England and Henry's court. On the other hand, Anna may have had barely any concept of her new home and husband. Perhaps Anna began learning English in fits and starts before she departed the United Duchies. There were people at court who could speak English, though these were gentlemen and the rules surrounding socialising among unmarried noblewomen and men were strict. What is known is Anna could communicate quite well in English by summer 1540, even if she chose to have important documents translated for her into German. As was noted by Wotton, Anna was no fool.

Anna was resting at Rochester on 1 January 1540 when she was informed of a visitor. Anna had met many of her new subjects and was surely exhausted by the time she arrived in Rochester, and less attentive than usual due to her fatigue. Anna encountered hundreds of English people who were appointed to meet her, including numerous peers of the realm and their personal entourages. Perhaps she was spending some of her time at Rochester daydreaming about meeting Henry or going over how she would greet Henry in the English language. She would not have the opportunity to follow through with any of those plans. Anna received that unexpected visitor on 1 January 1540, and the

German and English accounts of the first meeting between Anna and Henry differ from each other.

Olisleger, an eyewitness, dispatched a letter to Duke Wilhelm within a few days following the meeting. According to Olisleger, while Anna was at Rochester watching a bull-baiting with her German lords, Henry came to call on her after lunch with ten or twelve of his gentlemen. This presumably included Sir Anthony Browne, Henry's Master of Horse, who was deposed at the annulment trial later on that year. It was New Year's Day 1540, and the excited groom could not wait to meet his bride. Henry and his men were dressed as private persons. Henry entered the room and greeted Anna, which may have unsettled her. After all, Anna was used to the culture of the *Frauenzimmer*, so having strange men come into her presence without proper preparation could have caught her off guard.

Anna invited this private person, a representative of the King, to dine with her. Afterward, he presented Anna with a gorgeous gift 'from the King' for New Year: a crystal goblet, the lid and foot of which were completely gilded and inlaid with diamonds and rubies. Another golden band encircled the goblet, also with inlaid rubies and diamonds. Afterward, Henry and Anna enjoyed banqueting together. Henry stayed over to the next day, 2 January 1540, though at a separate location so as not to offend Anna's virtue. He and his men broke their fast with Anna and her gentlemen. Henry then returned to Greenwich. Anna herself departed for Dartford with her train later that day. It is unclear at what point Henry made his identity known to Anna.

Hall's Chronicle described the meeting:

the king which sore desired to see her Grace accompanied with no more then [sic] 8 persons of his privy chamber, and both he and they all appareled in marble coats privily came to Rochester, and suddenly came to her presence, which therewith was somewhat astonied: but after he had spoken and welcomed her, she was most gracious and loving countenance and behavior him received and welcomed on her knees, whom he gently took up and kissed: and all that afternoon, communed and devised with her, and that night supped with her, and the next day he departed to Greenwich, and she came to Dartford.

The chronicler Edward Hall wrote contemporaneously. He was trained as a lawyer and so paid attention to the details as he learned them, and provided excellent information on Anna's interactions with Henry and her first few days in England.

Anna's Official Reception

On 2 January 1540, the Black Heath was prepared for Anna's formal reception and meeting with Henry. The Black Heath was reported to be by the foot of Shooter's Hill, and there was a second location named Black Heath Hill, upon which a cloth-of-gold pavilion and other tents were pitched. The air was made sweet with perfumes and fragrant fires, and all bushes and such were cut away between the pavilion and the Park Gate of Greenwich.

For Anna's arrival in Dartford,

> The earl of Rutland, who is to be her lord chamberlain, Sir [Thomas] Denys, chancellor, Sir Edw. Baynton, vice-chamberlain, Sir John Dudley, master of her horse, and all others appointed to be of her Council, and also the lady Margaret Douglas, the duchess of Richmond, and other ladies which shall be her 'ordinary waiters,' 30 in all, shall meet her, and be presented, by the [Archbishop] of Canterbury, and the dukes of Norfolk and Suffolk, as her own train and household, and so wait upon her till she approach the King's presence, when all the yeomen and meaner sort shall avoid.

Anna was finally meeting the officers assigned to her as queen. They included Henry's niece Margaret Douglas, whose mother was Henry's elder sister Margaret Tudor, once queen consort of Scotland, and mother of James V.

The grandest public event for Anna would be this official meeting with Henry set for Saturday 3 January 1540, where she was received on Black Heath Hill outside of Greenwich. The instructions for 3 January stipulated that 'On the hill there shall be ... the King's rich pavilion, and others for other noble personages to retire to ... and there shall be prepared wine, fruits, and spices, in manner of a banquet.'

Before the official meeting, Henry's men were to go out into the field surrounding Black Heath Hill and 'range themselves aloof'. The gentlemen were 'to ride in two wide ranges on either side that His Majesty may have only such as shall be assigned before and after him'. The Earl Marshall, Duke of Norfolk, would use staves to keep the streets down to Greenwich's gate clear, through which Anna and Henry rode until they reached the late Friars church, close to the water gate. Greenwich Palace and the surrounding area was further set in order for the reception of Anna:

> The said door leading out of the lane where the stables be into the church of the late Friars, and all other strait places, to be enlarged. The streets to be graveled, paved, made clean, and put in as good order as may be; barriers to be made all along the Thames side, that no man be in danger of drowning by press of people.

A large crowd was expected for the event. While Henry awaited Anna in his pavilion, the King's Guard and the Vice Chamberlain went to Greenwich to secure it against the crowd. The plans set out that when Henry left the pavilion for Greenwich, 'all gentlemen not named in a special list to ride before him, shall stand on the heath in two ranges for his Grace and train to pass'. Once arrived at the gate, the gentlemen and lords were to dismount, then walk to court. Henry, Anna, and the ladies would ride. Barges on the Thames would carry the Lord Mayor of London and the aldermen. Musicians would fill the air with sweet sounds. All these people would remain on the barges, and not come into the court.

Gentlemen appointed to receive Anna with the Lord Admiral included the lords William Hawarde, Hastings, and Talbois; Henry's former brother-in-law Sir Thomas Seymour, Sir Francis Bryan, other miscellaneous gentlemen, Thomas Cromwell's son Gregory; Sir Francis Knollys, who married Anne Boleyn's niece Catherine Carey, and Anne Boleyn's brother-in-law William Stafford who was married to Mary Carey, née Boleyn; Anne Boleyn's uncles Thomas Howard and James Boleyn; Charles Brandon, Duke of Suffolk and his wife Catherine Willoughby, Duchess of Suffolk. The most important ladies of the realm greeted Anna: her new stepdaughters, the Lady Mary and the Lady Elizabeth, Mary Tudor's daughter the Lady Frances Brandon, and the Lady Margaret Douglas.

This was a tremendous panoply of all the important nobles in England, the ladies sent to attend their new queen, and the lords to attend her husband. Anna's train numbered around 263 distinguished persons from the United Duchies, including Overstein and Saxon Elector Johann Friedrich's marshall.

Anna arrived at around seven o'clock in the morning with her retinue of about one hundred horse, escorted by the dukes of Suffolk and Norfolk. An oration in Latin was delivered to Anna, and her brother's secretary gave a response. Anna was then greeted by the Lady Margaret Douglas and the Lady Frances Brandon. Anna was finally able to leave the chariot in which she rode from the United Duchies. Anna, 'with most goodly demeanor and loving countenance gave to [the ladies] hearty thanks and kissed them all, and after all her councilors and officers kissed her hand ... she with all the ladies entered the tents, and there warmed them a space.' It is not specified whether Anna took an interpreter with her into the tent. By this time, having been in English territory for more than three weeks, it is not far-fetched to think that Anna was able to exchange basic pleasantries in English with her new ladies. Henry was notified of Anna's arrival.

Henry rode through the surrounding park toward the tents with his company. Henry's trumpeters were at the front, followed by his counselors, then, 'the Gentlemen of the King's Privy Chamber, some appareled in coats of velvet embroidered', on horses likewise richly trapped. Next came the barons, ranked from youngest to oldest, including the Lord Mayor of London. After that were all the black-satin-clad bishops. Behind them were the earls, and Duke Philip of Bavaria and the Count Palatine of Neuburg. Next were the various ambassadors visiting the English court. After them came Thomas Cromwell, Lord Privy Seal, followed by other lords, 'for the most part ... appareled in purple velvet'.

After this long train, 'followed the King's Highness mounted on a goodly courser, trapped in rich cloth of gold traced lattice-wise square, all over embroidered with gold damask, pearled on every side of the embroidery, the buckles and pendants were full of fine gold.' Henry's mount must have looked Pegasus-likel with its glorious gold trappings in the January early morning light. Henry himself

> ...was appareled in a coat of purple velvet, somewhat made like a frock, all over embroidered with flat gold damask with small lace mixed between the same gold, and other laces of the same going traverse-wise, that the ground little appeared, about which garment was a rich guard very curiously embroidered, the sleeves and breast were cut [and] lined with cloth of gold, and tied together with great buttons of diamonds, rubies, and orient pearl, his night cap garnished with stone, but his bonnet was so rich with jewels that few men could value them.

As if that were not enough, Henry also wore a collar decorated with pearls. Behind Henry came Sir Anthony Browne and other gentlemen.

When Anna learned that Henry was approaching, she stepped out of her tent wearing 'a rich gown of cloth of gold raised, made round without any train after the Dutch fashion, and on her head a caul, and on that a round bonnet or cap full of orient pearl of very proper fashion'. The cap full of 'orient pearl' may be the very same cap Anna is wearing in the Rosenbach portrait. If so, Anna probably chose to wear it knowing that Henry and his court had seen her wearing it in that portrait. Anna also wore a, 'cornet[28] of black velvet, and about her neck she had a partlet set full of rich stone which glistered all the field'. Once outside, Anna mounted her splendidly trapped horse. Anna's footman wore clothing that bore the black lion of Jülich on one shoulder and on the other the gold escarbuncle of Cleves. Anna adopted these as her personal seal in later life.

Anna and Henry then approached each other. Henry and Anna rode to Greenwich as planned. When they arrived at the outer court of Greenwich,

> They alighted from their horses, and the King lovingly embraced and kissed her, bidding her welcome to her own, and led her by her left arm through the hall which was furnished beneath the hearth with the King's Guard, and above the hearth with fifty pensioners and their battle axes, and so brought her up to her privy chamber, where he left her for a time.

To celebrate Anna and Henry's entry into the court, another great volley of guns was shot from a tower at Greenwich and in the surrounding area.

A letter written 4 January 1540 to Lady Lisle details Anna's first steps in England, and her first meeting with Henry. Anna, referred to as 'the Queen's Grace', first arrived 'upon the Downes, and so lay at Dover Sunday all day. Upon Monday [her] Grace removed to Canterbury with my Lord of Suffolk and [my Lord Warden] and a great company of ladies and gentlemen, and three miles from [Canterbury] there met with her Grace my Lord of Canterbury.' In the great chamber assigned for Anna's stay in Canterbury on 5 January 1540, there were more gentlewomen and ladies to wait upon her. The letter to Lady Lisle provides a little more detail about Anna's actions when she arrived at Blackheath. Anna, 'there met with her …[the] Lord Chamberlain' and more gentlemen, and 'the duke of Suffolk's daughter', one of Henry VIII's nieces through his beloved little sister Mary, 'with many other ladies that I name not'. Next, Anna 'saluted them, Dr. Day made a goodly

---

28 A headdress made of delicate fabric with lappets.

oration, after which [Anna] went into the pavilion and shifted her wondrous gorgeously in cloth of tissue, and a rich attire upon her head of her own country fashion. When the King was within half a mile of her pavilion her Grace took horse.'

Anna and Henry delighted those gathered to witness their public meeting before the couple made for Greenwich. Anna rode upon 'a goodly palfrey or gelding, wondrously rich appareled'. Anna's Master of the Horse, Sir John Dudley, followed behind Anna, in front of her ladies. He led Anna's 'Horse of Honor'.

Anna's Letters Patent; and the French Account

While at Greenwich, Henry signed letters patent on 5 January 1540, which granted items to Anna to partially satisfy her dower. Their wedding took place the next day. The value of Anna's new lands was 4,367 marks. Specifically, Anna received

...the site of the priory of St. Margaret, near Marlborough, Wilts, lands in Marlborough, East Kennet, Manton, Yeatesbury, Lokeryche, Monkton, Puthallam, within the parish of Mildenhall and Alyngton, co. Wilts; also the rectory of East Kennet, the manors of Baberstokk and Fooffownte, otherwise Fovent; also the manors of Ha ... [Hanyngton] Sutton Scotney, Moundesmere, Old Fishbourn, Demmedmoleme, Prior's Dean, Culmere, Stubbington, and Hoo, in co. Southampton, late of the priory of Southwyke; also the manor of Bulborne, in Bremmere, with the site of the priory of Bremmere, Barnes Grange, the manors of Heywoode, Rokkestede, and Langley in co. Southampton, late belonging to the priory of Bremmere; the premises being valued at 327 marks 5s 1¼d. [And] the manors of Great Waltham, Maysbury, Dunmowe, Great Leighes, Great Haddowe ... and Farneham, Essex, of the annual value of 312 marks 8s. 1¼d.

The new queen had a battalion of women to serve and attend her, and another of men. It must have been strange for Anna to have men allowed to wait on her, given that she was used to being surrounded by women. Anna was typically around men only if it was during public social hours, and even then, there was someone to mind Anna and the other ladies at court. The women appointed for Anna are listed as 'Lady Margaret Douglas, the duchesses of Richmond and Suffolk, the countess of Sussex, ladies Howard and Clynton'. Her Ladies of the Privy Chamber were 'the *Countess* of Rutland, ladies Rochford, Edgecombe, and Bayntun'. There were Anna's Gentlewomen of the Privy Chamber, 'Mrs. Harbert, Tyrwhitt, Lye, Gilmyn'. Her *'ladies and gentlewomen attendant'* were 'ladies Dudley, Arundel, Dennys, Wriothesley, Hennage, Knevett, Crumwell, Mrs. Mewtas, Mrs. Wroughton'. The maids were '*Lady* Lucy, Mrs. Bassett, Garnysche, Cowpledike, Stradlyng' supervised by Mrs Stoner, the Mother of the Maids.

The French Ambassador Marillac provides an apparently honest appraisal of Anna's reception and appearance in a letter to Francis I on 5 January 1540. We cannot be sure whether or not the description given by Marillac is meant to damn with faint praise and ensure the impression that Anna was less attractive than, say, a Frenchwoman. 'She looks about 30 years of age, tall and thin, of medium beauty, and of very assured and resolute countenance.' It is not known how close Marillac had come to Anna: across a room, across the field at Black Heath, or face to face. Marillac did not say Anna was ugly, though he did seem less than enamoured of Cleves fashion.

A second letter, also dated 5 January 1540 and to Montmorency, gives a more critical, second-hand observation: 'According to some who saw her close [the twenty-four-year-old Anna] is not so young as was expected, nor so beautiful as everyone affirmed. She is tall and very assured in carriage and countenance, showing that in her the turn and vivacity of wit supplies the place of beauty.' Who told Marillac this – or what that person's political (or religious) leanings were – is unknown. Anna is again reported as an intelligent woman. No mention is made of the smallpox scars on Anna's face from when she survived the disease in earlier years. Given the prevalence of the disease, smallpox scars were not uncommon and not always disfiguring. Marillac goes on to criticise Anna's clothing, and remarks that the dozen or so women she brought over from the United Duchies were so swathed in fabric that their features were too hidden to say whether they were pretty. Perhaps it was the same with Anna. Marillac wrote approvingly of the meeting outside Greenwich:

> [It] was well conducted with marvelous silence and no confusion, to the number of 5,000 or 6,000 horses. The dukes of Norfolk and Suffolk were with the said lady five miles from Greenwich and the King went to meet her on the way. She was clothed in the fashion of the country from which she came, and he received her very graciously and conducted her into his house at Greenwich to the chamber prepared for her.

Johann Friedrich's ambassador came over to England with Anna, and Marillac assumed it was to conclude things between Henry and Johann Friedrich at the next parliament. Apparently, Marillac thought there would be a 'great supply of money which this King means to demand. His ministers say he can get 1,000,000 crs. without difficulty.' This may explain why Henry was willing to bring Anna to England at his own cost. Even though Anna's brother Duke Wilhelm had no funds, her brother-in-law did.

The marriage between the Lady Mary and Duke Philip of Bavaria seemed to be moving forward. Marillac reported that the Duke of Bavaria was to become a member of the 'Order of England', which meant the Order of the Garter. Marillac took this as a sign that the Lady Mary would wed the Duke.

The Wedding

At around eight o'clock in the morning on Tuesday, 6 January 1540, Henry and his nobles went to a gallery next to his closets to wait for Anna. Henry wore, 'a gown of cloth of gold, raised with great flowers of silver, furred with black genets, his coat crimson satin all to cut and embroidered and tied with great diamonds, and a rich collar about his neck'.

Henry's lords 'went to fetch the Lady Anne, which was appareled in a gown of rich cloth of gold set full of large flowers and orient pearl, made after the Dutch fashion round'. The gleaming gold dress must have set off Anna's hair magnificently, worn 'hanging down, which was fair, yellow, and long'. Anna had taken after her mother Maria, who was also blonde. On Anna's head was, 'a coronal of gold replenished with great stone, and set about full of branches of rosemary, about her neck and middle, jewels of great value and estimation'. Anna was escorted by Olisleger and Hoghestein, who 'had the conduct and performance of her marriage'. Anna showed a 'most demure countenance and sad behavior' as she walked through Henry's chamber. Here 'sad' retains the original Middle English meaning of 'steadfast', 'serious' or 'sober'. At last Anna and her escorts, 'came to the gallery where the King was, to whom she made three low obeisances and curtsies'. Thomas Cranmer, Archbishop of Canterbury, performed the marriage ceremony. Anna was given away to Henry by Olisleger. About Anna's wedding ring was engraved, 'God send me well to keep.'

The newlyweds went to Henry's closet to hear Mass. After the Mass, Anna and Henry 'had wine and spices, and that done, the King departed to his chamber, and all the ladies waited on her to her chamber'. Sometime after nine o'clock that morning, Henry returned to his closet dressed in 'a gown of rich tissue lined with crimson velvet embroidered.' Anna came in her wedding gown, preceded by her officers, 'like a queen...' Thereafter, Anna and Henry 'went openly on procession and offered and dined together'.

After dinner (lasting from late morning to early afternoon), Anna finally changed out of her wedding clothes. She returned wearing 'a gown like a man's gown, of tissue with long sleeves girt to her, furred with rich sables, her narrow sleeves were very costly, but on her head she had a cap as she wore the Saturday before [on 3 January 1540], which cap was so rich of pearl and stone, that it was judged to be of great value'. It seems that Anna favoured wearing caps or hats over hoods. This is reflected in both the Rosenbach portrait and the sketch of Anna by Wenceslaus Hollar, after Hans Holbein.

Anna's ladies were dressed in fashions from the United Duchies, which included wearing multiple, sometimes large, gold chains. Thus dressed, Anna went to Evensong and later ate supper with Henry. After supper, Anna enjoyed 'banquets, masks, and diverse disports, till the time came that it pleased the King and her to take their rest'.

The Sunday following her wedding, 11 January 1540, Anna and her retinue from the United Duchies enjoyed the jousts. This time, Anna 'was appareled after the English fashion, with a French hood, which so set forth her beauty and good visage, that every creature rejoiced to behold her'. After more ceremony, most of Anna's company prepared to leave for the United Duchies. Her cousin the Earl of Waldeck, amongst a few others, remained behind in England with Anna. He would become an almost constant guest of Anna's for the rest of her life.

Copies of Anna's dower and letters patent created by Henry on 5 January 1540 were not received by Olisleger before he started back to Cleves. On 21 January, Olisleger wrote to Cromwell requesting that said copies be sent to Gravesend or Dover. Olisleger was loath to depart for Cleves without them.

Anna and Henry left Greenwich for Westminster on 4 or 5 February, travelling by boat. It was a grand affair, with vessels owned by the merchants escorting them. The royal couple was 'accompanied with many nobles and prelates in barges ... garnished with banners, pennons, and targets, richly covered and replenished with minstrelsy ... and by the way all the ships shot their ordinance, and out of the tower was shot a great peal of guns'. The event was 'more honourable than any magnificence made at the coming of the said lady'. Now Queen Consort of England, Anna would henceforth sign her name as 'Anne the Queen' rather than 'Anna, Born Duchess of Jülich-Cleves-Berg'. She was fully adopting her new country and position.

The rumour that Anna was ugly can first be traced back to Cardinal Alessandro Farnese, who feared that Anna was a Lutheran and encouraged Cardinal Pole to stop Anna passing through France if that rumour were true. He described her to Pope Paul III as unattractive – but acceptably Catholic: 'the new Queen is worthy and Catholic, old and ugly, so that when the King saw her he was not pleased with her in that German dress, and made her dress in the French fashion.' This rumour possibly started with Marillac's letter to Francis I, stating that Anna was of middling beauty, or at least, not known for her looks, and that Anna appeared older than she was. Farnese himself had not seen Anna of Cleves, and so was repeating court gossip. While it is true that Anna began dressing in the English and French style, this does not mean that Henry ordered it. She may have preferred to take on the fashions of her new court and kingdom.

Anna wrote a letter to her mother, Duchess Maria of Jülich-Berg, at the end of January. Henry's man Wotton was dispatched to Cleves with the letter on 25 January and he arrived, likely at Swan Castle, on 9 February. Wotton, '[saluted] the Duchess, in the Duke's absence, and gave her the Queen's letter. She showed great joy, and said her son the Duke had gone to [Jülich] and thence to Paderborn to meet her son-in-law, the Elector of Saxony, on the 4th February.' No doubt Anna reported to Maria the various receptions, fêtes, and feasts held in her honour, how Anna was getting along with her husband – and perhaps what Anna thought of being Queen of England. Duke Philip of Bavaria was in Cleves when Wotton arrived. Philip told Duchess Maria of the positive reception he enjoyed in England.

Wotton wrote to Cromwell about the reaction in Cleves to early reports of Anna's marriage:

> On telling ... how well the King liked the Queen's Grace, [the Cleves representative] rejoiced greatly that the affection was mutual, for lady Keteler had written that, on leaving the Queen, she was desired to report to the Duchess, her mother, and the Duke, her brother, that she thanked them most heartily for having preferred her to such a marriage that she could wish no better.

Anna seemed as happy as she could be with her new husband and country. She did not communicate any worries or concerns, which could mean that either there were none within the first few weeks of her marriage or that she was savvy enough not to complain about being a queen consort, and thus elevated over her sisters Sybylla and Amalia, and brother Wilhelm.

A copy of documents about the alleged pre-contract between Anna and Francis of Lorraine was sworn to by Olisleger on 26 February 1540. The original document, which discussed the pre-contract, was written five years earlier, on 15 February 1535. The document in Latin appeared to terminate the pre-contract.

Anna would find out that the language of the termination was just loose enough to cause her trouble that summer.

In March 1540, Anna moved to Hampton Court Palace. She and Henry remained there through Easter until Parliament was called around 26 April 1540. Henry took the opportunity to visit his children at Richmond. The people of England 'did turn their whole attention to the jousts, tourneys and pastimes they intend to make after Easter, before and after their Queen's coronation, which shall be about Whitsuntide'. Anna of Cleves was a happy, positive presence in England, and the English were embracing her.

Johann Friedrich wrote to Henry in early March 1540, congratulating him and Anna on their 'joyful and prosperous' marriage, The Elector, though pleased with reports about his sister-in-law's new life, was more interested in whether Henry indeed wished to join with the other members of the Schmalkaldic League against the Emperor. It can be gleaned from Johann Friedrich's letter that Henry was more interested in a military alliance than one based on religious doctrine. Religious matters could be tended to afterwards. So far as Johann Friedrich knew, the same was true of any agreement with Duke Wilhelm: military support first, religion would be worked out later.

Henry reasoned with Johann Friedrich that such an arrangement would be workable and had historical precedent. After all, England and Cleves had a history of making confederacies.[29] Unfortunately for Henry, religion was everything for Johann Friedrich and the other German princes. Johann Friedrich stated, 'this league of the German princes against the tyranny of Rome, comprehends no other causes than religion, and neither Hesse nor he can, without the others, make a covenant for other causes.' Henry and Johann Friedrich were at an impasse.

The Six Articles continued to infuriate Johann Friedrich. Nevertheless, he was willing to work with Henry on these religious issues, saying that he desired 'their new knot of affinity to profit

---

29 In the early 16th century, Cleves and England worked together to assist English merchants in the Low Countries, near the duchies of Jülich-Berg and Cleves-Mark.

the Church of Christ, and to that end desires God to bless Henry's marriage with the Queen'.

Honours for Cromwell and Wilhelm

Cromwell was appointed Great Chamberlain, and created Earl of Essex, on 18 April 1540. It was reported that he was 'in as much credit with his master as ever he was, from which he was near being shaken by the [Bishop] of Winchester and others'. There was no sign of the trouble to come over the summer. Cromwell was awarded 'a patent sealed with yellow wax ... by which he was created High Chamberlain of England. The King then went to the Queen's chamber to dinner.' All was well. Henry was choosing to dine with Anna and spend time with her on that April evening.

On 23 April 1540, St George's Day, Henry was at the Palace of Westminster with the Dukes of Norfolk and Suffolk, amongst others. They were gathered to install new members of the Order of the Garter. Duke Wilhelm of Cleves' name was put forward, but ultimately was not accepted. The feast to honour the new knights was set for 9 May, at Windsor Castle.

Katheryn Howard, part of Anna's court, was given a grant on 24 April 1540. If Anna learned of the grant, she might have been suspicious or at least concerned about the reasons. This may have been one of the first cracks in the union between Anna and Henry. The alternative interpretation is that Anna knew that Katheryn Howard was the niece of the powerful Thomas Howard, Duke of Norfolk, and that she had been living as an orphan in the care of the Dowager Duchess of Norfolk. Katheryn needed provisions made for her now that she was of a marriageable age to make her an attractive bride for any potential suitor. Logically speaking, it was all perfectly normal. Katheryn's grant was not the same extraordinary action as Henry took with her cousin Anne Boleyn back in 1532, when he elevated Anne to the position of Lady Marquess of Pembroke so that she would be a more suitable bride for himself.

Anna enjoyed the May Day festivities with Henry that year. Taking place at Westminster from 30 April 1540 to 7 May 1540, the first

German Queen of England took in the English tournament, which featured 'jousting, tourney, and fighting at barriers'. The first rounds began on 1 May. Anna enjoyed not just the spectacle, but also numerous banquets and suppers with Henry and various nobles.

An indication that Anna was desirous of being a good queen to the English and adapting to English culture was that she dressed in gowns more becoming to English taste. Perhaps, as Anna had shortly after arriving in England, she was wearing a French hood. Anna was doing all that she could to fulfil her duties and be a gracious lady to her English people. Judging by outward appearances, there was no reason for anyone to think that Anna's marriage was anything but joyful.

About a month later, in early June 1540, questions about the validity of Anna's marriage were raised. Anna was sent to Richmond Palace on 24 June 1540, ostensibly to protect her from the annual increase in the threat of disease in the city around this time. By all accounts, Anna trusted and respected Henry. She had no reason to doubt Henry, or fear for her own position.

7

TENSIONS ON THE CONTINENT

The Emperor Charles V grew increasingly agitated with Anna's brother over Guelders. On 15 January 1540, nine days after Anna's wedding, Maria of Austria, Queen of Hungary awaited her brother Charles V. Vaughan, who was present in Brussels, informed Cromwell that according to Chapuys, 'the duke of Cleves was mustering men, but denied that the Emperor meant to attack him, though he had "prested" 5,000 men to attack...' The Emperor was expected at Brussels by the end of January 1540. There was a firm belief that the Lady Mary had or would marry the Duke of Bavaria, or at least, Chapuys believed it in mid-January. Vaughan complimented Cromwell on his decision to press Henry's marriage to Anna, patting himself on the head at the same time – he was 'glad Cromwell found his judgment true of the Queen'.

A time later, Cromwell held a meeting with German dignitaries of the Landgrave of Hesse and the Duke of Bavaria in Cromwell's private home. Henry's main counselors were present for the mid-January meeting. It became known to the counselors and Cromwell that Charles V was moving men out of Spain and Italy up toward France. Meanwhile, the Germans were arming themselves. The German territory was now split into two main factions: the pro-Catholic, pro-Imperial and the pro-Lutheran, anti-Imperial.

Charles V indulged the Landgrave of Hesse and other German nobles wishing to travel across Imperial territory by issuing passports to allow the Germans safe conduct. This included Wilhelm's and Johann Friedrich's men who formed part of the delegation that accompanied Anna to England. Despite the Emperor's promise of safe conduct on the way from England to Germany, there was great fear on the part of the Landgrave of Hesse and the Duke of Bavaria that they 'might be shut in here if war broke out, for they think the Emperor and their ecclesiastical adversaries are working to no other end than to attack them, which is very likely,' or this was the impression of the French Ambassador Marillac.

Duke Philip of Bavaria wrote to Cromwell on 6 February 1540, one month into Anna's queen consortship, telling Cromwell that war with Guelders was imminent. Small bands of troops were already gathering. Duke Philip was on his way to Anna's brother Wilhelm, then her brother-in-law Johann Friedrich, to deliver Henry's business.

Henry sent Thomas Howard, Duke of Norfolk, to Francis I's court in January 1540 to gain a better feel for Francis's intentions toward the Holy Roman Emperor and England. During the audience the Duke was to 'declare the King's complete assurance of their mutual friendship, and that he trusts Francis will take in good part the advice he has to offer'. Norfolk should press the idea that any overtures from the Emperor would result in Francis's political isolation.

Henry wanted Norfolk to subtly remind Francis that the Emperor was continuing to try to take Milan from Francis and suggest that Henry could assist Francis in securing it. This seemed to be through giving Francis relief from his debt owed to England and possibly some further funds to be supplied. Norfolk was also to suggest that Francis join with Anna's relatives, the Duke of Cleves, and Elector of Saxony.

It became clear by early February 1540 that the Lady Mary was not married to, nor likely would marry, Philip of Bavaria. Wilhelm angered Charles V by sending out letters to the various towns in Guelders, Ghent, Bruges, and elsewhere, declaring Wilhelm's right to Guelders. Charles V reminded Henry that, despite his being Wilhelm's brother-in-law, Henry had agreed not to involve himself in the Guelders dispute. The United Duchies, including Guelders, were within the Holy Roman Empire and thus the Emperor's vassals.

Attempts to Settle the Guelders Matter;
English Efforts in France

At the same time as Norfolk was in France, Wilhelm and Charles V were at Brussels, attempting to hammer out an agreement over Guelders. According to the French Ambassador Marillac, a settlement or agreement between Henry's brother-in-law the Duke of Cleves and the Holy Roman Emperor was something which, 'the English much desire, in order to take away the occasion of assisting their new allies with money'.

Cardinal Farnese, at the French court, gave his view of the political situation:

> The enterprise of Guelders gets warmer, which is not against that Duke alone, but all the Lutherans and England; so that if France aids the Emperor ... in consequence of the peace, it could well be that after Guelders might follow the punishment of the English king... The Emperor's instances to the Pope to join the Catholic league seem to show that he has this enterprise of Guelders much at heart.

At this point, within a month of her wedding, it was clear that Anna's brother Wilhelm and sister, Sybylla, were going to war against Charles V. It was a matter of time.

Failings in the English system of gathering intelligence about the brewing Guelders conflict were obvious to Charles V, who said as much to Sir Thomas Wyatt during an audience. Charles V said of Cromwell, '[a]s to Cromwell's words to the King's ambassador [Sir Thomas Wyatt], the Emperor said the king of England seemed to have very bad spies, or rather thought himself very well informed.'

Trying to fill in the gaps, Henry VIII sent the Duke of Norfolk to France in hopes of keeping Francis's friendship. Marillac, still stationed in England, believed that Norfolk was sent abroad to stall any action the Emperor might take against Wilhelm. Norfolk barely spoke French, and had to request the presence of the Bishop of London to act as translator between Norfolk and Francis.

Francis dallied in granting an audience to Norfolk. Once the time finally came, Francis bemoaned the presence of the Bishop of London. As Norfolk later learned, the Bishop's endeavours while he was at the French court more benefitted Charles V than Francis I. Norfolk was to broach the touchy subject of Milan. Francis and Charles were evermore battling over this valuable duchy, each claiming rights to it. The Truce of Nice remained in full force, just waiting for either Francis or Charles to violate it. Francis warned Norfolk that the Emperor was determined to keep Guelders, and when it came to Anna's brother relinquishing it, he 'would allow no arbitration'.

Norfolk next had an audience with Francis's beloved sister Marguerite of Angoulême, Queen of Navarre. Norfolk found Marguerite to be, 'the most frank and wise woman he ever spake with'. She loathed the Emperor. Marguerite gave an insight into how Francis's mind worked, saying that once he got an idea in his head, he would pursue it doggedly. This allowed Norfolk to lead Marguerite to discuss the issue of Milan. Marguerite firmly believed that, despite Francis and Charles getting along well recently, the rapprochement between them could not last. Marguerite believed that military action over Guelders was coming, but that the Emperor probably would not win. That, of course, was yet to be seen, as no overtly bellicose acts had been committed by either Charles V or Wilhelm.

Around 21 February 1540, Henry advised Norfolk to urge Francis to speak of Charles V's hold on Milan. Norfolk was then to urge Francis to strike against the Emperor now while the Emperor appeared weak. It was suggested that Francis should ally himself with Henry, Duke Wilhelm of Cleves, Elector Johann Friedrich of Saxony, and the rest of the Lutheran-leaning German princes. That way, Charles V must give in to the demands of both Wilhelm concerning Guelders and Francis concerning Milan. The Emperor, at this time in Flanders, would be surrounded and have no choice but to capitulate without violence.

Undaunted, Charles V tested his guns and arranged for secret passage of his men into Flanders. More crushing to Anna's brother, the residents of Guelders were working out an agreement with the Emperor independent of Duke Wilhelm. They did not seem in favor of a war on their doorstep.

Wilhelm's Obfuscation

In February 1540, Wotton just missed Wilhelm and Elector Johann Friedrich at Paderborn. Olisleger was in Wesel, and it was suggested Wotton try to meet with Olisleger there instead of following after Wilhelm and Elector Johann Friedrich. On Ash Wednesday, 11 February, Wotton took off toward Hamm through foul weather and met with yet another one of Wilhelm's advisors. Neither Wilhelm nor Elector Johann Friedrich were there. Wotton gave King Henry's letter to the advisor. Apparently, the advisor had a gift for Wotton, but forgot it in Cleves.

Wotton learned that Wilhelm and Johann Friedrich finished their business on Shrove Tuesday. By the time Wotton learned this, Johann Friedrich was well on his way to meeting with the Landgrave of Hesse in Kassel, and the Duke of Cleves 'to Bylevelt to take possession of his county of [Ravensberg] and would also take possession of the county of [Mark]...' Wotton decided to head back toward Paderborn from Hamme, where Wilhelm and Johann Friedrich conducted their meetings, despite knowing no one of any import was there. Wotton was the very first 'to return to the Duke of all the company that conducted the Queen to England'.

Wotton followed Wilhelm all the way to Lippe, hoping to be there by Valentine's Day 1540. Being that it was winter and stormy, the roads were not good and he did not come to Lippe until the 15th. Around supper time Wotton finally met with Wilhelm and gave him letters from Anna and Henry. Wilhelm was pleased with the letters and received Wotton kindly. Things then took a politically deceptive turn.

Wilhelm told Wotton that he had no instructions for Wotton to deliver to Henry because Wilhelm had already sent an ambassador to England with Wilhelm's instructions. Wilhelm flattered Henry's emissary, saying 'that the King could have sent no one to him more acceptable than Wotton, and that the Duke was much bound to Henry for being so ready to promote his interests'. Wilhelm turned the conversation toward the articles of the Anglo-Cleves alliance, which he had not received yet. Apparently, Olisleger, who was slowly making his way back to Wilhelm, was supposed to have a copy for Wilhelm's review.

Wilhelm then departed for the city of Soste, inviting Wotton to follow, which Wotton did. Wilhelm led Wotton to believe that Wotton would be able to meet with Olisleger at Soste concerning the Anglo-Cleves alliance the very next day. Olisleger never appeared, and Wilhelm had to leave for yet another city in his domains.

The entire time Wotton was with Wilhelm at Lippe and Soste, Wilhelm never mentioned what was discussed between him and Elector Johann Friedrich, nor any news brought by Wilhelm's ambassador to France. Wilhelm evaded Wotton's questions by stating that the matters discussed involved only Germany, and that Elector Johann Friedrich was amicably inclined toward England. When asked if Wotton could deliver information to Henry on behalf of Wilhelm, Wilhelm told of how his messengers had been captured by Charles V in Brabant. When pressed further, Wilhelm admitted the messengers were not on their way to England. Wilhelm told Wotton, 'the letters contained nothing but friendliness to the Emperor and a desire for the settlement of controversies about Guelders, in which he desired the towns of Brabant to intercede'. Wilhelm suggested that Wotton go to Düsseldorf, where Wotton could expect Wilhelm in about a week. On 18 February, a Wednesday, Wotton made his way to Düsseldorf.

Wotton informed Cromwell of what happened with Wilhelm, concluding that 'the Elector and the Duke had made some straight league,' or that Wilhelm and Johann Friedrich 'only treated of the pacification of Germany to prevent the Emperor's interference'. At the same time, Wilhelm had around five hundred *Landsknechte*, mustered in Jülich to brace for what Emperor Charles V might do. The *Landsknechte* were professional mercenaries for hire.

When it came to Charles's threats, Wotton declared of Wilhelm and his men, 'Whatever the rulers be, the young gentlemen and the common people are not afraid of him.' Karl Harst was present in Düsseldorf and Wotton questioned why Harst was not yet in England. It emerged that Wilhelm ordered Harst to remain in the United Duchies until Olisleger and the other Cleves ambassadors returned from England. Harst relayed that Wilhelm had reviewed the articles concerning the Anglo-Cleves alliance, and sent his own to England. Wotton was skeptical that Wilhelm agreed to the proposed terms of the alliance as they were stated.

Norfolk's Return; Bad News from Cleves

Norfolk arrived in England on 1 March 1540, feeling triumphant about his efforts in France. Around 2 March, another attempt at keeping Francis I's friendship was made by Henry through the Queen of Navarre. The Queen was told she should remember that Emperor Charles V was merely human, and thus fallible and subject to failure, just as any other. Henry offered his opinion that if Francis's son, the Duke of Orleans, were invested with Milan, this would simply make the Duke of Orleans a vassal of the Emperor. This would create the possibility of later conflict between the Dauphin of France and the Duke of Orleans. Further, the Queen of Navarre should relay to her brother that Francis should consider 'what Henry ought to do for the Duke [of Cleves], whose sister he has married, if the Emperor attempt to win Guelders by force'. Henry had intelligence that Francis pledged his support to the Emperor, should the Guelders matter come to a head.

After having a more meaningful meeting with Wilhelm, Wotton wrote another letter to Henry on 7 March 1540:

> The duke of Cleves, having taken possession of his counties of [Ravensberg] and [Mark], came to [Düsseldorf] on Monday, 24 Feb., and Wotton, while he waited there for the promised answer, received, on the 28th, the King's letter to the Duke, with the part of the treaty sent to him by the Duke ratified under the King's Great Seal.
>
> Next morning delivered them to the Duke, who said he would consider the matters. On the 5th he sent for Wotton, and gave him a letter for the King, saying it was in answer to Henry's last, and that he had also written in cipher to his ambassador in England things to be declared to his Highness.
>
> Desired a further answer by mouth to his overtures at Lippe, and the Duke, after consultation, caused the Chancellor ... to tell him that the article last sent to him might be taken by the Emperor and the German princes [as somewhat against] them... After this [Wilhelm] very soon took horse, and rode to the Duchess [his mother] at Hambach [Castle]. In five or six days he

will be at Cleves, where he wished Wotton to follow him. He will remain about Cleves, Nijmegen, and Arnhem till after Easter.

Wotton gave Cromwell a different view than he gave Henry about Wilhelm's reaction to Henry's letter and the terms of the Anglo-Cleves alliance. Wilhelm was amused when he found out Charles V refused to 'hear the King's intercession for him'. Wotton admitted that Wilhelm's reaction to the letter led him to believe that Wilhelm was sorely disappointed. Wilhelm was not much in favour of the alliance as it was written. Wilhelm thought 'the article last sent might be worded less dangerously to him. He has been negotiating for the marriage of his sister Amelia to the Elector [Johann Friedrich's] younger brother [Johann Ernst].'

Updating Cromwell on the Guelders negotiations, Wotton said, 'The men of the country buy harness and weapons apace. The six Electors have promised to urge the Emperor not to proceed against the Duke by force but by law ... He has sent another ambassador ... to the Emperor, to demand the investiture of Guelders.'

Cromwell therefore either miscalculated or did not appreciate the danger of the Guelders situation when he started pressing for Henry to marry Anna.

Another Push for Peace

The Lutheran princes requested that Charles V ratify the conclusions of the Diet of Frankfurt, and that the Emperor leave the Germans alone when it came to faith. The Lutherans were fearful of the Emperor's arrival in their lands and what he might do. It was thought that if Charles V ratified the Diet of Frankfurt, this would provide some political protection and surety. However, if anyone spoke to Charles V or his brother Ferdinand, then King of the Romans, 'about the affairs of Cleves they would not listen; and so they should do in the demands of the Religion, this cause being no less important to them than the duchy of Cleves.'

While debates over religion continued between Henry and Johann Friedrich, Wilhelm was unwilling to give up Guelders and even continued to press for a marriage with Christina of

Denmark, Emperor Charles V's niece. Wilhelm expected 'to settle his differences with the Emperor, retaining Guelders by marrying the duchess of Milan'.

Around 17 March 1540, peace for Guelders looked promising. Anna may have been anticipating Christina of Denmark becoming her new sister-in-law. The marriage between Wilhelm and Christina of Denmark was expected be concluded by Easter. In addition, reports showed that Charles V was willing to surrender the Duchy of Milan to Francis I:

> The ambassadors of the duke of Cleves are with the Emperor, and an accord will probably be made between them. The estate of Guelders will remain with the Duke, but the Emperor will reserve the title. The marriage between the Duke and the duchess of Milan will take effect, and also between the prince of Araunges [Orange] and the daughter of the duke of Loreno [Lorraine], who consents thereto for the action he pretends to have upon the duchy of Guelders.

Wilhelm was adamant about keeping Guelders. It did not seem that Charles V would enter into Germany in spring 1540, nor did it seem likely that Charles was keen on starting a war with any of the German princes. Wotton, present in the United Duchies, admitted that he did not have much intelligence to give Cromwell because he was 'cut off from the news'. Wotton did share that proposals were being sought for Anna's little sister Amalia, but not much more than that.

Charles V received conflicting advice from his counselors about Wilhelm and Guelders. One gentleman advised him 'to make truces with the [German] Protestants, and meanwhile recover Guelders'. Another warned Charles V that he 'should not try the matter of Guelders by law, for none of the German princes wished him to have it'. Another point of view given to Charles V was that '[T]he Protestants will make no truce with the Emperor without including the Duke [of Cleves].' Effectively, both Charles V and Wilhelm were on unsure ground – neither had taken decisive action in the last year. To complicate matters, the Germans were meeting again at

Schmalkalden around 21 March 1540, and everyone was 'waiting to see what the Emperor will attempt, and prepared to resist him'.

A letter from Marillac written at the end of March 1540 illustrated Henry's position when it came to foreign wars fairly accurately. He wrote that the English had 'several conceptions all tending to the end which they most desire – to escape war for this year and remain at peace with their neighbours, especially France. Cromwell says a settlement is certain between the Emperor and the duke of Cleves.' Most importantly, should the matter be settled between Anna's brother and the Emperor, then Anna's new English subjects would not be obliged to assist Cleves, England's new ally.

The cordiality between Charles V and Francis I was swiftly falling apart. That meant trouble for England as well because any wars between France and the Holy Roman Empire, depending on where the theatres were, could seriously affect English trade routes and present other dangers.

At the end of March, on the 29th, the German princes held a meeting in Schmalkalden. They were emboldened enough to urge the Emperor 'to show himself a true prince, otherwise war will rage all over Germany'. Sybylla and Wilhelm were butting up against the line between agitating for war and open rebellion.

In early April 1540, Henry was closely focused on the events in Germany. Specifically

...if there be any likelihood of peace among the princes there [in Germany] and the Emperor, especially between him and the Protestants, and on what conditions; whether they expect the Emperor to come thither shortly; how they feel towards the duke of Cleves, and what they intend towards him.

No matter how delighted Henry was with Anna, continuing with her as Queen consort placed England at risk of being absorbed into a costly war on the Continent.

Wotton, in Cleves, met with Wilhelm on 10 April 1540. Wotton learned that Charles V's brother Ferdinand, King of the Romans and living in Austria, offered to mediate between Wilhelm and

Charles V. Wilhelm believed Ferdinand when he promised safe conduct should Wilhelm go to the Emperor, and that Wilhelm could leave whenever he desired. Wilhelm's council did not believe that Wilhelm should trust so easily, and they 'fully represented to [Wilhelm] the danger of trusting promises, and some had this very day, with tears running down their cheeks, prayed him not to risk them; but it was the Duke's own mind, and he was fully resolved.'

Worse still, Wilhelm did not bother to wait and consult with either Henry VIII or Elector Johann Friedrich. Wilhelm left around 10 April to meet the Emperor.

Possibly realising that he was acting the petulant little brother, Wilhelm 'writes of this to Henry and the Queen [Anna], and also to the Elector and Duchess [Sybylla] of Saxony'. A significant measure of Wilhelm's power stemmed from the marriages both Sybylla and Anna achieved, and without them, Wilhelm's military heft would be greatly diminished. He was behaving like a hot-headed, inexperienced twenty-three-year-old. Wotton told Cromwell as much, but adding:

> The country, and especially Guelders, marvels much at this matter, and fears the end of it. The magistrates of the Duchy, with weeping eyes, yesterday, begged the Duke not to put himself in such hazard, but the Duke seems fully resolved. If Ferdinand mean well, [I] cannot tell what to think of it unless [Ferdinand] means to make one of his daughters duchess of Cleves. It were a great marriage for his daughter, [Ferdinand] having so many children and so little to bestow them with.

Ferdinand had thirteen children that survived to adulthood, ten of whom were women. If such a match was truly sought, Wilhelm was tired of waiting for the Duchess of Milan, but interested in placating the Emperor. This was contrary to Henry VIII's desires in light of his amity with Francis I. And it was completely against what the anti-papist Elector of Saxony wanted with regard to the Catholic Holy Roman Emperor.

Wilhelm arrived in the Low Countries to meet with Charles V on 13 April 1540. By that point, it was a foregone conclusion internationally that accords were already completed between the two, just as it was assumed they were concluded between Henry and Wilhelm. It was widely believed that Wilhelm would marry Christina of Denmark. It was not yet common knowledge that Wilhelm was interested in Charles V's nieces.

Wotton, forever trying to catch up with Wilhelm, finally met him on 14 April in or around Ghent. When confronted over his lack of communication with Henry, Wilhelm became defensive and told Wotton that he had 'given notice of all important affairs to Henry, both by his ambassador in England and by Wotton, communicating the cause of the meeting at Paderborn and the news from his ambassador in France'. Wilhelm did admit to cutting short the time his ambassador spent in France, but not in any way to injure Wilhelm's relationship with Henry.

The men next discussed the articles of the Anglo-Cleves treaty, to which Wilhelm had not affixed his signature yet. Wilhelm believed that if he agreed to the document as written, it would 'displease his subjects and neighbors, but, if the case required it, he would fulfill the articles no less than if he were bound thereto'. Wotton expressed his displeasure with Wilhelm at not giving any straight answers, either directly or through counselors. Wotton believed that Wilhelm 'and all his council are anxious to avoid war with the Emperor, because, although the towns of Guelders are well fortified, [Jülich] and [Berg] lie open to any enemy. Thinks, however, he is sincerely inclined towards England.'

Wotton took an opportunity to meet with Sir Thomas Wyatt. They had long discussions with Olisleger about Guelders and Wilhelm's intentions. Wilhelm drew a line in the sand with Charles V, telling Charles V's brother Ferdinand that he 'would not come to the Emperor if he intended to raise any question about [Guelders]'. Charles V planned to convene another Diet in Speyer around 6 July 1540. Charles V wanted to continue addressing the religious disputes between himself and the German princes, and to further push his interests in Guelders. At Wyatt's behest, Wilhelm scribbled out a letter to Henry to explain how matters stood in the United Duchies, and what Wilhelm's intentions were with the Emperor.

Francis and Wilhelm were beginning to have something in common: the constant head-butting with Charles V over land to which Francis and Wilhelm believed they had lawful claim. The Emperor was trying to drive a hard bargain with Francis I, such that Francis could keep Milan if he handed over most of Picardy, plus adding French lands to Charles' Duchy of Burgundy. Moreover, the Emperor wanted Francis to be completely in league with him, meaning that France and the Holy Roman Empire would have the same friends and enemies, and would deal with the Protestants in the same way.

As for Wilhelm, who was consistently asserting himself against Charles V:

...the difference with the duke of [Jülich] and Cleves is not by any means settled, and … the marriage of the duchess of Milan and the said Duke is made on condition that the Emperor leaves him in possession of Guelders and gives him 100,000 florins rent on the duchy of Bar in Naples, to which marriage the king of England must have consented.

Wilhelm outwardly appeared in favour of a match with Christina of Denmark in spring 1540.

Henry, through Cromwell, tried to learn more about Francis I's intentions and relationship with the Emperor in mid-April 1540. An English representative was in Navarre to meet with Queen Marguerite. After receiving a letter from Henry, Marguerite 'said his Majesty did her great honour, and that she would keep her chamber purposely a day or two', to set an appointment with the English ambassador. Francis and his wife Queen Eleanor, Charles V's sister, were away and would not know of Marguerite's conversation with the English.

Marguerite reasoned that Francis was doing his best to be cautious, and she professed herself 'always ready to do the King what service lay in her power', and advised Henry not to declare himself too openly with the duke of Cleves and the princes of Germany, otherwise Francis would side with the Emperor against both him and the Germans, for fear that England and the Germans should agree with the Emperor and leave Francis isolated.

Marguerite made a point of requesting small portraits or miniatures of Anna, Henry, Prince Edward, the Lady Mary and the Lady Elizabeth. It is not known if these portraits ever made it to Navarre, or if they survived. Marguerite could not accept gifts from Henry, as it would be obvious that she was in talks with England. However, a simple request of portraits of the English royal family would not raise suspicion.

Jeanne d'Albret Enters the Marriage Market

The Emperor hoped that he could make a double-marriage between his children and the French royal offspring. He proposed a marriage between Queen Marguerite's daughter Jeanne d'Albret and the Emperor's son, plus a marriage between the Emperor's daughter and Francis's son, the Duke of Orleans. Of course, such marriages came with more strings than a marionette. The King of Navarre would transfer his title to Charles's son, and the Duke of Orleans would receive the County of Flanders if Francis also gave his son the parts of Burgundy that Francis controlled, plus other territories. Such an arrangement would leave France more or less surrounded by the Holy Roman Empire.

Henry was anxious for news from Francis, but there was not much to give (or discover by espionage). The marriage between Jeanne d'Albret and the Emperor's son was not likely if the King of Navarre had to sign over his title. This was an attempt by the Emperor to incorporate Navarre into Spain.

Thinking they were out of danger from the Emperor, the people of England rejoiced that their new queen's family had settled differences with the Holy Roman Empire. As reported by Marillac, 'the agreement of the duke of Cleves with the Emperor by the marriage of the duchess of Milan [was reported in England]. Both the Emperor's ambassador and the common report here say he will marry her. [One] can imagine the pleasure of the English at this for the fear they were in of war on account of their new ally.' As will be seen, the rejoicing was premature. The 'fervent amity' between Francis I and Charles V was beginning to cool.

Francis I was willing to agree to Charles V's terms of the Franco-Imperial marriages, but he refused to ratify the proposed treaties of Madrid and Cambrai. Francis pledged to observe the terms of the two treaties. The terms did not do much for Francis or his children. All Imperial territories granted to Charles V's daughter would revert to the Holy Roman Empire if she and Francis's son, the Duke of Orleans, died childless. Moreover, Francis would agree not to press his claim for Milan. Francis would be allowed to keep his claims to Savoy and Piedmont.

The negotiations between the Emperor and Francis, and between the Emperor and Wilhelm, broke down by the end of April 1540. Francis sent for *Landsknechte* out of Germany. 'On the French borders people sell all they can, expecting war.'

Breakdown of Negotiations

The relationship between Charles V and Wilhelm passed the breaking point. Wilhelm gave Charles's brother Ferdinand his declaration of right to the Guelders territory. Charles quickly gave reply in Dutch, which was read before the Duke and his Council, 'saying the case was so clear, [Wilhelm] had better follow the Emperor's mind and deliver Guelders to him'. Wilhelm, in response, said that he

>...could make very good answer, but if the Emperor must needs have Guelders it was needless to reason further, and seeing that he could do no more without the consent of the Duchess [Maria], his mother, to whom he had not spoken when he left the country, said he would return home to have her advice and that of the country.

This was not good enough for the Emperor or King Ferdinand, who urged Wilhelm to give an answer before he repaired to Cleves. Wilhelm refused at first, then went to King Ferdinand to give his answer. Wotton wrote Henry a letter on 30 April 1540 describing the incident between Wilhelm, King Ferdinand, and the Emperor.

>...the Duke, being sent for, came to king Ferdinand, who ... told him that he wished to see some good end between him

and the Emperor and had examined the claims of the Emperor and the Duke to Guelders with the reasons alleged on both sides ... that he thought the Emperor had better right to the Duchy than [Wilhelm] and that he recommended him to follow the Emperor's mind.

Wilhelm, though desperate to avoid war and keep the Duchy of Guelders, should have known better than to allow King Ferdinand to pass on any sort of opinion as to who had a greater right to Guelders. King Ferdinand was Emperor Charles V's brother, after all. King Ferdinand 'represented the danger of having such an adversary as the Emperor' to Wilhelm. Not willing simply to accept King Ferdinand's advice and relinquish Guelders, Wilhelm again went over all the reasons why he lawfully held title. Wilhelm appealed to King Ferdinand, asking for his help. If King Ferdinand did not help, Wilhelm would try to seek some sort of resolution at law. The Emperor was not at all moved by this and continued to demand possession of Guelders. Wilhelm was not prepared to give up Guelders before discussing the situation with his and Anna's mother, Duchess Maria, or with his council back in the United Duchies. The parties separated.

Later on, the Emperor sent the Duke of Brunswick to try and urge Wilhelm to give up Guelders. Brunswick tried to convince Wilhelm to suggest some kind of recompense for handing over Guelders. Wilhelm refused. Wilhelm did offer to relinquish his family's title to it upon his death and let the matter thereafter be decided by law, but only if Charles V allowed him to keep Guelders peaceably until then.

Brunswick departed, but returned after speaking with Emperor Charles V, King Ferdinand, and their sister Maria. The message Brunswick delivered was no longer girded about with fancy diplomatic language. The Emperor said that 'he would not enter into no conference till possession was given up, and that the Duke, in entering into possession of Guelders without the Emperor's authority, deserved to be deprived of all the rest he holds of the Emperor.' Wilhelm deserved to be deprived of not only Guelders, but also the United Duchies of Jülich-Cleves-Berg, Ravensberg, Barr, and Mark.

Wilhelm was astounded by the Emperor's words. Charles V seemed almost irrational about the Guelders matter; but Charles V had already put down an insurrection in Ghent, and on top of that, was preparing observations to honour the anniversary of his beloved wife's passing. His patience was worn thin.

To leave Ghent as quickly as he could, Wilhelm claimed that he needed to go home to discuss things with the Duchess Maria and his council. Wotton, believing Wilhelm to be in imminent danger, suggested to him, 'that though I doubted not but that the Duke would be suffered to leave, yet it would be not unwise to have horses ready in divers places and 2 or 3 ways; so that in case it chanced otherwise they might be able to save him.'

The imminent danger that Wilhelm was now in was clear to Olisleger, Wilhelm's vice-chancellor, who explained to Wotton:

> One day it was come to the Emperor's ears that the duke of Cleves' men said the Emperor would not lightly make war against the Duke, who, besides his own great power, was so allied with the king of England, elector of Saxony, and other princes, that he could well enough resist the Emperor. The Emperor was offended that the Duke should suffer his men to speak so. The Duke, on enquiry, found that none of his men had spoken such words; so that this seemed to be half a picking of a quarrel.

Even if it was bluff on the part of the Emperor, it did illustrate his attitude toward Wilhelm. Wilhelm did not write any letters to anyone until he returned to Cleves, where there was less chance of the letters being intercepted. In an instant, friendship with France and an alliance with Cleves was no longer safe for England.

Continued Overtures to the French; The Danger of the Cleves Marriage

By May 1540, not long after he was created Earl of Essex, Cromwell was scrambling to avoid the catastrophe that the Third War of the Guelderian Succession would bring. (The first had been fought from 1371 to 1379: see Chapter 13.) Cromwell desperately tried to regain the affections of the French. The French Ambassador Marillac wrote to Montmorency, Constable of France, about his interactions with Cromwell during the May Day celebrations:

> First Cromwell spoke of his master's singular affection for Francis, which he exaggerated as much as he could; adding that in the past he and some others had been more Imperialist than French, but having discovered the design of the Emperor (who only desires to hold people with fine words, and meanwhile do his own business, aspiring evidently to make himself monarch of Christendom) it has made them recognise their error and open their eyes to extinguish this fire, which would burn all the world.

The Dukes of Norfolk and Suffolk approached Marillac as well, and echoed all that Cromwell stated. Norfolk

> ...confirmed Cromwell's sayings, asking Marillac to test whether he was not now as French as formerly he had been Burgundian. Suffolk ... also held the same language, as if to impress it upon the writer, adding that they were being practised with to make a closer league with the Emperor, but were now as unwilling to listen as formerly they had been inclined to the devotion of the said Emperor.

Cromwell himself acknowledged on 11 May that 'the whole of Christendom hangs in the balance.'

Charles V now turned his attention to England, showing respect and civility to Henry's Ambassador Richard Pate, who replaced Wyatt as Henry's ambassador to the Low Countries. Charles V, King Ferdinand, and Regent Maria were at Mass on Ascension Day in Holland with all the ambassadors present and made a show of their goodwill toward Pate. King Ferdinand contrived to make polite eye contact with Pate. The Regent Maria kept her eyes lowered. It was said of the Emperor that day that he was never seen 'of better cheer, and that natural and not constrained'. Emperor Charles V behaved 'lovingly' toward the French ambassador after mass. He welcomed

Pate at the palace. Francis I felt that the situation with the Emperor was not completely broken down, but it was a vain hope. Francis told Marillac in mid-May that, 'difficulties have arisen; but they are not of a nature to alter the amity.'

Henry sent instructions to Wotton in Cleves in the early part of June 1540. Henry was unhappy that the letters Wotton sent to him and Cromwell around 30 April had not made it into Henry's hands until 30 May. It was now clear to Henry that Wilhelm was, inevitably, eventually going to war with the Emperor. Such a war would be potentially devastating to England, a small island country. Trade would be thrown into chaos, the English Channel would become dangerous; and the sheer numbers of troops which the Emperor could muster was terrifying. Marriage to Anna von der Mark, Duchess of Cleves, had just become a massive liability to Henry.

Cromwell received the news around the same time as Henry, as Wotton wrote Cromwell a similar letter and dispatched it at the same time. Cromwell's reaction is easily imagined: as the orchestrator of the Anglo-Cleves alliance, he was responsible for any danger in which England was placed. This time, he would not be able to find a way to work around his failure.

Wilhelm sent a request to Henry for his advice. Henry instructed Wotton 'to show and declare ourself at all times his most perfect friend'. Henry gave an audience on 31 May 1540 to Wilhelm's ambassador in England. At this audience, the Cleves ambassador 'delivered ... certain articles, tending chiefly ... to this one point, that the Emperor seemeth to desire to be once in possession of Guelders.' Henry was angry with the Cleves ambassador, lamenting that he had not sooner been informed of Wilhelm's situation and desired course of action. Henry did not think the articles he was sent concerning Guelders could be addressed quickly by Wilhelm. Henry wanted Wotton to approach Wilhelm and tell him

> ...that as we be right glad of his return again into his countries, even so we be right sorry that his and your letters ... desiring our advice for his answers to the Emperor, came so lately to our hands that we could not before this time thereunto make him answer.

Wilhelm's council carried on with no concern for the Anglo-Cleves alliance and without input from England. In effect, all this time, Anna's brother kept Anna's husband in the dark. Henry wished Wilhelm to know that

> ...before we can fully consider what should be meet for him, he should open to us the full state of his affairs; but we neither know the whole of his estate, nor any one special part of his said affairs. For when his ambassadors were here they told us of certain overtures which he made for Guelders to the Emperor as a mean to purchase peace and quiet, and whether he rest on them we know not... if he shall hereupon frankly [notify] unto us what...he purposeth and intendeth, we shall not fail to counsel him as we think most for his honour.

Judging by Cromwell's behaviour during the May Day celebrations, he may have known full well what was going on and delayed telling Henry. This is pure speculation. However, it is possible that Cromwell had either received Wotton's letters to himself and Henry earlier in May and delayed giving the letters to Henry, or he knew that the Guelders negotiations had fallen apart by some other means. Either way, Henry was aware by early June 1540 that Cromwell, instrumental in negotiating the Anglo-Cleves entanglements, had just forced England into the dangerous and unpopular situation of war with the Emperor. While the exact thoughts of Cromwell and Henry may never be known, some of these possibilities help explain what happened next.

On 10 June 1540, Thomas Cromwell, Earl of Essex, Lord Privy Seal, and Lord Chamberlain, was arrested on accusations of treason. Cromwell was attending a privy council meeting at Westminster during Parliament when the Duke of Norfolk and the Captain of the Guard approached him, a small audience in tow. Cromwell is said to have thrown his hat on the table, enraged at what he knew was coming. The Garter badge of St George was ripped from Cromwell's clothing, supposedly by Norfolk. Cromwell was then escorted to the Tower of London to await his fate.

Astonished, Thomas Cranmer, Archbishop of Canterbury, addressed Henry, expressing, 'his amazement and grief that he should be a traitor who was so advanced by the King and cared for no man's displeasure to serve him, and was so vigilant to detect treason... [Cranmer] Loved him as a friend, and the more for the love he seemed to bear the King.'

A Franco-Cleves Alliance

Foreign intelligence recorded around 13 June 1540 delves deeper into the danger England faced through any alliance with Cleves. Christina of Denmark refused to marry Wilhelm unless he gave up his claim to Guelders. Wilhelm turned his attention toward a French marriage. Wilhelm wanted Henry's blessing and advice before acting on this. It was of the utmost importance that the pending French match be kept secret from the Emperor. Wilhelm was surprised to learn that Henry felt in the dark about Wilhelm's attempts to negotiate with the Emperor, as he had thought that Sir Thomas Wyatt, the English ambassador to the Imperial court, was relating everything of import to Henry.

The *Landsknechte* mobilised by Francis I headed toward the Bishopric of Minden. About 5,000 strong, it was believed that many of the captains hailed from the United Duchies. The Diet of Speyer was about to begin, and Francis made sure to have one of his ambassadors in attendance. Wilhelm was not expected to be there, though representatives of Jülich, from the Duchess Maria's territories, would.

On 21 June 1540, Duke Wilhelm of Cleves concluded an alliance with Francis I of France. Wilhelm ratified the alliance in Düsseldorf. Thus France and Cleves asserted themselves against the Holy Roman Empire, with Francis desiring Milan and Wilhelm desiring Guelders. The day after the Franco-Cleves alliance was created, Henry sent instructions to his ambassador in France, John Wallop, who had semi-permanent residency in Paris:

The ambassador of Cleves has informed us that the Duke
... finding the Emperor has only practised with him for his

own advantage by overtures of marriage, intends to provide marriage for himself elsewhere, and ... that the Duke desired the King's advice in the matter [concerning a French match for Wilhelm] ... and wished Henry to write to Wallop to help them with his counsel.

Henry sent a member of his council who was educated in the law to help Wallop advise Wilhelm. Wallop was to 'grope and fish out all their purposes and commission, both with the King and other personages of honour there ... so that Henry may know what he is seeking, and how he is disposed to all parties, whether the French favour his suit, and whether he has that confidence in Henry which he pretends'.

On 29 June 1540, a Bill of Attainder was passed by Parliament against Thomas Cromwell. The Bill was predominantly founded on grounds of religion, including Cromwell's failure to enforce the Six Articles and sympathy toward Anabaptists. The Duke of Norfolk personally delivered the news to Cromwell in the Tower. At Norfolk's behest, Cromwell attested to a document, then wrote a letter that would haunt Anna, and then her reputation, down through the centuries.

8

DOUBTING THE THOMASES

Both Thomas Cromwell and Thomas Wyatt were in Henry's service during the vital final negotiations for Anna's marriage and her brief reign. Cromwell was Henry's most trusted official, and Wyatt had the key posting of ambassador to the Imperial court. Cromwell gave an account of Anna's relationship with Henry in two documents from June 1540. Wyatt sent a series of letters to Henry during his time at the Imperial court. The documents and letters from each Thomas paint very different pictures.

Thomas Cromwell's second-to-last document, a signed attestation, recorded the interactions between Henry and Anna, declaring that they contributed to the annulment of their marriage. This oft-quoted attestation was signed on 30 June 1540, and then a letter which reiterated the same information that was dashed off by Cromwell that same day,

> ...beseeching most humbly your grace to pardon this my rude writing, and to consider that I am a most woeful prisoner ready to take the death when it shall please God and your Majesty and yet the frail flesh inciteth me continually to call to your Grace for mercy and pardon for mine offenses and this Christ Salve preserve and keep you written at the Tower [of London] this Wednesday the last of June with the heavy heart and trembling hand of your Highness most heavy and most miserable prisoner and poor slave Most gracious Prince I cry for mercy mercy mercy.

Imprisoned in the Tower of London since 10 June 1540, a Bill of Attainder against Cromwell was drawn up and passed on 29 June. This desperate letter was written the day after. The letter is because of the meeting Cromwell had in Tower on 30 June with with the new Lord Chancellor, the Duke of Norfolk, and the Lord Admiral, who sought an official accounting of the relationship between Henry and Anna. It contains very similar information to the attestation. Cromwell gave this account, 'upon the extreme danger and damnation of my soul and conscience'. He was also commanded to draft the letter to Henry. Cromwell starts with Anna's arrival on English soil:

> First after your Majesty heard of the Lady Anne of Cleves' arrival at Dover and that her Jemeyes[30] were appointed towards Greenwich and that she should be at Rochester on New Year's Eve at night your Highness declared to me that ye would privily visit her at Rochester upon New Year's Day adding these words to nourish love, which accordingly your Grace did.

Cromwell writes of the response Henry gave him after Cromwell inquired of Henry's visit with Anna:

> The next day ... your Grace returned to Greenwich where I spoke with your Grace and demanded of your Majesty how ye liked the Lady Anne your Highness answered as me pleasantly nothing so well as she was spoken of saying further that if your Highness had known as much before as ye then knew she should not have come within this Realm.

The day after Anna's entry at Greenwich, she was taken to her chamber. Afterward, Cromwell writes, 'I then waited upon your Highness into your privy chamber, and ... you Saying to me these words or the like, "My Lord, is it not as I told you? Say what they will, she is nothing so fair as she hath been reported, howbeit she is well and seemly."'

---

30 Hackneys or jenets, pack-horses.

The letter continues that Henry ordered his counsel to be assembled to review the matters concluded in Cleves and the previous purported betrothal of Anna and Francis of Lorraine. The demand shocked Olisleger and Hoghestein. 'They were much astonied and abashed and desired that [they] might make answer in the next morning.' Speaking of the status of the treaty between England and Cleves, and the prior entanglement between Anna and Francis of Lorraine,

> They answered as men much perplexed that as touching Commission they had none to treat concerning the Articles sent to Mr. Wotton and as to the contracts and covenants of marriage they could say nothing but that a revocation was made, and that they were but spousals.[31]

Olisleger and Hoghestein promised to stay in England, even as prisoners, until Duke Wilhelm sent the signed and sealed treaty to them in England, along with a copy of Anna's and Francis of Lorraine's revocation. All this, it should be remembered, took place after Anna's wedding.

After this incident, according to the letter, Cromwell went to Henry's private chamber. At that time, Henry reportedly declared, 'I am not well handled.' Cromwell then clarifies his interpretation of the king's declaration:

> insomuch that ... your Highness was fully determined not to have gone through with the marriage at that time saying unto me these words or the like in effect that if it were not that she is come so far into my realm, and the great preparations that my states and people hath made for her, and for fear of making of a ruffle in the world, that is to mean to drive her brother into the hands of the Emperor and French king's hands being now together, I would never have ne marry her.

Notice that the reason given by Henry, according to Cromwell in this letter, has nothing to do with Anna's appearance or personality,

---

31 Celebration of engagement or engagement ceremony.

but rather Henry's fear of driving Anna's brother Duke Wilhelm into the arms of either the Holy Roman Emperor Charles V or Francis I of France. Cromwell chooses to clarify the position by giving his own opinion of Henry's statement: 'so that I might well perceive Your Grace was neither content with the person ne yet content with the proceeding of the agents.'

After this meeting between Cromwell and Henry, Henry complains at dinner about how displeased he was about the status of the revocation of Anna's betrothal to Francis of Lorraine. This issue had not come up before. Henry reportedly thought that 'it should be well done that she should make a protestation before your said counselors and notaries ... that she was free from all contracts.' According to Cromwell's letter, Anna did in fact make such a protestation. Cromwell informed Henry that Anna had done as she was asked, which was not good enough for Henry. Henry protested to Cromwell, 'is there none other remedy but that I must needs against my will put my neck in the yoke...' It is not known to which yoke Henry was referring: the alliance with Cleves or his marriage to Anna.

On Monday, 12 January, Anna was waiting to be escorted by Henry Bouchier, 2nd Earl of Essex, to hear a sermon with Henry. As Bouchier was late, Cromwell briefly reported to Anna in her chamber. After Bouchier arrived, Cromwell went to Henry's chambers. Henry left his privy chamber, then stopped in the middle of his presence chamber. Henry supposedly commented to Cromwell: 'My Lord if it were not to satisfy the world and my realm I would not do that I must do this day for none earthly thing...' It's a famous quote – but is it accurate?

Word was brought that Anna was finally on her way. Henry appeared to be annoyed with her tardiness, and went down the gallery toward his closet to wait for her. The new royal couple then went to church. That night Anna and Henry would officially lie together to consummate their marriage.

The next morning Cromwell reported to Henry in the latter's privy chamber. Anna and Henry had been married for one week. Henry must have had a sour look on his face, or otherwise came across as being in a bad mood. Cromwell writes in June 1540 of his surprise at finding Henry in such a state and that he was 'so bold to ask Your Grace how ye liked the queen whereunto Your Grace soberly answered saying that, "I was not all men, surely my Lord as ye know I liked her before not well but now I like her much worse."' Henry is said to have stated: 'I have felt her belly and her breasts and thereby as I can judge she should be no maid, which strake me so to the heart when I felt them that I had neither will nor courage to proceed any further in other matters...' He 'left her as good a maid as I found her'.

This has far-reaching implications. If Anna was in fact a virgin and her betrothal to Francis of Lorraine was indeed revoked, Anna would be free to marry as a maid even after her marriage to Henry was annulled. Cromwell reports that Henry tried more than once to consummate his marriage with Anna, and on one or two occasions between Candlemas and Shrovetide said that he was unable to gain carnal knowledge of Anna for the same reasons as before. Candlemas is celebrated on 2 February, and Shrovetide was from late February to early March in 1540, with Shrove Tuesday falling on 2 March 1540. According to Cromwell, Henry informed him that Henry and Anna were in bed together every night or every other night for a couple of months after 12 January, but to no avail. Henry's comment then being that Anna was 'as good a maid ... as ever her mother bore her'.

There was another conversation Cromwell sought to memorialise: one between Anna herself and Henry. Anna's behaviour is characterised as stubborn and wilful; she was 'ever lamenting your fate and ever verifying that ye had never any knowledge with her'. This reasserts that Anna was a virgin, something very valuable in the marriage market for a noblewoman – and useful for an annulment. According to the 30 June 1540 letter, Henry continued to complain to Cromwell. Henry declared around Easter and Whitsun Week that he and Anna never knew each other carnally. Cromwell writes that the greatest grief 'was that [Your Majesty] should surely never have any more children for the comfort of this realm if [Your Majesty] should so continue, assuring me that before God [Your Majesty] thought she was never your lawful wife'.

Henry apparently continued to try and warm his heart to Anna, but found himself unable to approach her romantically. Cromwell states that, effectively, the pair had gotten off to such a poor start that fateful New Year's Day at Rochester that the king never took any liking to Anna. Cromwell knows of course that he is at the mercy of Henry for his life and declares his veracity before God:

> If I have not to the utterest of my remembrance said the truth and the whole truth in this matter god never help me I am sure as I think there is no man living in this your realm that knew more in this than I did Your Highness ...and as I shall answer to God I never thought Your Grace content after ye had once seen [Anna] at Rochester.

Cromwell's account of Anna's relationship with Henry was the truth, the whole truth, and nothing but the truth, so help him God.

Cromwell gives a lengthy closing to the letter, heaping blessings and praise upon Henry, wishing for Henry's long life and happiness. Finally, Cromwell begs for relief for a couple more lines, praying to God to preserve and keep Henry, as quoted above, and ending with 'most gracious Prince, I cry for mercy, mercy, mercy'.

That letter, written the day after Cromwell was attainted for treason and faced death, written under the guidance of the Duke of Norfolk and Lord Admiral, has served as the factual account for the past several hundred years of Anna's marital relationship with Henry: that Anna was ugly, that Henry hated her from the start, that her body was repulsive to Henry; that Anna seemed not a virgin. Virginity was imperative for a queen consort, as there could be no question as to the legitimacy of the king's children. Henry really, really tried to like Anna. But sadly, having a great aversion to this wholly unattractive German woman, Anna's marriage to Henry must be annulled. Who better to write a factual account of all the king's woes with his foreign bride than Henry's formerly most trusted minister, the Lord Privy Seal Thomas Cromwell?

Anna was a German Princess, and a born Duchess of Cleves. As a born Duchess, if her line should fail through her brother and elder sister, then the Dukes of Cleves would descend from Anna. This makes

Anna a valuable potential bride for any suitor after Henry. How could Henry have his marriage annulled and preserve the honour of Anna, so she might marry again? By suddenly taking issue with the pre-contract for marriage between Anna and Francis of Lorraine.

What else was happening that caused Henry to so speedily reject Anna and pull out of their marriage and alliance with Cleves? Sir Thomas Wyatt, who was the ambassador to the Imperial from approximately December 1539 to April 1540, gives a valuable insight into to what was happening on the Continent. Wyatt's dispatches were addressed directly to King Henry. The sometimes-accompanying dispatches to Thomas Cromwell frequently lacked the level of detail and information contained in those sent by Wyatt to Henry.

Wyatt's Letters

Sir Thomas Wyatt the Elder narrowly escaped the downfall of Anne Boleyn and others in 1536, and went on to work as Henry VIII's ambassador to the Holy Roman Emperor Charles V. He was a member of Henry's privy chamber. Wyatt faithfully communicated directly to Henry via letter, and was allowed at times to speak to the Emperor in person. Wyatt maintained a contact or spy in Germany who provided him with information.

Wyatt wrote his first correspondence of note on 12 December 1539 from Amboise. He wrote to Henry about Charles V's concerns over the marriage alliance with Cleves, and how such an alliance might affect any diplomatic agreements between Henry and Charles:

> [Charles V] thought it not reasonable that any man should meddle between his subjects and him,[32] and saying roundly, that he trusted [Henry] would rather counsel Mons. De Juliers,[33] rather than aid [Wilhelm] against his Sovereign [Charles V].

This stems of course from the Emperor's desire to obtain control of Guelders, the rights to which he could claim through several different avenues. The exchange between Charles V and Wyatt continues:

---

32 The territories of the United Duchies of Jülich-Cleves-Berg were under the purview of the Holy Roman Empire.
33 'Juliers' is French for Jülich

Charles: 'What hath Mons. De Juliers to do with Guelders? I assure you, Mons. L'Ambassador [Wyatt], I shall show [Wilhelm] that he hath played but the young man.'

Wyatt: 'I know not the right that [Wilhelm] pretendeth, nor I have no commission of this purpose, but only as I have showed unto you: and I doubt not but Mons. De Cleves will put himself to all reason with Your Majesty.'

Charles: 'Yea, Mons. l'Ambassador ... he shall so.'

Wyatt: 'As for the King my master, I dare well assure you, that like as he would be loth [not] to show himself a good and loving brother to: Mons. de Cleves, so would he be as loth but to show to Your Majesty all fashions of friendliness.'

Charles finished off the exchange with a veiled threat to Henry, should Henry aid his future brother-in-law, Wilhelm:

'Well ... Mons. l'Ambassador, this is but as incident; I doubt not but the King [of England] Your Master would give [Wilhelm] good and wise advice how to order [Wilhelm] to his Sovereign; for I assure you Monsieur De Juliers shall do me reason;[34] and I shall do but well so to do.'

Charles goes on to issue his politically well-worded threat against Wilhelm, holding his hand over his heart and saying, 'I say he... [Wilhelm] shall; [he] hath of one a Sovereign, a neighbour, and a cousin; and otherways shall lose all three.'

Wyatt gave Henry his opinion on the situation regarding Guelders and Cleves:

It confirmeth me in the opinion ... that surely [Charles V] mindeth more Guelders in his heart, than he doth Milan and all Italy. And in my conscience, his coming out of

---

34 Charles V is alluding to using military force.

Spain in this haste hath been upon the news of your Majesty's alliance with Mons. de Cleves, to prevent things that might succeed.

As proof of the alarm experienced by Charles V over the marriage between Anna and Henry, Wyatt continued, 'And if that be so, the danger of [the Emperor's] person, the hardness of the winter, and the length of the journey, declareth therein his desire.' Another blow to Henry? The Duke of Lorraine and his son Francis, who was previously betrothed to Anna, were coming to court to press their own claim to Guelders through Francis's mother Philippa.

By Christmas 1539, Wyatt found it important to warn Henry again of Charles V's reaction to the marriage alliance of Anna and Henry:

And as for the Emperor's necessity, it was manifest that ... Your Majesty's sudden alliance with Guelders, always to him suspicious... And it is out of doubt, that the Bishop of Rome could not allow his coming through Italy, for then must he have come through Almain;[35] whereas he might peradventure have caught a persuasion not best for the Bishop's purpose.[36] ... So that there was left [to the Emperor] no way but other to come through France ... and leave his great desire of Guilders.

What does Wyatt say to Cromwell about the Guelders issue? In a letter of December 1539, not much at all. Wyatt only asks that the accompanying letters from the Ambassador of Cleves are delivered safely.

From Paris the day after Anna's wedding, on 7 January 1540, Wyatt penned another letter to Henry about the issues swirling around Germany, Guelders, and Henry's new brother-in-law, Duke Wilhelm of Cleves:

This I say for the purpose I note it for. The Emperor ... sayeth Your Majesty should join with the Almains; and ...

---

35 Germany, from the French, Allemagne
36 Sympathy toward the Lutherans/Protestants

declare unto you that he can, and hath the means to show you like displeasure, as ye may do him by joining with the Almains and Guelders: and the whilst he, holding Your Majesty in that neutrality, shall win time; and peradventure bear away Guelders; and so make his way more facile into Almaine.

Even worse, Charles V brought an army with him toward the Low Countries: 'And no doubt he intendeth something about the Low Countrie; for he hath done to come two thousand old soldiers, Spaniards out of Italy, that are already passed through Loraine.' Wyatt gives Henry his opinion that,

Some man of ancient wisdom and learning ... whom Your Majesty shall think meet [should tell the Emperor that] whereas Your Majesty hath been inclinable to all overtures of straighter alliance ... and that hitherto nothing hath ensued , but that ye have been holden in suspense, not hearkening to the other alliances[37] by reason that ye have reckoning yourself tarried with the treaties between you and [Charles V], nor yet being sure of his, by reason that he may think himself, since your just withdrawing from the tyranny of Rome, but at his pleasure bound, that Your Majesty cannot think in such bond of friendship any equality ... that though ye intend to keep your amities with him, yet unless he will come to new treaties, or, to confirmation of the old ... that otherwise your Majesty will not hang in such suspense ... but that ye would not refuse any such alliance as shall seem ye good...

This may, me thinketh, with power to treat and roundly to conclude if [the Emperor] will come to this, drive him to defend himself. And me thinketh also never better time than now, before he begins his enterprises[38] and so also shall ye set him in as great doubt of you, as you may seem of him.

---

37 With Cleves, Saxony, etc.
38 Military enterprises

As mentioned, Anna and Henry formally consummated their marriage (or didn't) on the night of 12 January 1540, five days after Wyatt wrote this letter. It conceivably had time to reach Henry before the 12th.

A month later, Wyatt was stationed in Brussels, from where he writes on 3 February 1540. This letter contains considerably more information about the intrigues in Guelders and Germany. Wyatt cuts to the chase immediately:

> ...I shall begin at the end, and ... in your request for the matter depending between the Duke of Cleves and [the Emperor Charles V]; ... And for the matter of the Duke of Cleves, [the Emperor] knoweth nothing to be in question or title, but taketh the matter for clear: and prayeth you not to meddle between [the Emperor] and his subject [Duke Wilhelm], no more than he doth with yours: and for all the rest of the request plainly, 'Je ne ferai rien.'[39]

Wyatt provided a summation of the conversation he had with the Emperor about who legally claimed title to Guelders:

> In the matter of the Duke of Cleves ... because I had spoken of the good will and favor that your Majesty must bear unto the Duke [Wilhelm], he inferred that the greatest favor that your Majesty could shew [Wilhelm] should be to advise [him] to submit him to his Sovereign... And with such incidents we came to such resolutions in this matter as above... Of the Duke of Cleves nothing at all, other than having from him the state of Guelders: and [Wilhelm's] only help is, as far as I can see, either at your Majesty's hands, or to join himself with the Protestants if he may, and that by times; or else both.

A gruff exchange with Charles V alarmed Wyatt, who reported,

> I must say that by all that I can perceive, either this man hath knowledge of some such your intent against him, whereby he

---

39 'I (the Emperor) will do nothing.'

hath no trust to have you for him: or else knoweth himself, not to merit your friendship; whereby he is in despair, which way it will; or else would provoke you to be the first breaker. I cannot else see what should move this rigor, this sharpness, and this unaccustomed manner in proceeding, unless I, peradventure, be unacceptable to him I wot not by what occasion.

Wyatt then touched on the topic of religion, one of Cromwell's reasons for pressing the Cleves alliance:

It may be also that [the Emperor] hath some imagination, that by such faces he might draw your Majesty again to the subjection of Rome; whereof peradventure he conceiveth a vain hope, in that he sees you not wholly addicted to the Germans: but that your institution is apart from theirs.

Candlemas was 2 February 1540. As per Cromwell's 30 June 1540 letter, Henry did not consummate the marriage between then and Shrovetide: Charles V's increasing agitation over Henry's new alliance and the Guelders matter may have cooled Henry's ardour, such as it was.

Wyatt remained in Brussels until late February, though the Emperor and his entourage departed for Ghent on or about Valentine's Day. Though the Emperor was allowed to enter, the residents of Ghent were not so welcoming to the Emperor's army, which was not allowed into the city. Wyatt sent Henry a dispatch dated 25 February 1540, in which he informed Henry of reports out of Cleves that Wyatt received from a man he sent there. The identity of this man is not stated. The man was of some standing, as one who 'penetrates far into matters of state'. Should the King so desire, he could have 'from the same place continual letters'.

Wyatt told Henry that an assembly would take place at Wittenberg, then part of Saxon domains, in a few days' time, on 1 March. Wyatt offered to send his man to the Wittenberg Assembly, 'if that it seem good that your Grace knew what were in that [Assembly] determined, I shall by my letters ... cause that same man to go thither, as it were upon my cost. And I doubt not that anything shall be hidden from him.'

Wyatt's man, able to infiltrate these German circles, is a great asset. Cromwell's men were unable to gain this sort of access or gather valuable intelligence concerning the matters of Wilhelm, Anna, and the United Duchies of Jülich-Cleves-Berg when they pressed for Anna's marriage in 1539.

Revealingly, Anna's marriage to Henry was not held in high regard in Germany. This same confidential source told Wyatt as much, which Wyatt then relayed to Henry:

> Furthermore, it seemeth that nowadays men set forward their matters wondrously with false rumors and noises, so that these things pass as much by appearance as facts, and I doubt not but that like as Your Grace's marriage (as he writeth) is falsely spoken of there, so been other of your notable deeds disguised, to alienate the Germans' minds.

That is information of great value. By early March 1540, when Henry probably received Wyatt's 25 February letter, Henry then knew that Charles V was willing to go to war with Henry's new brother-in-law over Guelders, that Charles V did not trust Henry because of his alliance with Cleves, and that the Germans were ill-disposed toward the English king. Wyatt suggested an attempt to salvage the situation: 'Wherefore, if it seem good that anything were published in justification, and declaring your Majesty's proceedings, I would undertake by the same man to cause the thing to be put into the Almain tongue and published ... and it should stop many things that upon such rumors, for lack of knowledge, would proceed.'

Wyatt did not really know what the rumours about Henry were: 'I will write to know plainly what things ... [are] in the people's ears, touching your things, that against those things may be made indirect provision.'

Between the 25 February letter and the next, Wilhelm sent his legal team to meet with the Emperor to establish why it was Wilhelm and not Charles V who could legally claim Guelders. Wyatt wrote from Ghent on 9 March 1540 to tell Henry that the

Cardinal of Lorraine and perhaps the Constable of France would arrive in Ghent shortly, 'at the uttermost to make appearance of amity among those Almain Ambassadors, than for any resolution that shall ensue further: as I gather, as well by passed things, as by those that here under I shall advertise your Majesty.'

Wyatt made light of another issue for Henry, that there could be some sort of plotting against him: 'And if I would make reckoning of these common drunkards talk, the people's common devises, yea! and the merchants' doubts and reports, I should minister unto your Majesty matter of great suspect toward some secret thing against your Highness.' Wyatt later said that he did not believe there was any plot against Henry. Offering a glimpse of hope to finally conclude the matters with Cleves and Saxony, Wyatt wrote:

Me thinketh I gather near at hand an accord with the Germans; a suspense, as it is still with the Frenchmen, and a time for the managing of the said accord, by the truce that shall yet last till the latter end of June. And if these things come to pass, your Majesty not comprehended with the Germans, then me thinketh were something to be suspected, that is here commonly bruited[40] against your Majesty. For if it be true ... that they have gotten to be passed already between the Emperor and the French King, that neither of them shall further treat any particular with your Majesty without the advice and consent of the other; then seemeth these things an appearance to leave your Highness destitute of any foreign assurance.

In March 1540, it seemed that Christina of Denmark, Duchess of Milan, might become Anna's sister-in-law. In Wyatt's opinion, Henry managed to avoid a scandal by not marrying Christina because she was carrying on a flirtation with the Prince of Orange.[41] Wyatt did clarify that though he could 'not but rejoice in manner the scape that you made there', he nevertheless supposed 'nothing but honour in

---

40 To voice abroad

41 Christina and the Prince of Orange carried on their flirtation for about eighteen months at the court of Christina's aunt, Maria of Austria, Regent of the Low Countries.

the lady'. Wyatt then returned to the issue of Germany, saying that he thought the Emperor would arrive there soon.

Three days later, on 12 March, Wyatt wrote to Henry again. From Ghent, Wyatt learned of an ongoing rumour that Wilhelm would marry Christina of Denmark, and that Cromwell's information from Germany did not give the whole story:

> Forasmuch as my Lord Privy Seal wrote unto me that the letters of advice out of Almaine did not mislike unto your Majesty, having yesternight received another, I send it unto your Highness; [and] write of the things that been here bruited, the fame of the accord with Cleves by the marriage of the Duchess of Milan, groweth still.

There was no source for the rumour about Wilhelm and Christina, so Wyatt then says, ' By all things that I can draw out here ... I remain of the same opinion ... that there would accord[42] follow shortly betwixt the Protestants and the Emperor, and this letter out of Almain doth not appaire[43] that opinion.'

Effectively, Charles V kept Anna's brother in hopes of a marriage to Christina of Denmark until Charles came to some sort of accord with the German Protestants:

> For upon that same protracting of the Duke of Cleves entering with the Protestants, the Emperor taketh occasion so to entertain him till he appoint with the Protestants, and feedeth him with some fame of marriage; yea, and useth his brother [Ferdinand, King of the Romans] to give the Duke's servant here good words, and delay of his answer.

The Emperor worked hard to turn the opinion of the peoples of Jülich-Cleves-Berg against Anna's marital alliance with England and against her brother Wilhelm. By mid-March 1540, Wyatt believed the Emperor's political machinations had made the German

---

42 An agreement
43 give

populace believe that he had pulled Francis I back to his side and out of league with the German princes, never mind what any of the French ambassadors had to say. The Emperor planted the seed of doubt in the Germans' minds as to whether Henry would in fact join them and give them aid. Finally, the Emperor persuaded them that Wilhelm, through failing to give answer in the Guelders matter, was willing to go to war with the Emperor over Guelders. Wyatt told Henry, 'This performed, [the Emperor] hath both time by the means, with the rank and commodity to assault the Duke; and then, dare I warrant, the Duke shall not find that facility[44] in him, that the King of Romans painteth here to his servant.'

On 14 March and from Ghent, Wyatt reported worrying news that troops were on the way to the Low Countries, numbering about 10,000 from Italy and Spain. Worse yet, letters from Spain confirmed those numbers. Given the close proximity of the Low Countries to Guelders and the Emperor's desire for it, this show of force was meant – at the very least – to intimidate Anna's brother. Wyatt restates his opinion that:

If your Majesty may not dispose with the French King as you would, and that the Emperor may assure him there better than you, if the Almains accord with the Emperor, your Majesty nor the Duke of Cleves comprehended it, it cannot be but to your prejudice; at the least the Duke of Cleves, I warrant him, shall feel it; and I doubt not but the state of Guelders would make the Emperor go as near the brink as he may to please the Almains.

Negotiations over who held proper legal title to Guelders continued into April 1540. Wilhelm came out of his territories to meet with Charles V about the issue. Wyatt, in Ghent on 16 April and toward the end of this particular period abroad, wrote to Henry,

On Tuesday[45] last [Wilhelm] arrived here, and [there] was sent against him to receive him the Prince of Orange, the Great

---

44 Ready compliance, easy manner
45 6 April

Master, and other. He arrived about six of' the clock at night. I found the means that same night to speak with him secretly, unknown. And the Thursday after I went to him to do my duty in public, and for because I judged it in Your Majesty's service that he concluded nothing suddenly without Your Majesty's knowledge, whereof was thought great appearance by his coming, I did insure all that in me was to dissuade him from any conclusion, as well by declaring him the state of things of this Court ... the poverty of the Emperor ... whereby he might be better [drawn] to stand awhile till your Majesty were advertised ... His coming hath some appearance of good reason to justify his duty, and avoiding of force; which he pretendeth to desire, if so be it had been consulted with his friend; but since that is done, he desireth greatly to be excused...

Having made his point, Wilhelm was done with meeting.

I have moved [Wilhelm] to write to your Majesty particularly and at length the order of his coming, and his determinations resolute; which he hath done. Where upon it seemeth unto me, if he persist there is no hurt done, if his friends been not offended. And for because he writeth more particularly I shall not in that point enlarge longer; for that in substance his letter [gives] his answer to the marvel, and proposes that I purposed unto him, with the determinations that he saith he is finally resolved in. It seemed here to most men the matter concluded before he came.

But they allirm, and also it appeareth, that nothing not word was mentioned of any particular before; nor yet hath he but spoken with the King of Romans, and only protested that he is come with neither word nor mind of the sequestration, of the state of Guelders. And I think if he persists in that, as he saith, that he shall not speak with the Emperor; so stands he sometime upon such points of greatness.

Although his replacement Mr Pate was there, Wyatt desired to stay longer in Ghent; and that others present at court and various German Electors, 'do write to the Emperor, remembering him of his oath to do no violence where law is offered; which letters the Duke of Cleves looketh daily for'.

As seen by the series of letters which Wyatt sent to Henry from December 1539 through April 1540, tensions between Wilhelm and the Holy Roman Emperor Charles V were edging ever closer to boiling over. Some of the events between Anna and Henry that Cromwell described may indeed be true, and when taken together with the intelligence Henry was receiving from Wyatt, explain why Anna's marriage to Henry fell apart so quickly. But which was the more decisive factor? Henry's dissatisfaction with his new bride or the dire position of an alliance with Cleves? War between England and the Holy Roman Empire was daily becoming a more distinct possibility now that Henry was married to Anna, and Anna's brother was resisting the Emperor's attempts to regain Guelders. Had Henry known that a war was coming, he would not have married Anna. Amongst other apparent shortcomings, Cromwell failed to recognise the danger in which England was placed through an alliance with Cleves.

9

THE ANNULMENT

Anna may or may not have known the exact situation the United Duchies were facing when she was sent to Richmond in June 1540. She was aware of the Guelderian Succession crisis because it was part of the basis for Anna's engagement to Francis of Lorraine. Only men could inherit land in German and French areas. Anna saw that with her own mother, Duchess Maria of Jülich and Berg. Francis of Lorraine's mother was Philippa of Guelders; Philippa was the twin sister of Duke Karl of Guelders. Duke Karl left Guelders to Anna's brother Wilhelm when Duke Karl died. Had Anna married Francis of Lorraine, Francis would inherit Guelders, as would Anna's male children through Francis. It is doubtful that Anna did not understand the political reasons behind the proposed Lorraine match.

Anna maintained correspondence with her mother, brother, and her elder sister Sybylla while she lived in England. She likely wrote letters to her younger sister Amalia, though Amalia was not of much diplomatic importance. Anna's family wrote back to her and informed her to the best of their respective abilities what was happening back home. Though communication about issues facing the United Duchies was not always direct; Wilhelm had his ambassadors present in England who kept Anna informed, too.

Anna's trek from Cleves to England had required the permission of the Holy Roman Emperor Charles V. Anna's elder sister Sybylla and her brother-in-law Elector Johann Friedrich were already starting trouble with the Emperor long before the English marriage became a possibility. Anna would have been aware of that. Now here she was, sent away from court to the Palace of Richmond to await her fate.

Anna was sent to Richmond around 24 June 1540, ostensibly to avoid falling ill. Sweating Sickness was a very real, very dangerous infectious disease peculiar to England. The disease was most active between summer and early autumn, with almost annual outbreaks from 1485 to 1551. Sending Anna to Richmond for the safety of her health was an excellent diplomatic cover-up for what was to come.

Parliament was in session, and the men were working very quickly and secretly on creating a legal basis to annul the marriage. The annulment had three bases. First, that Henry did not inwardly consent to the marriage; second, that the marriage was not consummated and third, that Anna had a pre-contract with Francis of Lorraine. Specifically, the document in Latin which the Cleves ambassadors produced bore the word *sponsalia*, or betrothal. The document did not say whether the *sponsolia* was *de præsenti* or *de futuro*.

The annulment proceedings were meant to preserve Anna's honour and extricate England from the political mess Cromwell created. Bishop Gardner and Wriothesley, enemies of Cromwell's, put together a plan of action for the annulment. They wanted to select men in secrecy about the matter, willing to quickly affix their signatures to any resolution created by this proposed secret council.

The Secret Council

The Secret Council informed the King of the best legal steps to take to affect the annulment. A search at the behest of the Secret Council of Cromwell's house for the marital contract between Anna and Francis of Lorraine to determine whether the contract was *de præsenti* or *de futuro* was necessary. If *de præsenti*, the contract would create a binding legal marriage between Anna and Francis of Lorraine as soon as it was signed, whereas *de futuro* would not become legally binding until all conditions precedent of the contract were met. Next, the renunciation of the Lorraine marriage that was produced or created when Anna was in England needed to be located. Finally, the Secret Council needed to determine how, when, where and by whom the news should be broken to Anna.

The Secret Council wanted to ask Henry to appoint individuals to examine Cromwell about the matter, and finally to determine 'How the King's Majesty shall order himself as using his liberty from matrimony or otherwise in the meantime [t]his to be deferred [to] the determination of the clergy'; and 'A remembrance that as much proof as may be had be prepared and in a readiness to declare the King's Majesty's misliking, his Grace's dissent and abstinence *a carnali copula*, and also her confession thereof if it may be attained.'

The overall plan was that someone had to write a memorandum about Henry and Anna's marriage saying that Henry did not like Anna and thus did not engage in conjugal relations with her. Anna would confess that these things were true. Thomas Cromwell, the disgraced Earl of Essex, was just the man for the task.

The Secret Council waded through several legal issues. One legal task for the Secret Council was sorting out the difference between a marriage contract *de futuro* and *de præsenti*, and whether either or both sorts of contract created an impediment to a second marriage arrangement. If a legal hurdle caused the marriage between Anna and Henry to be declared void, did it matter that they consented to it? The reasoning was that neither Anna nor Henry could genuinely consent to their marriage if Anna was technically the wife of Francis of Lorraine.

If the parties were not free to marry and did anyway, then failed to consummate the marriage, would that, 'be matter [sufficient to] declare, upon a marriage not *heartily* [consummate as] afore, the insufficiency thereof without [further process]'. The Secret Council needed to decide whether the Beer Pot Document was legally sufficient to free Anna from the marriage contract with Francis of Lorraine (or more accurately, prove that it wasn't). A determination had to be made as to whether there was any legal impediment to Anna and Henry's marriage since the only documentary evidence available concerning the rescission of the

Lorraine match was a letter from 1535. Finally, the Secret Council had to review how many witnesses needed to be deposed in order to show that Henry, and perhaps Anna, did not 'heartily' or genuinely enter into the marriage.

The Secret Council pondered solutions to the question of consummation. This included requesting an inspection of Queen Anne to see if she remained *virgo intacta*. A declaration of maidenhood would also suffice. The Council thought that securing a statement from several witnesses saying that Henry was quite displeased with Anna's character and appearance would help reinforce that she was a maiden, making it easier to annul the marriage. The status of Anna's maidenhood was important because if their marriage was consummated, then Henry must petition for a divorce.

The argument concerning Anna's pre-contract was based on the letter dated 15 February 1535. As described earlier, a copy of this letter, sworn to by Olisleger, was delivered to Henry on 26 February 1540. The letter was from Heinrich de Groff, the Guelders ambassador. In it, de Groff wrote that the betrothal was terminated by Karl of Guelders because Anna's father Johann could not make the necessary payments.[46] The letter was defective enough for the Secret Council because it was missing the vital *de præsenti* or *de futuro* language. It simply declared the *sponsalia*, or betrothal, terminated.

It is easily discovered from the 15 February 1535 cancellation that the betrothal was *de futuro*. Certain conditions precedent, namely the payment of monies by Anna's father Johann III to Duke Karl of Guelders, were necessary before the betrothal took effect. The money was never paid, so the pre-contract was terminated, meaning that Anna was free to marry Henry: but the Secret Council was tasked with annulling the marriage and Anna was never given the chance to represent her interests.

---

46 In the Latin, '*Sponsalia illa progressum suum non habitura, ex quo dictus Dux Carolus admodum doleret, et propeterea quædam fecisset, et amplius facturus esset...*' Johann III's ambassador wrote to him from the Guelders court, '*Illustrissimum Ducem Gueldriæ certo scire prima illa sponsalia inter Domicellam Annam fore inania et progressum suum non habitura.*'

Going a step further, the Secret Council combed over the Beer Pot Document for other possible defects. After reviewing the document, the Council found that there was no formal cancellation of the Lorraine contract. Given what is now known about the lack of an enforceable pre-contract, it makes sense that the Beer Pot Document made no mention of Francis of Lorraine or prior marital negotiations. Furthermore, the Beer Pot document is imperially notarised. This means that it was valid throughout the Holy Roman Empire, which in 1539 included the United Duchies and Lorraine. Again, neither Anna nor any of her counselors, ambassadors, or lawyers were allowed to represent her at the impending convocation.

Wriothesley's Involvement

Sir Thomas Wriothesley worked for Cromwell as his personal secretary and chief clerk. Before entering the employ of Cromwell in the early 1530s, Wriothesley worked for Stephen Gardiner, Bishop of Winchester. In April of 1540, Wriothesley was appointed by Henry to the joint position of principal secretary of state, a position which Cromwell formerly held. Wriothesley became the Secretary to the Privy Council, a politically powerful position. Wriothesley was a friend of Gardiner's and was not supportive of Cromwell's efforts with the Lutherans.

As a member of the Secret Council, Wriothesley created an outline of questions for the deposition of Thomas Cromwell. They were all leading questions, meaning that Cromwell could really only answer yes or no. There was no room for Cromwell to contribute his own perceptions. Cromwell could not fail see what the 'correct' answers were.

The first question devised by the Secret Council and recorded by Wriothesley was 'Whether [Cromwell] asked the King, coming from Rochester, how he liked the Queen and was answered, "Nothing so well as she was spoken of, and that if his Highness had known so much before, she should not have comen hither; but what remedy now?"'

Cromwell should declare that 'he said he was sorry.' Next, Cromwell had to comment on Henry's first impressions of Anna. Cromwell was supposed to recall that:

On her entry to Greenwich, after the King had brought her to her chamber, Cromwell waited upon his Grace in his, who said, 'How say you, my Lord? Is it not as I told you, say what they will, she is nothing fair; the personage is well and seemly, but nothing else?' Cromwell replied, 'By my faith, you say truth, but me thinketh she hath a queenly manner withal.' 'That is truth,' quoth his Highness.

Here is more support for the idea that Henry was not attracted to Anna, despite her 'queenly manner'. The inclusion of Anna's noble and fitting demeanour let the poor Duchess of Cleves keep some of her dignity: a classic case of it's not her, it's him.

Of legal import, the Council wished Cromwell to profess that the Cleves ambassadors who accompanied Anna to England were not properly authorised to consent to any treaties or covenants between England and the United Duchies. Cromwell would then claim that Henry commanded Cromwell to declare to the ambassadors Henry's displeasure over their lack of authority, and his concern that Anna did not properly 'assent and consent' to the marriage.

The Council came up with the following:

[o]n this Cromwell came, the back way, to the King to 'declare' the same, and asked again how he liked her. The King answered, 'If it were not that she is come so far into England, and for fear of making a ruffle in the world and driving her brother into th' Emperor and the French king's hands, now being together, I would never have her; but now it is too far gone, wherefore I am sorry.'

This statement devised by the Council clings to every legal obstacle surrounding the marriage; it argues that some of the conditions requisite for the marriage were not concluded. The Anglo-Cleves treaty was not completed before Anna came to England, which was part of the marriage negotiations.

The Council decided that there was doubt that Anna wished to or, more importantly, legally could, consent to the marriage.

The lack of Anna's legal ability to consent is twofold in this declaration. First, that a condition precedent was not met because the treaty was not concluded, and second, that Anna was already lawfully married to Francis of Lorraine.

Most telling are the phrases 'making a ruffle in the world' and driving Anna's brother 'into th'Emperor and the French king's hands'. Henry did not want the powerful United Duchies, Holy Roman Empire, and France allied against him. For that matter, Henry preferred that the United Duchies were allied with England only, which would create bookends to the Kingdom of France, and provide a militarily strategic allied location within the Holy Roman Empire if the Emperor decided on aggression. The United Duchies bordered part of the Low Countries, which could only assist the English merchants located there.

Another inspired tale manufactured by the Secret Council was that

> On [t]he eve of the marriage Cromwell told the King that the ambassadors and commissioners were agreed. His Grace asked, 'How do you with the assurance which was made by her to the duke of Lorraine?' and added that she must make a renunciation herself. This Cromwell caused her to do and returned to tell the King. 'Then is there no remedy, quod his Majesty, but put my neck in the yoke?'

Anna was likely requested – if she was at all – to make this renunciation after Henry received the notarised copy of the de Groffe letter. If Anna truly did make this renunciation, it must have seemed an extraordinary request. After all, the 15 February 1535 letter specifically said that prior negotiations for her betrothal were terminated.

For purposes of the annulment contrived by the Secret Council, Anna must be shown to be unable legally to consent to the marriage on 6 January 1540. Her renunciation had to be given quickly, and arguably a second marriage after the renunciation would have been necessary to make Anna and Henry legally married. This episode could be a complete fabrication by the Secret Council.

Again, Anna had no one present at the resulting Convocation who could state whether such a renunciation was ever made, or was even legally necessary if it had been.

Then the most insulting description of Anna was devised. The Council wished Cromwell to declare that the day after their wedding night, Henry could divine that '"by her breasts and belly she should be no maid; which, when I felt them, strake me so to the heart that I had neither will nor courage to prove the rest." Doubtless Cromwell remembers how that often, since, the King has said his nature abhorred her.'

This description of her breasts and belly was the contemporary way of saying that Anna did not come to Henry's bed a maiden, based upon not a scintilla of physiological reality. Note that it does not say that Anna herself was unattractive, but that Henry found her not to have a maidenly body. Henry could claim not only that he had absolutely no carnal knowledge of her, but also that he had never seen Anna nude. Her shift need not be off for Henry to touch Anna's body. This continues to support the idea that Anna was already married to Francis of Lorraine and consummated her marriage with Francis, while leaving her attractiveness or lack of same out of the discussion. Again, Henry is claiming that his marriage with Anna was not consummated, leaving the way open to an annulment.

The overall theme in these statements crafted by the Secret Council? It was all Cromwell's fault.

Wriothesley and the Secret Council first decided that Cromwell would write, or at least attest to, a memorandum concerning Henry and Anna's relationship. They determined what was needed legally to effect the annulment: how to prove that Anna was another man's wife, that Henry's morally upright princely heart would not allow his body to fall into sin, and if all else failed, neither Anna nor Henry heartily, genuinely consented to the marriage. Approaching the annulment in this way rather than having Henry divorce Anna would maintain diplomatic stability. Wilhelm, now focused entirely on Guelders, was too busy to worry about his sister. By annulling the marriage with at least part of the grounds being non-consummation, Henry would not offend Wilhelm. Anna would be free to marry again.

Turning to the two documents written, or at least signed, by Cromwell on 30 June 1540, the first one is written in a fairly solid, confident hand and is more or less a copy of the points decided by the Secret Council. It is possibly Wriothesley's handwriting, as he was the Secretary to the Privy Council. It is attested to by Cromwell, who was informed either the day before or moments before of the Bill of Attainder passed against him on 29 June. In his attestation of this letter, Cromwell declares that 'All these articles be [true by the] death I shall die, and ... as more plainly [appears by a] letter written with my [own hand] sent by Mr. Secretary [unto] the King's Highness.' He not only agrees with the veracity of the attestation, but also that a letter written by himself and delivered to Henry through Wriothesley would confirm all.

The Duke of Norfolk, and probably Wriothesley, called upon Cromwell on 30 June at the Tower for the purpose of securing Cromwell's attestation and to inform him of his imminent execution. Cromwell even swore upon his certain death in the attestation. The second letter, written in a more frantic hand by Cromwell himself, contains very slight deviations from the formally attested document. It is not known if Cromwell scribbled off his own letter with the Duke of Norfolk looking over Cromwell's shoulder or if Cromwell wrote the letter later in the day. What is obvious is that Cromwell was under duress and was trying to save his life by appeasing Henry.

The Depositions

Henry's own declaration about his marriage with Anna paralleled the attestation by Cromwell but is in contrast to news out of England during the period of Anna's marriage. Henry's declaration showed the political reasoning that led to him consenting to Cromwell's idea of the Anglo-Cleves alliance.

> When the first communication was had with [Henry] for it he was glad to hearken to it, trusting to have [some assured] friend, as he much doubted the Emperor, France and the [Bishop] of Rome, and he had also heard so much of [Anna's] beauty and virtue. But when he saw her for the first time at

Rochester, he was glad he had kept free from making any [pact or bond] till then; for he liked her so ill he was sorry she had come and he considered breaking it off. The Great Master, the Admiral that now is, and the Master of the Horse can bear witness of his misliking. The lord of Essex, if examined, can or has declared what he said to him after his repair to Greenwich. As he is condemned to die he will not damn [his soul, but declare what the King said, not only at the time but continually till] the day of [marriage] and many times after, whereby his lack of consent will appear; and also lack of the will and power to consummate the same; 'wherein both he, my physicians, the lord Privy Seal that now is, Hennage and Denny can, and I doubt not will, testify according to truth; which is, that I never for love to the woman consented to marry; nor yet, if she brought maidenhead with her, took any from her by true carnal copulation. This is my brief, true and perfect declaration.

Henry's declaration needs analysis. First, Henry needed allies. He could not rely on Charles V or Francis I, who consistently used Henry as a catspaw (though one with potentially dangerous claws) throughout the three reigns. Henry needed an ally against the Pope, because he had broken away from the Catholic Church a few years before. Both Francis I and Charles V were Catholic and themselves allied with the Pope at various times to various degrees of commitment. They were not reliable in the event religious matters came to a head.

Anna of Cleves' family was at the very least tolerant of Reformist religion. Sybylla and her husband the Saxon Elector Johann Friedrich were openly Lutheran, and Wilhelm was anti-Catholic. Amalia, though having no political import, was herself a Lutheran. Anna was a Catholic as she was very close to her mother, the devout Duchess Maria of Jülich-Berg. Despite her Catholicism, through marriage to Anna Henry was supposed to have access to the anti-Catholic faction of German princes, and to the powers of the Schmalkaldic League. Anna was reportedly beautiful and virtuous, and certainly regarded that way in the United Duchies.

Henry says that he disliked Anna from the time he first laid eyes on her at Rochester. This, of course, conflicts with German reports from around 6 January 1540, which relayed that he stayed overnight not far from Anna, then came again in the morning to dine with her and spend time with her. It is true that Henry was concerned about the state of the Anglo-Cleves alliance, and of his standing with the Schmalkaldic League, when Anna arrived in England. The requisite documents had yet to be executed, and Johann Friedrich's attitude toward Henry being allowed into the Schmalkaldic League had cooled. He was considering breaking it off right around when Anna arrived, or shortly after, because the pledged alliances and military support were not forthcoming.

Depositions of 'diverse noblemen' were taken before the Convocation gathered to hear the matter of Anna's marriage. The first deponents issued a collective statement. Amongst these nobles were 'the right honorable Thomas Awdley, Lord Chancellor, Thomas Archbusshop [sic] of Canterbury, Thomas [Howard] Duke of Norfolk, Charles [Brandon] Duke of Suffolk, William [Fitzwilliam] Earl of Southampton, and Cuthbert Bishop of Durham'. These men jointly said that the main issue facing Anna's marriage was the contract with Lorraine, that it was not properly cancelled. Because of Henry's doubts, the marriage was delayed by two days. Wishing to rid himself of those concerns, Henry requested that the ambassadors from Cleves bring a copy of the contract with them to England. Henry married Anna despite his misgivings. It was important for the joint deponents to claim that Henry was unhappy that the ambassadors sent with Anna did not have the authority to enter into any agreements or execute documents that would bind the United Duchies.

The second deposition was given by Charles Brandon, Duke of Suffolk. Charles Brandon was a brother-in-law to Henry VIII through marriage to Henry's younger sister Mary, who died in 1533. Brandon was a life-long close friend of Henry. Brandon claims that Henry 'constantly affirmed' he would not marry Anna without the Lorraine pre-contract being cleared. Henry relied on a promise from the ambassadors of Cleves and Saxony that the document would be brought to England with Anna. Brandon echoes the group in claiming that the solemnisation of the marriage was delayed by two days, from 4 January 1540 to 6 January. Brandon asserts that Cromwell had set to work on the situation, possibly without Henry's knowledge. In Brandon's opinion, Henry never liked Anna and would have been happier not to marry her. Henry felt he had to marry Anna, 'than to the world have been disappointed'. The Lorraine pre-contract was cleared in 1535 – but the more grounds for the annulment presented to the Convocation, the better.

Some of the other depositions presented during the convocation repeatedly stated that Henry was not attracted to Anna. The depositions even went so far as to call Anna ugly, in so many words. The purpose of saying Henry was not attracted to Anna at best, or that she was ugly at worst, was to support that Henry did not, and could not, consummate the marriage.

The Earl of Southampton, the new Lord Privy Seal after Cromwell, testified that he praised Anna's beauty because Southampton thought it was too late to give an honest assessment to Henry. Anna was already in Calais. Later, Southampton saw his half-brother, Sir Anthony Browne, at court. Browne told Southampton that Henry did not like Anna. Afterwards, Cromwell met with Southampton and 'laid sore to his charge' that Southampton so praised Anna in letters. Cromwell threatened 'malicious purpose' against Southampton and to do 'displeasure' to him. Cromwell threatened to make Southampton shoulder the blame for Henry finding Anna unattractive.

Southampton continued that he thought he was doing the right thing, especially since the marriage was a foregone conclusion. Southampton was sorry to see Henry marry Anna. He made the same comments about the wedding being delayed owing to the Lorraine issue. However, Cromwell somehow ended the Lorraine controversy during a private conversation with Henry. Eight days after the wedding, Cromwell told Southampton that Anna was yet a maid. Henry had no attraction to her, did not like her body, and so on. Southampton asserts that a little before Easter 1540, Henry told him that Henry had not known Anna carnally.

Lord Russell, the new Lord Admiral, stated that when Henry first saw Anna at Rochester, he was 'astonished and abashed' at her appearance. After returning from Rochester the next day, Henry asked Russell if he thought Anna was 'fair'. Russell responded that Anna was of a 'brown complexion'. Fair could mean either blonde or attractive. There is obvious ambiguity here. Anna was indeed a blonde, though Henry may have been expecting a lighter blonde and the paler skin that accompanies it, similar to his third wife, Jane Seymour. Continuing with his deposition, Lord Russell tells of how Henry felt that he could not trust anyone and said, 'I like her not.' Henry repeated this sentiment to Lord Russell on many occasions. Russell told Sir Anthony Browne of the king's concerns. Russell stated that Browne confirmed Henry also made the same statements to him. In Russell's opinion, Henry was always unhappy with the marriage.

The fifth deponent, Lord Cobham, said simply that a man named Palant lamented that Henry married Anna.

Sir Anthony Browne's Imagination

Sir Anthony Browne, Henry's Master of the Horse, gave the longest deposition. It echoes the same lamentations as the other deponents. Browne's statement begins with Henry and Anna's first meeting at Rochester, with Browne providing details that differ from the German account written around 6 January 1540. Browne's statements, and the purpose for which they were given, are not reliable.

Ultimately, Browne's statements did achieve Henry's goal of assisting in the annulment based on non-consummation. Browne begins with recalling that Henry ordered Browne to go to Anna on New Year's Day with a gift and ask Anna if she would like to see it. Browne entered the room where Anna was and, 'having conceived in his mind, what was by pictures and advertisements signified of her beauty and qualities, at the general view of the ladies [Browne] thought he saw no such thing there ... when [he] was directed unto [Anna], and advisedly looked upon her, he saith, he was never more dismayed in all his life.' A dramatic disappointment: not so much a *coup de foudre* as a *coup de boule*.

Browne continues that he did not tell Henry how unattractive he believed Anna to be. Browne recalled that 'when the King's Highness entered to embrace her, and kiss her [Browne] saw and noted in the King's Highness' countenance such a ... misliking of her person, as he was very sorry for it.' Browne states that Henry barely spoke with Anna. 'The King's Majesty had brought with him a partlet furred with sables and richly garnished, sable skins garnished to wear about her neck with a muffley furred, to give the Queen, and a cap,' but Henry changed his mind and did not hand over the gifts. In fact, according to Browne, the next morning Henry 'sent [the furs] by the said Sir Anthony Browne with as cold and single a message as might be'.

This statement by Browne is completely at odds with the report given by Olisleger to Duke Wilhelm. The letter by Olisleger of around 6 January 1540 tells of how Henry dined with Anna, gave her a crystal goblet encrusted with rubies and diamonds, and called on her the next morning. One of two things can be gleaned from these extreme variances. Either in January 1540 Olisleger was completely misrepresenting everything to his master, Duke Wilhelm, or in late June to early July 1540 Browne wove a tale that would suit Henry's purpose.

It is possible that Henry did have the furs as an additional gift for Anna. It is also possible that Henry chose not to give them to her. Why, then, give her the goblet? Why did Browne fail to mention it? Why did Browne say that Henry barely spoke to Anna, when the German account gives the impression that the King of England and his new Queen Consort got on just fine? The pressing issue in July 1540 was that Henry needed the marriage annulled, and one way of annulling the marriage was by proving he and Anna never consummated it.

Sir Anthony Browne continued the deposition along the same lines as those before and after him: Henry saying on a barge to Greenwich, 'I see nothing in this woman as men report of her, and I marvel that wise men would make such a report as they have done.' Browne even pressgangs his wife, who was appointed to wait on Anna; she apparently thought her unattractive. On the evening of 5 January 1540, Browne says Henry declared that he had a 'great yoke to enter into'. And on the morning of 6 January, Henry outwardly displayed his displeasure when preparing for and going to the wedding. Overall, Browne stated, at no time did

Henry heartily consent to the marriage. The lack of hearty consent was another ground for annulment. 'Hearty' here does not of course mean cheerily – 'heartfully' is closer.

Five More; and a Conversation with Cromwell

The seventh deposition was given by Sir Thomas Hennege, echoing the others: mainly, that Henry did not like Anna before or after the marriage, and was unable to consummate it. The eighth deposition was given by Anthony Denny, Gentleman of the Privy Chamber. Denny repeats Henry's complaints about Anna's breasts and belly being loose and 'non-virginal'. Again, Henry was unable to consummate the marriage.

The ninth deposition is very different from the other ten in that it focuses more on Cromwell. Thomas Wriothesley, the man who composed Cromwell's attestation from the Tower, discussed events that occurred shortly before Cromwell's arrest. On 6 or 7 June 1540, Wriothesley 'chanced ... to go into [Cromwell's] gallery' at one of Cromwell's houses. Cromwell was pensively leaning on the sill of a window. The following exchange took place:

'Have we any news?'

'None, Sir,' replied Wriothesley, 'but that I would be glad to go to my house nearby, to devise how to make it fit for me, unless you shall command me to do any other business.'

'Nay,' replied Cromwell, 'I have no business now: but one thing resteth in my head, which troubleth me, and I thought to tell it you. The King ... liketh not the Queen, not did ever like her from the beginning. Insomuch as I think assuredly she be yet as good a maid for him as she was when she came to England.'

Wriothesley responded, 'Marry, Sir, I am right sorry that his Majesty should be so troubled: for God's sake devise how his Grace may be relieved by one way or the other.'

'Yea, how?' asked Cromwell.

'I cannot suddenly tell,' Wriothesley said. 'But standing in the case as you say it doth, I think some way may be devised in it.'

'Well, well,' Cromwell said, 'it is a great matter.'

'So it is,' Wriothesley finished.

The men then parted ways. Wriothesley testified that he ran into Cromwell the day after this alleged exchange. At that point, Wriothesley said to Cromwell, 'Sir, I have thought somewhat of the matter ye told me, and I find it a great matter; but Sir, it can be made no better than it is. For God's sake devise for the relief of the King; for if he remain in this grief and trouble, we shall all one day smart for it. If his Grace be quiet, we shall have our pasts with him.'

'It is true,' Cromwell responded, 'but I tell you, it is a great matter.'

'Marry,' Wriothesley pleaded, 'I grant, but let the remedy be searched for.'

'Well,' said Cromwell, who wandered off before completing his thought.

It is entirely possible that some form of this conversation about which Wriothesley testified took place. What is odd is how Wriothesley encountered Cromwell in the first place. Why was Wriothesley at Cromwell's house? And why on earth is Henry telling almost everyone in his company how much he disliked the Queen, and that he simply could not bring himself to consummate the marriage? Again, the attestation from the Tower was likely drafted by Wriothesley, then in a purely political position as Secretary to the Privy Council. Wriothesley's deposition is about specific conversations he chanced to have with Cromwell. The conversations were no more than three or four days before Cromwell was taken to the Tower.

The last two formal depositions were given by Henry's physicians, Doctor Chamber and Doctor Butts. The doctors say almost identical things, namely that Henry did not consummate the marriage with Anna on their first night together, nor any night thereafter, and that Henry, 'found [Anna's] body in such a sort disordered and indisposed to excite and provoke any lust...'

Anna's Conversation with her Ladies

The final piece of recorded evidence given at the Convocation was contained in a letter from Cromwell to Henry. In it, Cromwell reported to Henry about a conversation Anna had with her ladies at Westminster. The conversation occurred on 22 or 23 June 1540, the Tuesday or Wednesday before Midsummer. Cromwell was in the Tower by then. Anna and her ladies discuss how Anna is not pregnant, though Anna sorely desires it. Lady Catherine Edgecomb asks the Queen, 'How is it possible for your Grace to know that, and lie every night with the King?' Anna replied, 'I know well I am not.'

'I think your Grace is a maid still.' Anna responded to the observation with a laugh. Lady Jane Rocheford, former sister-in-law to Anne Boleyn, said, 'By our Lady, Madam, I think your Grace is a maid still indeed.'

'How can I be a maid,' Anna said, 'and sleep every night with the King?'

'There must be more than that,' Lady Rocheford responded, 'or else I had as leave the King lay further.'

'Why,' said Anna, 'when he comes to bed he kisses me, and taketh me by the hand, and biddeth me, "Good night, sweetheart"; and in the morning kisses me, and biddeth me, "Farewell, darling." Is this not enough?'

Lady Eleonore Rutland then suggested, 'Madam, there must be more than this, or it will be long before we have a Duke of York, which all this realm most desireth.'

'Nay,' said Anna, 'is not this enough? I am contented with this, for I know no more.' Anna then reportedly told Lady Rocheford that the first four nights that Henry and Anna were together, the royal couple was unable to consummate the marriage.

This last piece of evidence at the convocation is impressive. It happened on 22 or 23 June 1540, when Parliament was already debating how to annul Anna's marriage. One of the women, Lady Rocheford, probably already had experience of giving evidence for Henry. Some historians believe Lady Rocheford gave evidence against Anne Boleyn in 1536. True or not, Lady Rocheford certainly assisted Katheryn Howard, Anna's successor, with the trysts between Katheryn and her lover. The alleged conversation was somehow communicated to Cromwell in the Tower. He decided to write a letter to Henry about it.

While all the depositions and evidence presented at the convocation could be completely true, the timing militates against this. When compared with German sources, some details vary hugely from the ones given at the Convocation. Henry needed to have the marriage to Anna annulled quickly and seamlessly to keep England out of the burgeoning war between Duke Wilhelm of Cleves and the Emperor. To accomplish that, the Secret Council was created.

The Secret Council's Conclusions

The Secret Council determined the best grounds under which the marriage could be annulled, and for which testimony would be needed. A letter was then drafted with input from the Secret Council, who made sure that Thomas Cromwell attested to it. Cromwell attested to the letter under watch from the Duke of Norfolk the day after Parliament passed a Bill of Attainder against him. Cromwell provided further support for the claims that Henry was unable to consummate the marriage with Anna, and that Henry did not heartily consent to the marriage.

Testimony was taken from many of Henry's closest servants and members of the Secret Council, to whom Henry allegedly constantly bemoaned his fate in having to marry Anna, how ugly he found Anna, and how unattractive Anna's body was. Finally, the Secret Council relied on the declaration of 15 February 1535 written by an ambassador of Guelders, and a letter written 17 April 1535 written by a Cleves Ambassador, to prove that Anna was pre-contracted to Francis of Lorraine.

All that the declaration and letter proved was one of two alternatives. First, that there never was a pre-contractual document because Anna's father had to fulfil certain conditions and failed so to do. The second possibility was that the pre-contract did exist but was *de futuro*. The documents of 1535 served as proof that the pre-contract, whatever its form, was cancelled.

Curiously, the Convocation received a notarised document describing the denunciation and letter of 1535. The notarised document attested to by Henry VIII states that on 5 January 1540, Henry and Cromwell were at Greenwich. Olisleger and other

Cleves officials discussed the Lorraine pre-contract. The Cleves officials did confirm that a pre-contract was created between Anna and Francis, and that Anna was not more than ten years old at the time. Francis was no older than eight. Neither one of the children could be lawfully married because of their minority, again pointing to any possible pre-contract being *de futuro*. The pre-contract was declared null in the presence of Olisleger, a doctor of laws, and others. The letter of April 1535 was drafted later and reinforced the cancellation of any pre-contract between Anna and Francis.

It was promised to Henry that the denunciation and letter of 1535, and the pre-contract, would be delivered to him before May 1540. In late February 1540, only the denunciation and letter were produced. It is not clear why the pre-contract was not presented, or whether the pre-contract did indeed exist.

A second notarial instrument, also allegedly created at Greenwich but on 6 January 1540, states that Olisleger and other Cleves officials, in Duke Wilhelm's name and theirs, 'acknowledge Henry VIII as a Catholic and Orthodox king unjustly dealt with by the Pope'. This is a fascinating document. Should details of the trial be known by Emperor Charles V, he would be aware – taking the document at face value – that Henry VIII was at least Catholic-leaning and not in favour of the Protestantism and rebellion sweeping Germany, including the United Duchies and the Electorate of Saxony.

A third document previously mentioned and dated 26 February 1540 was created in the presence of Duke Wilhelm. The Cleves archives were to be searched for proof of the denunciation. Thereafter copies of the denunciation and the 1535 letter were created and sent to Henry. The 1535 letter was written in Duisburg, to the northwest of Düsseldorf and between there and Cleves. Olisleger was present when the 1535 letter was drafted.

The Convocation ignored this evidence, or otherwise tried to use it to prove there was a pre-contract at some point. No one provided evidence on Anna's behalf to support the legality of her marriage, whether she was still a maid, whether she heartily consented to the marriage, or whether she was legally bound to the Lorraine contract. The Imperially notarised marital document signed by Anna concerning her marriage to Henry was legally sufficient in the Holy Roman Empire, and there were no impediments to her marriage under Imperial jurisdiction, which included Lorraine.

Now the only thing standing in Henry's way was Anna's consent to the annulment.

10

POLITICAL REFUGEE

Anna reportedly wailed and screamed when Henry's representatives came to deliver the news of the annulment. A few days before, Henry covered his tracks by ordering Wallop to provide 'counsel learned in those laws and experimented in treaties to be sent thither for the matters of the duke [of Cleves]'. Wallop was supposed to ask the Cardinal of Lorraine about the termination of Anna's alleged pre-contract with the Cardinal's nephew, Francis. Henry requested a copy of the 'pact', too. By this time, though, it was already decided that Anna's marriage would be annulled.

On 4 July 1540, a few days before Anna learned her fate, Henry ordered his ambassador at the Imperial court, Pate, to

> ...obtain access to the Emperor on Thursday [8 July 1540] morning, and say he has ... received instructions to inform him that the Lords and Commons, perceiving some doubts in the King's last marriage with the daughter of Cleves, and considering the great effusion of blood heretofore from doubtfulness of titles to the Crown.

The 'doubtfulness' of the Lords and Commons was about Anna's children by Henry being declared illegitimate because of her alleged pre-contract.

That there is 'but one imp' [child, Prince Edward] of [Henry's] body, have petitioned him to commit the examination of the matrimony to the bishops and clergy. Knows that calling the matrimony into question is a matter of some importance, and that people 'will diversely speak after their own fantasy.' Hopes the Emperor will conceive a good opinion and restrain slanderous tongues.

Henry was asking the Emperor to ignore and avoid spreading any gossip about the annulment. Pate was not supposed to tell the Emperor how the annulment came about. Henry would tell Emperor Charles V later.

It was common knowledge in the Low Countries on 4 July 1540, two days before Anna's annulment was declared, that her brother Wilhelm was engaged to Jeanne d'Albret, Francis I's niece. This allied Cleves with France and Navarre, and against the Holy Roman Empire. Francis was preparing for war. The people of Flanders were ill-disposed toward the Emperor at this time, too, because of his rough handling of Ghent.

Another Imperial Diet was planned. Again, the hope was to restore peace in the Emperor's German territories. The German princes intended to send their attorneys. This meant that, though negotiations could be undertaken, very little could be properly resolved. The Imperial Diet came to naught. Only the Catholic German princes showed up. Wilhelm was of course absent, as was Johann Friedrich of Saxony, and the Landgrave of Hesse.

The news of Wilhelm's engagement to Jeanne d'Albret was sent to Henry on 5 July 1540. Rumours of Wilhelm's coming to the French court were rife at the end of June, so the news was not a complete surprise. Wallop had an opportunity to meet with Francis I. The Cleves ambassador was already at Francis's court. Cromwell's demise (though he remained alive in early July) pleased many people at the French court. Francis told Wallop, 'he would gladly make alliance with the duke of Cleves, as Henry approves of it, and was glad that Henry was sending another ambassador to conclude the affair.' Francis was keeping the Cleves ambassadors

...in the Cardinal of Bellie's palace to keep them secret. They said the French king was contented to treat for a defensive league, and would be glad for the Duke, their master, to marry the King of Navarre's daughter, and desired them to go the next day to the said King and Queen.

A new Franco-Cleves alliance was definitely moving forward.

The Annulment Takes Effect

On 6 July 1540, the clergy of England were asked to determine the validity of Anna's marriage. Henry sent to several archbishops and bishops letters of commission under his Great Seal. At the chapter house of St Peters, Westminster, the letters of commission were read to the amassed clergy on 7 July. Stephen Gardiner, the Bishop of Winchester, then 'explained the causes of the nullity of the marriage of the King and lady Anne of Cleves in a lucid speech'. The Bishops of Winchester, Durham, London and Worcester, amongst others, were appointed to 'receive and weigh all the evidences in the case and explain them to the Convocation'. The depositions referred to in the last chapter were taken at this point. All the deponents gave their statements under oath and affixed their signature. An additional deposition was taken from John Chamber, M.D. This deposition was given at Dr Chamber's home in Canon Rowe.

Also on 6 July 1540, Henry's ambassador to the Imperial court at Bruges, Pate, received news from Henry about his doubts over the legalities of the marriage. Pate straightaway went to speak with Emperor Charles V, who asked the causes of those doubts. Pate replied, 'As the doubts took success by the laws of God, justly resolved, the King would make him partaker of them.'

After hearing this, the Emperor, 'professed that the King would always find him his loving brother and very friend, according to the old accustomed amity'. Those present in the Emperor's privy chamber stood up as the English ambassador exited and 'made him as great reverence as possible'.

A final deposition was taken from Philip Hoby on 8 July, in the vestibule of the chapter house of Westminster. After the final deposition was collected, the Convocation reassembled. Four doctors of law were present. The Bishop of Winchester presented the depositions to the group appointed to hear the matter. The Convocation discussed the depositions and other evidence. No one was present at the Convocation on Anna's behalf. Then the Archbishop of Canterbury prorogued the rest of the Convocation until 3 pm the same day.

At that time on 8 July 1540, 'it was agreed in full Convocation that the King and Anne of Cleves were nowise bound by the marriage solemnised between them, and it was decreed to send letters testimonial of this to the King.' On Friday, 9 June 1540,

> ...after much discussion, the letters testimonial, containing the judgment of the nullity of the marriage, made on parchment in the form of a public instrument, was subscribed with their names and signed and sealed by the prothonotary, &c., and sealed by the remembrancers of the archbishops.

The Judgment of Nullity was witnessed by the four doctors of law and made public on 9 July 1540. Written in Latin, it stated,

> The clergy of both provinces have received the King's commission (recited), dated Westm., 6 July 32 Hen. VIII. After mature deliberation, they have found the marriage null by reason of a precontract between lady Anne and the marquis of Lorraine, that it was unwillingly entered into and never consummated, and that the King is at liberty to marry another woman, and likewise the lady Anne free to marry.

The speed with which the annulment went through is astounding. Henry, the clergy, and Parliament treated Anna's case much differently than those of Katherine of Aragon and Anne Boleyn. Both Katherine and Anne had hearings, albeit of different kinds. Both Katherine and Anne were allowed to testify. Not so for Anna of Cleves. None of her lawyers, advisors, or others were present at the Convocation to represent Anna's interests. No one was there to speak on Anna's behalf about whether Anna and Henry consummated the marriage, or whether the contrived statements in the various depositions were true. No one was there to speak about the lack of a pre-contract with Francis of Lorraine, the letters cancelling the betrothal, or the validity of the Imperially enforceable marriage contract between Anna and Henry, or to point out that Henry used Prince Arthur's and Katherine of Aragon's consent to their marriage in 1502, unconsummated though it may have been, as sufficient proof in English law for a marriage to be valid: Henry had used the widowed Katherine's marriage to Arthur and testimony about its consummation in order to have his subsequent marriage to Katherine declared unlawful.

This set a dangerous precedent. If someone, in this instance Henry, unwillingly entered into an agreement or treaty despite all outward appearances, it could later be invalidated. Henry learned from the annulments of his marriages to Katherine of Aragon and Anne Boleyn that it was best not to give Anna a chance for formal protest.

Henry Defends Himself

It was much rumoured on 9 July 1540 at the Imperial court in Bruges that an alliance was forming between the Empire and England. The Emperor had 'not a little praising the realm of England, for the pleasantness and benefits thereof, to such Italians and Spaniards that hath praised these his own countries'. Meanwhile, Francis I was slowly gearing up for the Sixth Italian War with Charles V. At this time, the French were constructing a castle at Ardes, not far from Calais.

Henry wrote a letter to his ambassador at the Imperial court:

> ...tell the Emperor that ... the clergy began to examine the King's marriage on Wednesday morning, and this Saturday gave their judgment that, 'the said marriage neither was at the beginning vailable, nor by any act done since is yet of that sort as doth bind us to continue the same, but leaveth us both in our former liberty.' If the Emperor asks the grounds ... the clergy of England, being so many virtuous, learned, and

grave persons, would determine nothing but on substantial grounds, which they can defend against the whole world.

In the first half of July, Henry received additional intelligence about Wilhelm's betrothal to Jeanne d'Albret, niece of Francis I. It was clear that Wilhelm and Francis now had, or were very close to having, a defensive alliance. As part of the negotiations, Jeanne d'Albret's inheritance of Navarre would go to both Francis and Wilhelm. Francis and Wilhelm would defend each other's dominions.

As was already known, the Emperor offered Wilhelm a marriage with Christina of Denmark in exchange for Guelders. The word in early July 1540 was that the Emperor wanted Guelders so much that he would give Wilhelm the Kingdom of Denmark by virtue of Wilhelm's marriage to Christina, once the current, childless king died. Christina's elder sister Dorothea, married to the Count Palatine, had a childless marriage. Despite the promise of the Kingdom of Denmark, Wilhelm refused to give up Guelders. This idea seems more based in rumour than any genuine conversation between Wilhelm and the Emperor.

What was more likely, and in fact already conveyed to Henry, was that Wilhelm wanted the matter of his right to Guelders tried by a court of law. The Emperor agreed, so long as his brother Ferdinand, King of the Romans, presided. Wilhelm wanted the case tried by the German princes. They could not agree.

Upon meeting with Francis I, Henry's ambassador opened the conversation by expressing his hope that Duke Wilhelm was completely free from any betrothal to Christina of Denmark. After all, Wilhelm failed to fully clear Anna from the Lorraine union. Francis was informed of the Convocation. He expressed astonishment. After the ambassador confirmed that the Convocation was indeed about Anna, Francis heaved a great sigh. He had nothing to say.

Henry hoped that Francis believed Henry's actions were just, legal, and equitable. Francis gave the diplomatic answer that he would not turn away from their friendship. However, Henry must live with his conscience. Francis would continue to call Henry friend, and make up his own mind about Anna's fate.

Francis's sighing of course was prompted by the fact that he was expecting the same thing as Wilhelm: that the marriages between Cleves and England, and Cleves and Navarre, would strengthen his position against the Emperor. Now that plan was partially undone. Would Francis have betrothed his niece to Wilhelm if he knew of Henry's plans to annul the marriage to Anna? The speed with which Henry and the clergy forced through the Convocation and judgment meant he had no time to react.

The Path to Sisterhood

On 11 July 1540, Anna sent a letter from Richmond to her former husband. In it, Anna stated she was aware of the doubts surrounding the legality of their marriage. She knew that the matter must be examined by the clergy and stated that she consented to the examination. Anna expressed her sorrow over the situation and that she had a great love for Henry. Ultimately, Anna left the matter up to God, though she accepted the earthly judgment. She then requested of Henry that he regard her as one of his humble servants. Anna also asked leave to see Henry from time to time. She signed the letter as 'Your Majesty's most humble sister and servant Anne, Daughter of Cleves'.

Anna was asked to write to Wilhelm about the situation. She responded,

> What, should I write to my brother before he write to me? It were not meet. But when he shall write the King's [Grace] shall know what he writeth, and [as he answereth] him so will I answer him with the [best will] and pleasure. And I trust, [howsoever he] or the duke of Saxe take this [matter, his] Grace will be good to me, for I [remain at] his pleasure.

Anna's response accomplished several things. First, she bought herself time before having to tell Wilhelm what had transpired. Second, she put the responsibility on Henry to inform Wilhelm. Third, she declared her loyalty to Henry despite what either Wilhelm or her brother-in-law, Elector Johann Friedrich of Saxony, might do.

'Unknown Woman'. Possibly Amalia of Cleves. Likely by Barthel Bruyn or from his workshop. *c.* late 1530s, possibly 1538. (Courtesy of the Master and Fellows of Trinity College, Cambridge)

Wilhelm V of Cleves. Likely by Barthel Bruyn or from his workshop. *c.* 1538. (Courtesy of the National Museum of Stockholm)

Anna of Cleves. Likely by
Barthel Bruyn or from his
workshop. *c.* 1538. (Courtesy
of the Rosenbach Museum,
Philadelphia, PA)

Anna of Cleves. After Barthel
Bruyn. *c.* 1560s–1570s. (Courtesy
of the President and Fellows of
St John's College, Oxford)

Sybylla of Cleves. Lucas Cranach the Elder. 1526. (Courtesy of Klassik Stiftung Weimar)

Johann Friedrich's engagement portrait when contemplating the marriage to Sybylla, *c.* 1526 by Lucas Cranach the Elder. (Courtesy of Schloss Weimar, Germany)

Sybylla of Cleves. Lucas Cranach the Elder. 1531. (Courtesy of the Bemberg Foundation, Toulouse)

Above left: Johann Friedrich, Elector of Saxony, *c.* 1532 by Lucas Cranach the Elder. (Courtesy of Veste Coburg, Germany)

Above right: Three-quarter length portrait of Anna by Hans Holbein the Younger, 1539, in the collection of the Musée du Louvre, Paris.

Mural at Schloss Burg in Solingen completed *c.* 1900, showing Anna's parents Maria of Jülich-Berg and Johann III. of Cleves-Mark. What is significant about this depiction is that the portraits of Maria and Johann were likely based on original portraits that existed before World Wars I and II, making these very good likenesses. (Author's collection)

Mural at Schloss Burg in Solingen completed *c.* 1900, showing the coats of arms that comprised the United Duchies in 1524, when Anna was roughly nine years old. (Author's collection)

Above left: Painting completed *c.* 1900 depicting the engagement of Maria von Jülich-Berg and Johann III von Cleves-Mark. (Courtesy of Schloss Burg, Solingen, Germany)

Above right: Great Hall in Schloss Burg. Anna, her mother, and her sisters would have spent time in this room. (Author's collection)

Another room in Schloss Burg, Solingen. (Author's collection)

The courtyard of Schloss Burg, Solingen. (Author's collection)

Above left: Düsseldorf City Hall. The original building was built in 1573 at the direction of Anna's brother Wilhelm. It was expanded in 1749. The building suffered heavy damage during the Second World War and was rebuilt between 1958 and 1960. (Author's collection)

Above right: The only remaining portion of the Ducal Palace in Düsseldorf; this tower is now a maritime museum. (Author's collection)

15th-century baptismal font with bronze lid made in 1978 by K. M. Winter, called 'The Creation'. Within the Basilika St. Lambertus, Düsseldorf. (Author's collection)

Above: View of the rebuilt Swan Tower of the Swan Castle, Cleves. (Author's collection)

Right: View of the rebuilt Swan Tower of Swan Castle, Cleves. (Author's collection)

Left: Wilhelm V of Cleves by Heinrich Aldegrever, 1540. (Courtesy of the Rijksmuseum)

Below: 'Wilhelm's Surrender'. The image shows Wilhelm V of Cleves in the bottom right and Emperor Charles V on the throne, *c.* 1543. (Courtesy of the Rijksmuseum)

Henry VIII *c.* 1537 by Hans Holbein the Younger, in the collection of the Museo Nacional Thyssen-Bornemisza, Madrid.

Francis I of France *c.* 1530 by Jean Clouet, in the collection of the Musée du Louvre, Paris.

Charles V at the Battle of Mühlberg, *c.* 1548, in the collection of the Prado Museum, Madrid.

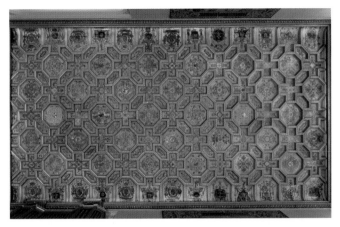

Ceiling of Chapel Royal at St James's Palace, London; the altar and windows are to the right of the image. (Courtesy of the Royal Collection Trust/© Her Majesty Queen Elizabeth II 2018)

Above left: Detail of the ceiling of the Chapel Royal showing Anna of Cleves' coat of arms depicting left to right, top: Cleves, Jülich, Guelders, and Berg; across the bottom left to right are Mark, Zutphen, and Ravensberg. (Courtesy of the Royal Collection Trust/© Her Majesty Queen Elizabeth II 2018)

Above centre: Detail of the ceiling of the Chapel Royal showing intertwined 'H & A' for Henry and Anna. (Courtesy of the Royal Collection Trust/© Her Majesty Queen Elizabeth II 2018)

Above right: Detail of the ceiling of the Chapel Royal showing a fleur-de-lis centre, and clockwise from top right: intertwined 'H & A'; Henry's motto, 'Dieu et Mon Droit'; Henry's name as 'Henricus Rex 8'; and the archaic German, non-Anglicised, non-Gallicised spelling of 'Cleve' or Cleves. (Courtesy of the Royal Collection Trust/© Her Majesty Queen Elizabeth II 2018)

Below: Detail of the ceiling of the Chapel Royal from the portion over the altar, closest to the windows, showing left to right: Anna's coat of arms, 'H R' for Henricus Rex, and Henry's arms. This would place Anna's arms over where she would have stood during a marriage ceremony and Henry's arms over where he would have stood. It is not known if the Chapel Royal at St James's Palace was intended as the setting for the Von der Mark–Tudor marriage. (Courtesy of the Royal Collection Trust/© Her Majesty Queen Elizabeth II 2018)

Right: Jeanne
*d'*Albret, *c.* 1565.
(Courtesy of the
Bibliothèque nationale
de France, Paris)

Below: Coin from
the United Duchies
of Jülich-Cleves-Berg.
1574. (Courtesy of
the Rijksmuseum)

Jeanne d'Albret, F. d'Antoine de Bourbon et mère de Henry IV.

Above left: Folio 1r of the Prayer Book of Anna of Cleves. The escarbuncle of Cleves can be seen in gold, top right. *c.* 1541. (Courtesy of the Kantonsbibliothek Appenzell Ausserhoden, Switzerland, CM Ms. 9)

Above centre: Folio 2r of the Prayer Book of Anna of Cleves. Pastiche with crowned letters A. *c.* 1541. (Courtesy of the Kantonsbibliothek Appenzell Ausserhoden, Switzerland, CM Ms. 9)

Above right: Folio 4r of the Prayer Book of Anna of Cleves. Arms of England in the left margin and red, crowned A in the bottom left corner of the margin. (Courtesy of the Kantonsbibliothek Appenzell Ausserhoden, Switzerland, CM Ms. 9)

Below left: Folio 12r of the Prayer Book of Anna of Cleves. In the bottom margin, the arms of England are displayed in the dexter (male/husband) side and the arms of Cleves are displayed sinister (female/wife) side above a blue crowned letter A. (Courtesy of the Kantonsbibliothek Appenzell Ausserhoden, Switzerland, CM Ms. 9)

Below right: Folio 15r of the Prayer Book of Anna of Cleves. In the left margin, a red crowned letter A within a wreath. (Courtesy of the Kantonsbibliothek Appenzell Ausserhoden, Switzerland, CM Ms. 9)

In Anna's letter to Henry was a telling detail. Members of Henry's Council and some of his lords were present when Anna wrote it. She wrote that their presence and the information they brought comforted her, and that she was happy to be considered as Henry's sister. Though it makes sense for Henry's men to be present when Anna wrote the letter to verify she wrote it, this sounds suspiciously similar to Cromwell's attestation from the Tower. What choice did either Anna or Cromwell have but to acquiesce to the King's will?

A notarial instrument that accompanies the 11 July 1540 letter shows that Anna wrote this letter at the Palace of Richmond in the Queen's Inner Chamber. Charles Brandon, the Duke of Suffolk, was present along with other lords. Anthony Huse notarised the instrument. The instrument indicates that Anna did write and sign the letter consenting to the annulment. Also present were Jane Rocheford, Catherine Edgecomb, and Eleanore Rutland. Those were the same ladies who provided valuable testimony for Henry's case.

The very next day Henry wrote from Westminster to Anna. He was very pleased with Anna's compliance and her apparent desire that Henry adopt her as his sister. He sent that letter along with 500 marks in gold as a token of his new fraternal affection.

Right dear and right entirely beloved sister,

By the relation of the lord Master, lord Privy Seal and others of our Council lately addressed unto you we perceive the continuance of your conformity, which before was reported, and by your letters is eftsoons testified. We take your wise and honourable proceedings therein in most thankful part, as it is done in respect of God and his truth, and, continuing your conformity, you shall find us a perfect friend, content to repute you as our dearest sister.

We shall, within five or six days, when our Parliament ends, determine your state after such honourable sort as you shall have good cause to be content, [we] minding to endow you with 4,000*l.* of yearly revenue. We have appointed you two houses, that at Richemont where you now lie, and the other at Blechinglegh, not far from London, that you may be near us and, as you desire, able to repair to our Court to see us, as we shall repair to you.

When Parliament ends, we shall, in passing, see and speak with you, and you shall more largely see what a friend you and your friends have of us... Thus subscribed, Your loving brother and friend, H.R.

Henry asked his new sister, the Daughter of Cleves, to be quiet and merry. Anna must have been relieved – at least, to some extent. It is difficult to know her true feelings about her situation. We can speculate on Henry's own state of mind: relief on his part certainly, but also a certain amount of surprise. As Elizabeth Norton suggests,[47] the king was probably 'still under the impression that he was the handsome prince of his youth', which he most emphatically was not. He writes to his ambassadors at Cleves about Anna's pain, due to the 'great love and affection which she seemed to have only to our person'. Is this real concern about the woman's feelings, or middle-aged preening?

It was actually reported to Henry that Anna took the news well. However, this was not how it was reported by Olisleger, as previously mentioned. The interpreter who translated Henry's business did a poor job of it. This interpreter may have been Anna's receiver general, Sir Wymond Carew. Either that, or she was in such great shock that she broke down. It was determined to be a better course of action for a letter in German to be given to Anna, to clarify Henry's intentions.

Anna wrote her reply in German, though she had an excellent command of the English language by this time. It is reasonable to assume that Anna chose to write to Henry in her first language to ensure that her thoughts and intent were conveyed clearly – and for the record – and not scrambled by an amanuensis. One of Henry's interpreters had already caused her anguish. Also on 12 July, Henry wasted no time in writing to his ambassadors to

---

47 For more information on Anna's time in England, Norton's *Anne of Cleves: Henry VIII's Discarded Bride* (Amberley, 2010) comes highly recommended.

the French court. Henry informed them that Anna accepted the annulment, and that a notarised instrument recorded events. The ambassadors were to inform Francis I.

Solid proof of Henry's need for Anna's acquiescence exists in a letter he wrote to the Duke of Suffolk, Earl of Southampton, and Wriothesley. It is harsh. After Henry reviewed Anna's letter with his council, it was determined that more was needed from her so that she could not plead ignorance of the situation later on. The Duke of Suffolk and others were ordered to move Anna to write to Wilhelm. A translation of Anna's 11 July letter to Henry was to be attached to any letter Anna sent to Wilhelm. Henry was worried that Anna would change her mind and Wilhelm advise her to press for recourse with Charles V. Henry believed that the annulment was not fully settled with Anna's promise alone. She was a woman, and Henry did not think it wise to rest on her promise 'to abandon the condition of a woman'. Anna was reassured that things would not go worse for her with Henry if she wrote to Wilhelm sooner rather than later. There is an implied threat here that if Anna did not do as Henry asked, things would not be quite so amicable.

Henry visited Anna twice before the annulment was declared. As he did with his first wife, Katherine of Aragon, Henry wanted to maintain the appearance of a loving husband while the Secret Council and Convocation were working out the matter. And, as in Katherine's case, no one was fooled by Henry's cordial visits to Anna.

Anna's letter of 16 July 1540 to Henry simply reiterated her acquiescence. Though she did not sign her name, she did sign as Henry's 'servant and sister'. This letter may have been dictated to Anna, as the handwriting of Wriothesley exists on at least one of the three versions, with Gardiner's handwriting found on one of the others. She sent one of her rings as a gift. After that, Anna's servants were changed from those befitting a Queen Consort of England to those of the King's sister.

Anna told the Duke of Suffolk, the Earl of Southampton, and Sir Thomas Wriothesley that she would send all correspondence she received from her brother Duke Wilhelm, her mother the Duchess Maria, or any other of her relatives, to Henry. Though this may seem like an offer free of coercion, it is possible that Henry wanted to make sure Anna was not giving out nor receiving any sort of intelligence that would go against the interests of England. As England was more closely aligned with the Holy Roman Empire at this point, this made the United Duchies of Jülich-Cleves-Berg potential enemies.

On 21 July 1540, the Duke of Suffolk, Earl of Southampton, and Sir Thomas Wriothesley were sent once more to check on Anna. Henry wanted to ensure that his new sister's household was properly established, and he ordered a gift of jewels to be delivered to her. The gifts may have been part of the effort to persuade Anna to send her brother a letter stating that all was well. The men brought along letters from Wilhelm and John Clerk, the Bishop of Bath, who was Henry's ambassador to Cleves at the time.

The notarial instrument goes on to say that Anna wrote a letter in German to Wilhelm explaining her situation. Olisleger's nephew was in the service of Henry and it was determined that he should deliver the letter to Wilhelm. (Olisleger felt that Anna was mistreated throughout her ordeal.)

The instrument states that once Anna found out who was taking the letter, 'she had him called in, and desired him to commend her to her brother, and say she was merry and well entreated. This she did with such alacrity and pleasant gesture that he may well testify … that he found her not miscontented.' If Anna did behave this way, it was another attempt to placate Henry.

'After she had dined, she sent the King the ring delivered unto her at their pretensed marriage, desiring that it might be broken in pieces as a thing which she knew of no force or value.' This was a subtle ploy – even potentially a risk. By breaking the ring and declaring it to be of no value, Anna was with a single gesture declaring the marriage null and implying that Henry's promise was valueless – a brilliant example of *courtoisie* at its most artful. Lastly, Anna sent a letter she received from Wilhelm. After reading the letter, Henry returned it to Anna.

Breaking the News to Wilhelm

Anna was certainly under pressure when she wrote that letter to Wilhelm on 21 July 1540 explaining the situation. The twenty-five-year-old Daughter of Cleves originally wished to inform Wilhelm in the natural course of their correspondence; but she was pressured by Henry's representatives to write the following:

Brother,
Because I had rather ye knew the truth by mine advertisement than for want thereof ye should be deceived by vain reports, I write the present letters unto you, by which ye shall understand, that being advertised how the nobles and commons of this realm desired the King's Highness here to commit the examination of the matter of marriage, between me and his Majesty, to the determination of the clergy: I did the more willingly consent thereunto, and since the determination made, have also allowed, approved, and agreed unto the same, wherein I have more respect, as becometh me, to Truth and good Pleasure, than any worldly affection that might move me to the contrary.

I account God pleased with that is done, and know myself to have suffered nor wrong or injury, but being my body preserved in the integrity which I brought into this realm, and I truly discharged from all band of consent, I find the King's Highness, whom I cannot justly have as my husband, to be nevertheless a most kind, loving and friendly father and brother, and to use me as honourably, and with as much humanity and liberality as you, I myself, or any of our kin or allies could wish or desire; wherein I am, for my own part, so well content and satisfied, that I much desire my mother, you, and other mine allies so to understand it, accept, and take it; and so to use yourself towards this noble and virtuous prince, as he may have cause to continue his friendship towards you, which on his behalf shall nothing be impaired or altered for this matter; for so hath it pleased his Highness to signify unto me, that like as he will show me always a most fatherly and brotherly kindness, and has so provided for me.

So will he remain with you, and other, according to such terms as have passed in the same knot of amity which between you hath been concluded, this matter notwithstanding, in such wise as neither I, nor you, or any of our friends shall have just cause of miscontentment. Thus much I have thought necessary to write unto you, lest for want of true knowledge ye might otherwise take this matter than ye ought, and in other sort care for me than ye should have cause. Only I require this of you, that ye so use yourself, as for your untowardness in this matter, I fare not the worse, whereunto I trust you will have regard.

It should be borne in mind that there were no 'knots of amity' formally concluded between Wilhelm and Henry. The two never finished their negotiations.

Around 24 July, Henry dispatched a letter to Wotton and Clerk. It contained instructions as to how Wilhelm should be handled. After reciting the events of the annulment and how Henry wished for Anna's consent in the matter to be expressed, he informed Clerk and Wotton that Wilhelm sent letters to Anna and Henry, indicating that he 'would be content with justice...' Then, as has been seen, Anna sent her letter of 21 July to Wilhelm and now Olisleger's nephew was on his way to deliver it.

Henry noted his surprise at Anna's conformity, as he expected otherwise when Clerk was dispatched. Henry instructed his men to avoid discussing any offers Henry initially made to Wilhelm. Now that the marriage was annulled, any money offered by Henry to Wilhelm 'should rather be bestowed on the Lady, and the cost of her traduction to Calais is recompensed by her present endowment'. Formally, any monies previously promised to Wilhelm would be kept by Henry so that he could maintain Anna in England. Henry would keep any monies Wilhelm sent with Anna to reimburse him for the cost of bringing her to England.

Henry wished it conveyed to Wilhelm that he wanted to maintain friendly relations with the young Duke of Cleves. On the other hand, Henry was displeased that Wilhelm did not trust Henry or the Convocation. Wilhelm referred the matter of Anna's annulment to his own relatives and states. Henry used Wilhelm's distrust as another justification for not giving him any money. Aside from simply keeping his cash, Henry was depriving Wilhelm of money that could be used to fund troops and fortifications against the Emperor.

Henry told Clerk and Wotton to accompany Olisleger's nephew to Cleves. They were to give Wilhelm Anna's letter 'and declare the causes of separation as in the King's letter to the Duke'. The men were then to gauge Wilhelm's reaction. Henry directed that if Wilhelm was 'mild, gentle, and desirous of quietness and silence in the matter, with a demonstration that he would gladly have something for his own profit, they must not put him in despair thereof, but refer to the King, and enter into capitulations for mutual aid'. However, if Wilhelm was incensed at how Anna was treated, or showed himself 'intractable and high couraged, Clerk shall say he was not sent to render an account of the King's just proceedings, but friendly to communicate them, and desire licence to depart, while Wotton shall remain'.

Reactions

Wilhelm's and Anna's countrymen were already snubbing Pate, the English ambassador to the Imperial court at Bruges, by 12 July 1540. One of Anna's servants was travelling to England from Cleves, and he tarried at the Imperial court of Bruges for three days. The entire time there, he never once bothered to greet Pate. At the same time, some of the Emperor's nobles were mobilising to woo Henry and flatter the English king. Members of Emperor Charles V's court and chamber were travelling with Don Francisco de Ferrara to visit Henry. Another rumour being passed around in summer 1540 was that Henry intended to put Anna in an abbey.

The papal nuncio to the Imperial court confirmed that the Emperor was surprised by the events in England. Initial international reactions to Anna's annulment were that it was a dishonourable action on Henry's part. Or at least, it did not make Henry look good.

Thomas Cromwell was beheaded on 28 July 1540. On the same day, Henry wed the young Katheryn Howard, his fifth wife and former servant to Anna of Cleves. Katheryn Howard made the perfect bride following the annulment. As the abandoned-child-turned orphan of Lord Edmund Howard and Joyce Culpepper, she had no male relative to protect her; that is, no one except Thomas Howard, 3rd Duke of Norfolk. The Duke of Norfolk took Cromwell's place and so was in a perfect position to recommend his niece. Katheryn also had the Howard pedigree and was from a Catholic family; so no Lutheran complications.

By marrying Katheryn so quickly after the annulment, Henry created an extra impediment to reviving any supposed commitment to Anna. Even if Anna's marriage were reconsidered on the Continent and the marriage considered valid, enforcing Anna's marriage now that Henry and Katheryn were together would prove more or less impossible. Even more so because at the end of July 1540, it was little more than a rumour on the Continent that Henry had repudiated Anna. There was not much Anna or Wilhelm's counselors could do.

When Henry's representatives arrived to inform Wilhelm of what had happened, he was hunting in the area around Utrecht. This served as an excellent excuse to delay his response to Henry's ambassadors. Wilhelm did not react well to the annulment. Henry sent along a prepared response, to be delivered by Clerk, the Bishop of Bath to Wilhelm or his counselors. Clerk was to say that if Wilhelm 'had given [Clerk and Wotton] a hearing from the first you would have had the lady [Anna] whom you so greatly desire here present or at least not far off on the way hither'. Wilhelm's contumacious behaviour, including his insistence 'on consultations and on quarrels with friends ... compelled the King to adopt a new policy, which I [Clerk, the Bishop of Bath] greatly regret'.

If Clerk was unavailable, Wotton was to deliver a similar speech. They were to accuse Wilhelm of going back on his word to be content with justice: '[t]his showed little conformity, for an enemy might say it. It seemed only an excuse for meanwhile consulting other people.' Because of Wilhelm's reaction and other difficulties, they were to say that Henry resolved to keep Anna in England. That was because, '[h]aste was required as the approbation of Parliament, the dissolution of which was at hand, was necessary.'

In contrast, if Wilhelm was content, Clerk and Wotton should inform him of the settlement given to Anna for the maintenance of her dignity in England. Henry did not want Wilhelm 'to feel aggrieved, nor to despair of the kindness of the King, who has shown his desire to content him by sending ambassadors and letters and offering friendship and treaties'. Wotton and Clerk were then to ask Wilhelm for his thoughts on creating a league with Henry, and offer that Henry would provide funds for 3,000 soldiers. The funds would be enough to maintain the soldiers for over two months, in case the United Duchies were invaded. Clerk and Wotton were to ask what Wilhelm would offer in return.

More Legal Manoeuvrings; Anna's Settlement

The Statement of the King's case from earlier in July 1540 explicitly laid out that 'a matrimony non-consummate is made void by a second matrimony consummate as the bishops of Rome, when it suited them, have judged.' If Henry married Katheryn Howard and consummated the marriage, then the non-consummated marriage with Anna was void. There was nothing Anna could do. This was in line with previous decisions of the papacy.

The inspiration for this could have come from the canon law issues surrounding Henry's first marriage to Katherine of Aragon. Originally a papal legate was sent from Rome to preside over Henry's Great Matter. At the time, Emperor Charles V held the Pope hostage. With the papacy issuing a ruling that Katherine's first, non-consummated marriage to Prince Arthur was voided by her subsequent, obviously[48] consummated marriage to Henry VIII, the papacy's intention was to make it even more impossible for Henry to leave Katherine.

More importantly, Henry's current adherence to the papal decree about void marriages gave Henry better standing with the Emperor. Katherine of Aragon was Charles V's maternal aunt, making Henry the Emperor's uncle. By using papal precedent quietly to reinforce and legitimate the deceased Katherine's marriage to Henry, Henry accomplished two things. First, that made it easier for the Lady Mary to be legitimate royal offspring. The Lady Mary was twenty-four in July 1540, and Henry had her marital value on his mind. Second,

---

48 Henry and Katherine had at least six children together, of whom only the future Mary I of England survived.

Henry was offering a *mea culpa* of sorts to the Emperor. Just as importantly, by choosing to follow previous papal rulings, it made it very difficult for most of the Catholic lands of the Holy Roman Empire, Scotland, or France to argue against the annulment.

The Statement describes how 'lawfulness of the marriage might have been always called in question, whenever the son of Lorraine might make his claim by the laws of the Bishop of Rome.' This seems logical. Lorraine was part of the Holy Roman Empire, as were the United Duchies. It seems unlikely that a legally binding document in one part of the Empire had no effect in another. The Statement says, 'If any allege that in the solemnization the King consented, it is to be answered that a conditional consent is no consent unless the condition is fulfilled.' Weasel words. Effectively, this made Henry's consent *de futuro*, after a fashion. Even though Henry consented at the actual wedding, the marriage's validity was based on the condition precedent of consummation. Per the Statement, this made Henry and Anna's marriage *de futuro*, despite those words not appearing in the Beer Pot Documents. Unfortunately for Anna, this bit of reasoning could only be used by Henry. Anna could not state that the Lorraine contract, which was almost certainly *de futuro* anyway, was not consented to by her because not all the conditions were fulfilled.

Henry gave Anna the manors of Bletchingley and Richmond as part of her settlement. The manors included parks and houses. Anna received a gift of 8,000 nobles and was promised more money to sustain her household until she could appreciate income from her new properties. A good deal of pearls, jewels, plate,[49] furniture, and hangings were provided, too. Henry ordered that Anna have an appropriate number of officers and servants for her new station. He formally declared that Anna was his sister, 'and have precedence over all ladies in England, after the Queen and the King's children'. Such largesse must have comforted Anna despite losing her position as Queen Consort.

---

49 In the buttery of Hampton Court Palace is a lead platter owned by Prince Arthur Tudor that was subsequently given to Anna. Her seal, the Lion of Jülich, is imprinted on it.

When being so generous with Anna, Henry may have recalled the poor position his first wife, Katherine of Aragon, was in between 1502 when her first husband Prince Arthur died and when Henry married her in 1509. Katherine was borderline-destitute whilst her father, the Catholic monarch Ferdinand, and father-in-law Henry VII debated what to do with her. Henry VII did not want to lose Katherine's sizeable 200,000-ducat dowry to Spain. He already received 100,000 ducats, and would be required to return that money should Katherine be sent back to Spain. Katherine spent several miserable years at Durham House in London, waiting for Henry VII and Ferdinand to sort out her situation. Perhaps Henry did not wish to see Anna suffer as Katherine had.

France

Francis I spent the month of July 1540 courting the German princes to estrange them from the Emperor. It was becoming more obvious that Francis had no intention of adhering to the June 1538 Truce of Nice. Francis's accord with the Ottoman Turks, something used against Charles V before the Truce of Nice, was extant. Charles continued refusing to give Francis the Duchy of Milan. In the two years after the Truce of Nice, the Emperor gained more and more influence in Italy. Francis was at breaking point.

In the middle of July 1540, Francis was formally told of the annulment. The Cleves ambassadors at the French court ceased communicating with Henry's after 7 July. They were completely focussed on the engagement of Wilhelm and Jeanne and spoke with Francis and the King and Queen of Navarre almost exclusively. The English ambassadors were equipped to discuss an alliance with Cleves. One must wonder if Henry was relying on the possibility that Wilhelm would be so displeased that he would not further pursue such an alliance.

At the French court, few could figure out why Henry annulled the marriage. Francis met with Henry's men around 15 July 1540, in part to learn the reasons. No answer was forthcoming, the excuse being that details of the case had not yet reached the ambassadors.

The English ambassadors and Francis dined together, after which the King was informed of the determination. Still, there were no specifics. Francis wished to know more, but all he was told was who presided over the Convocation. Francis was concerned about whether the annulment was because of a prior pre-contract. He also wanted to know what would happen to Anna. Was she sent back to Cleves? The best the English ambassadors could do was promise to send Francis the particulars of the annulment, and assure him that Anna was being treated honourably.

At first it seemed uncertain whether Wilhelm was betrothed to Francis's daughter Marguerite or to his niece Jeanne d'Albret. Jeanne, as the sole heir of her parents, expected a sizeable inheritance, which included Navarre under Salic law. It was widely believed that Francis would not allow Jeanne to marry outside France or areas under French control. It seems that Francis's and Wilhelm's desperate times called for desperate measures.

Francis finally learned the grounds of Anna's annulment from his ambassador, Marillac. A letter dated 21 July 1540 goes over the details of Henry's and the Convocation's actions. Francis learned that Anna consented to the annulment, though he knew well enough that Anna had little or no choice. Marillac conversed with one of Wilhelm's ambassadors, possibly Olisleger, who was very disappointed by Anna's choices. She consented to the examination, the Cleves ambassador telling Marillac:

> He had often warned her to grant nothing to the prejudice of her own rights or her brother's estate, but could get no answer except that she would obey the King her lord, pointing out the great kindness he had used towards her and her firm intention to endure all he thought fit and to remain always in this country and not return to her own.

Why did Anna consent? Did she did not know what was going on? Did she not believe her marriage would be annulled? Or was she simply frightened of the man historian John Matusiak called 'England's Nero' (quoting Melanchthon), a man with a potentially deadly habit of changing things to suit himself and with one beheaded wife in his wake?

England

There are any number of reasons why Anna wished to stay in England. She may have felt ashamed to face Wilhelm. Between signing her marriage contract with Henry in September 1539 and leaving for England, Anna boasted to Wilhelm that she was of a higher station than either him or their sister Sybylla; no longer. Though Henry gave her properties, she held far less than Wilhelm and Sybylla. It is unknown how Amalia felt about all this.

Anna may have truly loved England. She was known to enjoy English ale and the culture in general. She led a more sheltered life in Germany by virtue of her station as a duchess. In England, Anna was elevated over most of the population, save for four or five people in the kingdom. She could come and go as she pleased. The people of England loved her. Losing Anna as Queen Consort of England was 'to the great regret of this people, who loved and esteemed her much as the sweetest, most gracious and kindest queen they ever had or would desire'.

A more politic reason for why Anna stayed in England might be that she knew about the tensions over Guelders. A passport for Anna's journey through Imperial territory was secured back in 1539, but it was not safe to assume that Charles V would grant the same for the return home. Should Anna be captured whilst travelling back to Germany, she would make a valuable hostage. It was safer for her to stay in England, where she was well provided for. If she stayed, Henry did not have to take responsibility for her safe conduct.

Around the same time as the annulment, Marillac relayed to Francis that Parliament had 'concluded although not yet published ... that all strangers [foreigners] dwelling in this realm shall depart before Michaelmas next, except only those engaged in commerce, who shall not keep house unless they be married or have letters of naturalization.'

A large part of this population were Flemings, who were citizens of the Holy Roman Empire, and neighbours to the United Duchies.

The motivation for expelling them is unclear. Perhaps Henry wanted to eject the citizens from rebellious Imperial territories to further appease the Emperor.

The Holy Roman Empire

The Duke of Lorraine's daughter married René of Chalon, Prince of Orange, on 20 August 1540. René was the apple of Christina of Denmark's eye until this marriage. She herself, as mentioned before, married Francis of Lorraine on 10 July 1541. There was no legal impediment under Imperial law to Francis marrying Christina, which further underlines the fact that one of the bases for Anna's annulment was manufactured. The final Lorraine child, Nicolas Duke of Mercœur, was devoted to ecclesiastical life in the early 1540s, and thereafter married the first of three wives, Marguerite of Egmont. These marriages and appointments successfully kept the Von der Mark family away from any inheritable claim to the Duchy of Guelders during the tumultuous early 1540s.

The Cleves ambassadors left the French court by 23 July 1540 without uttering a word to Henry's ambassadors. On the same day, ambassadors from Guelders were in Paris. There was some confusion as to Anna's annulment because Wilhelm had not said anything about it in Cleves. It was widely believed by the Guelders embassy that Wilhelm was already engaged to Jeanne d'Albret and that things were 'in a manner concluded'.

Charles V was encouraged to bring Henry back to the Catholic Church. Peace negotiations between the Empire and Cleves were over for a while. Cleves was now aligned with France, and it was time for England to choose a side. If the Emperor could succeed in bringing England back to Catholicism at the same time as securing an ally, even better.

The Diet of Hagenau,[50] held around 8 July 1540, was mostly fruitless. Any concession given to the Lutherans 'would be a bad example to give in Germany, in presence of their Majesties [the

---

50 Hagenau, Haguenau in French and known to English speakers as Hainault, is in the Bas-Rhin of France. Though Bas-Rhin means Lower Rhine, the area is actually in the Upper Rhine. Hagenau is about 450 km or 280 miles south of Cleves, and about 100 km or 65 miles west of Stuttgart.

Emperor and king of the Romans], now when the king of England has taken a turn in the right direction'. The German Protestants were directed either to restore the items taken from Catholic persons and establishments, or set them aside until religious differences were settled. It was determined that the peace established at Nuremberg would only apply to those 'who gave in their names at the time of the diet at Augsburg', but not anyone who 'accepted the confession subsequently'. No one new could be admitted to the Schmalkaldic League. It was agreed that the Protestant Germans would maintain peace in the Holy Roman Empire, or suffer the consequences.

The German Protestants responded by claiming any goods seized were already disposed of, for 'godly uses according to the Scriptures and to old canons'. The Germans wanted the Pacification of Nuremberg to apply to 'all who agreed with them in religion as shown by the Emperor's rescript', which was given before the Diet of Hagenau. The Germans refused the Emperor's demand that no new members should be admitted to the Schmalkaldic League, so long as the new members 'would embrace true religion'. The Germans represented that they were 'always ready to keep peace, and will give securities if necessary'. The Diet was prorogued until around 28 October 1540. It would then resume in Worms.

Parliament

Soon after Anna's annulment, on 16 July 1540, Parliament was presented with a bill that amended the Six Articles. Specifically, the proposed bill changed the condition placed upon priests: non-adherence to the Six Articles would result in forfeiture of goods and chattels instead of death. The forfeited items, including ecclesiastical promotions and rents, now reverted to the King. The bill changed the position on priests marrying or having sexual relations with women. The bill quickly moved through its required three readings in the House and went down to the Commons. The bill was returned to the House on 21 July and passed. Of interest are two clauses in the bill, which would allow for hearings related to those clauses to be heard by secular, and not ecclesiastical, judges.

A further 'Act Concerning Archbishops, Bishops, their Chancellors, Commissary, Archdeacons and their Officials', also from July 1540, was a coup for Catholic-leaning members of Parliament and for Catholicism in England. No wonder the Pope believed now was a good time to return England to the Catholic fold.

Parliament passed another curious bill during that session. It applied to marriages annulled 'during the time of popery' because of pre-contracts or degrees of consanguinity. Anne Boleyn's marriage to Henry was annulled in part because of her pre-contract to Henry Percy and because Anne's sister Mary Boleyn was his mistress. That made Henry's marriage to Anne incestuous. This new bill stated, 'after a marriage was consummated, no pretence of any pre-contract, or any degrees of kindred or alliance, but those mentioned in the law of God, should be brought or made use of to annul it,' so long as the marriage was 'duly solemnized, and consummated; and that no degrees of kindred, not mentioned by the law of God, should be pleaded to annul a marriage.'

This new bill 'softened' the illegitimacy of the Lady Elizabeth. Of more immediate concern, it allowed Henry to marry Katheryn Howard despite Katheryn being Anne Boleyn's cousin. Under the laws of Scripture – not canon law – Katheryn and Anne were not within the prohibitions of consanguinity.

At the end of July 1540, the Emperor continued to maintain Pate, English ambassador to the Imperial court, as 'his Englishman ... the Emperor entirely loves the King, and trusted that the [Tudors and Hapsburgs] would continue friends against all adversaries forever.' Pate was invited to a banquet with Maria of Austria, Regent of the Low Countries. It was said about the Imperial court at The Hague, where Pate then was, that Anna's annulment 'alienated the hearts of the Electors ... one of the King's council said that the marriage, if heard in an indifferent place, could be but legitimate.'

Anna spent the rest of 1540 away from court.

11

THE SLOW MARCH
TOWARDS WAR

Although Anna kept to herself at Richmond for the rest of 1540, the fallout of her marriage dogged Henry. Clerk and Wotton did not make good progress with Wilhelm in the United Duchies. Henry was unhappy with the pair, who immediately gave to Wilhelm the more cordial response that Henry dictated. The ambassadors were supposed to wait and gauge Wilhelm's response over time. It was represented to Wilhelm that Henry was willing to help him with his fortifications.

Clerk and Wotton had an audience with Wilhelm on 5 August 1540. Olisleger's nephew finally arrived with Anna's and Henry's letters to him. Wilhelm read the letters, then withdrew to discuss the situation with Olisleger. Wilhelm was none too pleased. Clerk and Wotton asserted that the decision by the clergy was enough to effect the annulment. Wilhelm disagreed. He stood off from the English ambassadors and ordered Olisleger to tell them that the annulment needed consideration by himself and his council.

Olisleger interrupted Clerk and Wotton at dinner to tell them that Wilhelm was willing to maintain his amity with Henry. Wilhelm was not at all pleased with Henry keeping Anna in England. Olisleger asked if she could be conducted back to Cleves; the response was that it was her choice to stay or return. Wilhelm was aware of the Emperor warming to Henry. Aside from wanting his sister back so he could secure another marriage for her, Wilhelm surely saw that Anna's being kept in England potentially made her a hostage to Wilhelm's good behavior. Unless Henry consented to conducting her back to Cleves, Anna could not safely travel through Imperial territory.

Wilhelm gave his final response to the letters he received from Anna and Henry on 9 August 1540. As far as he knew,

> ...there never was any matrimony between the lady and the young marquis of Lorraine; that he is sorry it is otherwise found, but he trusts the King will order the matter to his honour, and desires to continue the amity and league.

Clerk and Wotton pressed for Wilhelm's consent to the annulment decree, but Wilhelm refused to give it. Clerk then withdrew from the United Duchies and Wotton stayed behind. Discussions with Wilhelm were over. Henry's ambassadors encouraged him to give Wilhelm a large sum of money in the event Wilhelm came around to seeing things Henry's way. If Wilhelm were content, then so too would be the Elector of Saxony and the other German princes.

Anna's New Life

Meanwhile in England, Anna was reportedly having a grand time. Through her cupbearer Anna sought a licence to order 800 tuns of beer for her new household, and wore new clothes practically every day. A tun is equal to about 252 gallons. Thus, Anna's request was for about 201,600 gallons of beer. Anna also sought a licence to export, presumably wanting to use the beer as another form of income. In fact, this must be the case – such a huge quantity could not be drunk in one location before it went off. Marillac, the French ambassador, remarked that, 'far from pretending to be married, she is as joyous as ever ... which argues either prudent dissimulation or stupid forgetfulness of what should so closely touch her heart.' The argument for prudent dissimulation is stronger.

As described earlier, the life of a German noblewoman was strictly guarded. Anna spent her days in the United Duchies under the watchful eye of a governess in the *Frauenzimmer*. When Anna was allowed to engage with the court, it was only at specific times of the day, and again, a governess was usually present. It was important to protect a noblewoman's virtue. Anna enjoyed excursions like hunting at her family's German court, but there was always some degree of supervision. Otherwise, Anna learned the skills of running a household with the other women in the *Frauenzimmer*.

Anna made the most of her new-found freedom, whatever her motivation. Her behaviour distressed the Cleves ambassador, who was trying to receive guidance from Wilhelm as to the next steps for her. The Cleves ambassador encouraged Marillac to keep Francis I abreast of events involving Anna, too.

Not everything was pleasant for Anna in England. She did not have any official permanent status in the kingdom yet. Her receiver-general Sir Wymond Carew, originally appointed to the post in 1537 in the service of Jane Seymour, was vexed by the Lady of Cleves. Carew probably gained the position through his brother Denny, who was a favourite of Henry's. Carew spoke German, making him a valuable source of information.

Anna learned that Carew had the task of reading and copying all letters received or sent between her, her siblings, mother, or countrymen. Anna viewed Carew and his wife as inferior to her own steward. In Germany, that may have been so, but not in England. Anna's attitude was insulting to Carew and his wife. Carew wrote, 'The lady Anne of Clevelond [sic] is bent to do me displeasure. I think she has heard how I procured the knowledge of such letters as were sent to her ...which of truth at the beginning she denied.'

Anna was not inclined to send all of her letters from Wilhelm to Henry. Carew reported that Anna received correspondence around 17 August 1540 and asked the Cleves ambassador for the letters. The ambassador stated they were congratulatory letters from Wilhelm. Carew stated that all letters must be sent to Henry. Eventually Carew was able to cajole Anna into sending along the letters.

The Hated Henry

On 14 August 1540, the Act or Statutes Against Strangers were published. All foreigners, with narrow exceptions, had to leave the country by Michaelmas in late September 1540. The Act's provisions were not well drafted and, in some ways, directly conflicted with extant treaties that were of concern to Marillac.

In Saxony, Henry was hated. Melanchthon, still an important figure at Sybylla of Cleves, Duchess of Saxony's court, said of him:

> Let us cease to sing the praises of the English Nero. I know not whether you have heard of his cruelty to the Queen. If you know anything about that business you can judge with what mind our people will read these panegyrics.

Sybylla's husband Elector Johann Friedrich, who was ever suspicious of Henry, felt vindicated in his earlier warnings and unhappy with the treatment of his sister-in-law. Henry now had no hope of an alliance with Saxony or of ever being welcomed into the Schmalkaldic League.

Over in France, Henry's ambassador Wallop was ordered to tell Francis of Henry's continuing friendliness toward the disillusioned Duke of Cleves. Now that Francis's niece was marrying Wilhelm, Henry was even more happy to remain friendly with him. Francis probably saw right through these political niceties.

The marriage of Anna of Lorraine, cousin to Marie of Guise, Queen Consort of Scotland, was discussed between Marie and Montmorency in late August 1540. Anna of Lorraine, whose children would enjoy a potential claim to Guelders, was also tied to Scotland through her relation to Marie. The Auld Alliance between Scotland and France was revisited with the marriage of Marie to James V of Scotland. So too was Scottish interest in French and Imperial politics. Marie of Guise was the granddaughter of Philippa of Guelders through Marie's father Claude of Lorraine, second son of René II, Duke of Lorraine. This meant that Marie's male children by her husband James V could potentially lay claim to the Duchy of Guelders.

Over in Saxony, Melanchthon was cursing, 'May God destroy this monster!' Unable to hide his outrage, Melanchthon ranted about the 'atrocious crimes' being committed in England. Enforcement of the Act Against Strangers was stayed from Michaelmas 1540 to Easter 1541. The Act was further modified to exempt foreigners 'in the service of the King's family and Anne of Cleves'. The official writ was issued on 1 September 1540. Marillac noted that the Act required all foreigners either to become naturalised or be 'in service with the English'. The Act affected about 400 or 500 Frenchmen, but upwards of 15,000 Flemings. Marillac noted that the Act disproportionately affected poor persons who had lived in England for a long time. Ultimately, the Act did not violate any treaties, so far as Marillac could tell.

Henry was trying to keep in with Francis. While out hunting, he sang Francis's praises in front of Marillac. Henry predicted that Charles V would not long be favourably inclined toward Francis. Henry wanted Marillac to know the Emperor was making overtures to him. But talk was cheap, or so he told Marillac. Henry was warning Marillac that though he had a friendly disposition toward France for the time being, he may switch to being in league with the Empire.

In early September 1540, despite feeling spied on by Carew, Anna was reported as being 'unusually joyous'. She continued to dress splendidly and indulge in pastimes. She not only had the money to buy new clothes – she didn't have to mend the old ones, as she had in the *Frauenzimmer*.

Katheryn Howard made an appearance at a progress. She was described as, 'graceful more than beautiful', and short. Katheryn favoured dressing in the French fashion, and Henry doted on her, to say the least. Despite the triumph of the new queen consort, Anna persisted in her cheerful disposition.

Chapuys, the Imperial ambassador, arrived back in England. He was not well received. He did not have access to Henry or important persons about court. He did press Marillac for details about the Cleves-Navarre match, but Marillac demurred and feigned ignorance. Meanwhile, Francis established a connection with Johann Friedrich in Saxony and was continuing to work with the Turks. The Turkish faction was invaluable to Francis at the end of the Third Hapsburg-Valois war from 1536 to 1538, before the Truce of Nice was signed.

On 10 September 1540 the defensive treaty between Jülich-Cleves-Berg and France was ratified by Francis I. Francis and his counselors knew they were flirting with violating the 1538 Truce of Nice by entering into this treaty. Part of the Truce stated that Francis would refrain from interfering with the Guelders matter to the detriment of the Emperor's interests. To get around it, the Cleves-France treaty only used Wilhelm's titles to the United Duchies and omitted calling Wilhelm the Duke of Guelders. While the Truce of Nice was not technically violated, it was obvious that Francis was openly disregarding portions of it. This document was certified by an Imperial notary, much the same as Anna's Beer Pot Documents had been.

In England there were rumours that France and the Holy Roman Empire were already embroiled in war. That was not true, yet. What was true was that Wilhelm was leaving for France any day, and Henry wanted to know what his plans were. Wotton, in attendance on Wilhelm, was ordered to discover what was happening with the Navarre match. Wotton was to offer to go with Wilhelm to France and give advice to Wilhelm along the way. If Wilhelm did not want Wotton's company, then Wotton was to learn which of Wilhelm's advisors were going to France. The names and any other pertinent information should be passed on to Henry and his council.

Dorothea of Denmark's husband, Fredric the Count Palatine, was angered and frustrated by Henry by October 1540. Count Frederick visited Henry's court throughout 1539 and in early 1540, hoping to secure assistance in seizing back the thrones of Denmark and Norway from the usurper, King Christian III. Henry promised some monies and other assistance, mostly through Cromwell. The assistance was not forthcoming. Henry maintained a correspondence with Christian III during 1539 and the early part of Henry and Anna's marriage. That relationship was now cooling: Dorothea was Emperor Charles V's niece and supporting Christian III conflicted with friendly overtures toward the Emperor.

Fallout and Fortifications

In early October 1540, Charles V was on his way to Ghent. He set in motion improvements to the castle there that cost in excess of 500,000 ducats. The issue over Guelders was to be heard at the next Imperial Colloquy of Regensburg (sometimes called Ratisbon). This Diet, following so closely the one at Hagenau, irritated the Pope and his legate.

On the way to Germany, Charles V extended an invitation to Pate to visit him in Brussels, to find out how things stood with Henry regarding himself and Wilhelm. From the Emperor's perspective, Anna's brother was a usurper and had wronged Henry.

Unpleasant things were said about Henry by the pro-Cleves faction at court in Brussels. They estimated his age to be around 60 when he was not quite 50, noted he had grown fat, and that he embraced 'tyranny for riches'. One of Anna's relatives, who wanted her to return to the United Duchies, 'trusted to see the day that the King would repent of her repudiation'.

Meanwhile, the French were strengthening fortifications. In early October 1540 in France, 'there is more fear of war than hope of agreement between the French king and Emperor.' The Deputy of Calais was ordered not to allow people from the French-controlled town of Ardes to enter Calais. Francis ordered repairs to Cowbridge during the summer, and the English were prohibited from crossing the bridge. As early as mid-October, there was a real worry that skirmishes between the French and English would break out. Anxiety was high in England, as there was a general feeling that Anna's treatment 'offended all the world except France'.

Worried that the French were going to attack Calais, a spy was sent to learn whether French troops were gathering at Boulogne. The port, lying 22 miles southwest of Calais, was frequently occupied by the English during times of war with France. Correspondence from Cleves was being carefully reviewed before going on to its intended recipient. It is safe to assume that this means Anna's private correspondence was subject to perusal and copying too. Letters to the Cleves ambassador in England were intercepted and reviewed by Henry and his Council before being sent along.

Anna's brother and the Emperor were even then trying to settle the Guelders issue. Frederick, the Count Palatine, offered to bring Wilhelm to Charles V before Charles came to Germany. Charles V might have hoped to try for a match between his niece Christina of Denmark and Wilhelm, with appropriate capitulations from Wilhelm, as the information at the Imperial court was that Wilhelm was slowly turning away from his betrothal to Jeanne.

Surely to Anna's distress, Henry's council antagonised the French by bringing up France's various friendly overtures to the strong naval territories of the Venetians and the Turks, plus the amity with Cleves, and the Pope. There was even some talk of the Lady Mary marrying the widowed Emperor Charles V, despite the two being cousins. They were betrothed at one point when Mary was just a girl, but Charles opted not to wait for her to come of age and instead married Isabella. Now that Mary was twenty-five, she was certainly old enough to marry.

On 1 November 1540, Henry sought taxes for war. Hiding from the plague at Windsor Castle, Henry fulminated that London was not paying enough: its citizens 'should be punished as traitors; and the mayor and magistrates had no remedy but to cry for mercy'. Needless to say, Henry got his money. The French citizens living in England at the time were being taxed at extortionate rates, so much so that Marillac complained to the Council. This appeared to breach extant treaties between the countries.

Wilhelm had not given an official response to the matter of Anna's annulment. Clerk, the Bishop of Bath was yet to return from Cleves, in part because Clerk was sick and resting at Calais before crossing the Channel. Meanwhile, 'The new Queen has completely acquired the King's grace, and the other [Anna] is no more spoken of than if she were dead.'

Marguerite, Queen of Navarre, believed her daughter would marry Wilhelm. She passed this along to Henry. Wilhelm's envoy was delayed until early November 1540 because the Turks were attacking Hungary and causing consternation in Germany over where they would go next. Marguerite made certain to sing the praises of Henry for his 'good and honourable treatment of my lady Anne'. Matters were still being settled for Anna by the Privy Council.

In the middle of November, Henry sent new representatives with a retinue to the Imperial court. This was a company designed to impress, 'a hundred horsemen, all in grey velvet, with great gold chains on their necks'. The excuse for this display was the replacement of the current ambassador to the Imperial court, Pate, with Sir Edmund Knyvet and Winchester.

Winchester had assisted Cromwell in bringing about the Cleves match. Henry wished to explain the apparent changes in church doctrine that allowed him not only to marry Katheryn Howard, but to have that marriage completely void Anna's marriage. Henry was worried that 'in the German Diets, it might be said he only observed the law of marriage at his pleasure, and innovated nothing in religion but what served ambition and avarice' – perhaps not an idle speculation.

Henry's overall goal was to keep Francis and Charles V at odds with each other. To that end, the idea of a marriage between the Lady Mary and Charles V was kept alive by this elegant embassy headed toward the Imperial court. Even though this rumour existed, it was surely dismissed by any attentive listener. Emperor Charles V refused to wed the Lady Mary because she was illegitimate. And Henry did not want to match Mary with someone outside of England, which could result in England returning to the Catholic Church. Though Parliament did make a half-hearted attempt at making Mary legitimate, she could not attain fully legitimate status without England admitting the authority of the papacy. Members of the Emperor's court nonetheless supported the idea of her marrying her cousin Charles V.

More Debates over Religion and Territory

Ramparts continued being fortified and built along the English coast. Marillac noted that the English seemed 'to be preparing for war, but rather defensive than offensive'. Henry went to London from Windsor to review the war machines being manufactured. Henry ordered the construction of 'six swift galleys, similar to those at Marseilles, for crossing to Calais and coasting'. Skirmishes between English Calais and French Ardres continued. Cowbridge, the actual bridge between Calais and Ardres, was captured, torn down, recaptured, and rebuilt.

Charles V prepared to attend the religious colloquy at Regensburg. Henry continued to agonise over his reputation with the German princes, and the French knew it. Henry's act of sending Winchester and Knyvet to relieve Pate at the Imperial court was questioned. It was explained at the French court that Henry believed it best to have someone attend the Colloquy of Regensburg who had a good knowledge of why Anna of Cleves was no longer Queen Consort of England; and possibly to explain why, in mid-November 1540, she remained in England.

Meanwhile, in Cleves, Wilhelm returned to Düsseldorf from a stay at Hambach, the castle that was so damaged by fire in 1512. Wotton remained as the English ambassador to Cleves. He had his work cut out for him. Rumours about Henry were spreading around the United Duchies like wildfire, and Wilhelm did not make an earnest attempt to stop them.

Wotton told Henry that the Cleves council deemed Henry's actions to be based on an 'abominable and devilishly invented lie … also it did tend to the derogation of [Henry's] honour.' Wilhelm promised to try to 'extinguish the rumor', nothing more than lip service. Anna's brother had more pressing concerns swirling about him than how the United Duchies felt about Henry and England. Wilhelm proceeded with negotiations for his marriage to Jeanne d'Albret. Even though Wotton knew about it, he was kept in the dark about the specifics of the marriage plans.

By 28 November 1540, the German princes were gathering in Worms to prepare for the next Diet. At the previous one, in Hagenau, eleven German princes were chosen to compile and present their disagreements. Wilhelm was one of those princes, and sent his counselors to assist in preparing the reasons for dissension.

By December 1540, things had cooled off between the Emperor, Francis, and Wilhelm. Francis and the Emperor were able to come to some sort of agreement. This could have been influenced by the fractious Italian states under Imperial control. Those states were threatened by the Turks, who were in league with Francis. Wilhelm was not in a rush to marry Jeanne d'Albret, though his lack of urgency could have been because he was preparing for the Colloquy of Regensburg.

The Emperor looked into another match for Christina of Denmark, and set his eyes on Francis of Lorraine, Anna's former betrothed.

Through Francis, Christina of Denmark's male children could inherit the Duchy of Guelders. By marrying Anna of Lorraine to Prince René of Orange and Francis of Lorraine to Christina of Denmark, the Emperor was doing everything he could to ensure that children of the Holy Roman Empire could assert a lawful claim to Guelders. Christina was delighted that she had avoided marrying Henry.

The Colloquy of Worms, begun in November 1540, ran through December. It was unsuccessful. Wilhelm was noticeably absent. The parties could not decide the order in which debates were presented. Alesius, a Scot, did his best to represent the interests of Catholicism. The representative sent by Anna's brother attempted flattery, but he was largely opposed to the Imperial position. The matter was convened with a planned Imperial Diet in April 1541 at Regensburg.

An anti-English book written by the Saxon Melanchthon was intercepted in England by late December 1540. It criticised Henry's religious stance and gave Melanchthon's view of the tyrannical behaviour of Henry in abandoning his marriage to Anna.

Things were at a standstill on the Continent during Christmastide. The Emperor was ill, possibly suffering from hemorrhoids, though he feigned something far worse. The Emperor's sister, Queen Consort of France Eleanor of Austria, sent the Emperor a couple of horse litters to help him in travelling around his huge territories. The Emperor used his illness as an excuse not to attend the current religious debates, and instead sent an ambassador whom he thought would better be able to influence the Germans. Anna's brother was not making much progress toward marrying Jeanne d'Albret because Jeanne's parents wanted to see how things between Wilhelm and the Emperor developed. Wilhelm resumed being persistent in pursuing the match.

The Emperor and the Regent were showing support for Marie of Guise's family by the end of December. Marie's younger sister, Louise of Lorraine, also a granddaughter of Philippa of Guelders, prepared to marry Charles II de Croÿ, Second Duke of Aarschot, amongst other dignities. Again, this would allow the male children of Louise of Lorraine and Charles II de Croÿ to lay claim to Guelders, to Wilhelm's disadvantage. Louise died young, however, in 1542.

The Emperor saw to it that all his eligible female family members, plus the descendants of Philippa of Guelders, were quickly being wed. It is worth considering that Emperor Charles V was doing all this, at least in part, to further undermine Wilhelm's claim to Guelders and build up a Continental army that could attack or defend against the United Duchies.

Anna remained at Richmond and away from court through the end of December. Henry sent her gifts. The gift-giving boosted the ever ebbing and flowing rumour that Henry would discard Katheryn Howard and return to the Daughter of Cleves. The speculation quickly fizzled out owing to Henry's ongoing public affection shown toward the young Katheryn.

The 1540 Diet of Worms saw the Germans voicing their displeasure at the Emperor delaying yet again. The Lutherans, including Melanchthon, had already prepared an answer to one of the questions of faith. There was concern amongst the Germans that by delaying the Diet further, it would allow the Emperor's Catholic theologians more time to refute the German position. Debate stemming from the 1540 Diet continued into January 1541. At Hampton Court, where Henry was spending Christmastide with the not-yet-pregnant Katheryn Howard, it was believed that nothing much would happen at Worms. Chapuys promised Charles V that he would do his best to 'indirectly thwart' any reconciliation between Anna and Henry.

Anna and the New Queen

Anna decided she would send Henry and Katheryn a token of her goodwill for New Year. On 3 January, Anna made her way from Richmond to Hampton Court with a gift of 'of two large horses with violet velvet trappings'. Anna and her suite ran into the Duke of Norfolk's brother while on their way there. Upon arrival, Anna was received by the Duchess of Suffolk and other ladies, who conducted her to her lodgings and then to the Queen's apartments. During Anna's interview with the new queen, she 'insisted on addressing [her] on her knees, for all the Queen could say, who showed her the utmost kindness'.

Henry came into the room and 'after a low bow to lady Anne, embraced and kissed her. She occupied a seat near the bottom of the table at supper, but after the King had retired the Queen and lady Anne danced together and next day all three dined together.' From the sounds of things, Anna and Katheryn got along just fine. It is an extraordinary scenario. When the three were dining, Henry gave Katheryn a present of a ring and two small dogs, which she passed over to Anna. Anna accepted the gifts with good grace. On 4 January 1541 Anna returned to her lodgings at Richmond.

Frequently, Anna's visit to Hampton Court for New Year and the gifts given to Henry and Katheryn are viewed quite simply as an attempt to mend things with Henry. Anna accepts Katheryn as her new queen and has no outwardly discernible feelings of ill will toward either Henry or Katheryn. What is overlooked is the context of gift-giving between German princesses.

As mentioned in Chapter 1, it was a common form of competition, albeit a playful one, for German princesses to send increasingly grand gifts to each other. The motivation was not unalloyed kindness: a gift showed a potential rival one's financial or domestic superiority. For example, exquisite pieces of embroidery were a common item exchanged amongst German princesses. The embroidery itself showed how skilled a princess was, and the materials used illustrated the wealth of the court.

In January 1541, there is no mention of the violet velvet trappings being embroidered, but the sheer cost of the horses and trappings must have been substantial. Anna was surreptitiously showing Katheryn how well-placed she was, and perhaps how accomplished. Katheryn, who only had two small dogs and a ring to give Anna, could not compete with Anna's beneficence. Even worse, the presents were actually from Henry. Katheryn herself did not have the wherewithal to give Anna a gift. By contrast, Anna was a duchess in her own right, and had property and an income at her disposal that allowed her to purchase the lavish horses and trappings. All Katheryn had was her Howard pedigree.

When Anna spoke to Katheryn whilst kneeling, one can imagine that Katheryn felt unsettled, flustered. Katheryn was a former lady-in-waiting to Anna, and now the former queen was forcing Katheryn to acknowledge her humility. This show by Anna of dedication to Katheryn as Queen Consort not only pleased Henry and showed the English that Anna really was accepting of her new position, but was also an ironic dumb show, a very subtle mockery of Katheryn and the absurdity of the situation.

Early 1541

On 9 January 1541, Anna became a denizen of England. The official paperwork declared:

> The lady Anne, daughter of John, late duke of Cleveland, Guligh, Gelder and Barre, and sister of William, now duke of Cleveland, Guligh (Jülich), Gelder and Barre, count Marke, Rauesborough (Ravensberg) and Sutfin (Zutphen), and lord Rauesten (Ravenstein), a native of Cleveland. Denization, subject to the condition that she shall not leave England without licence.

It was reported in early January that Anna's visit was not 'a sign that Anne of Cleves is to be restored to her former state; for the King would rather have two than leave the present one, who is so much in his favour.'

On 19 January 1541 during a meeting of the Privy Council at Hampton Court, the Archbishops of York and Canterbury requested that a book of attestations reviewed by both archbishops be added to the register concerning the Convocation. These attestations were probably the various depositions from June 1540 used during the Convocation to show that Henry and Anna never consummated their marriage and so on.

The Turks were amassing a great fleet to invade Hungary, which was a threat to the eastern border of the Holy Roman Empire. At the moment of attack, it was thought that Francis would be able to seize Milan in Italy. The bulk of the Emperor's forces would be tied up in defending against the Turkish fleet, which intended to sail up the Danube.

This made Guelders even more strategically important for Charles V. If Wilhelm chose to block the rivers in Guelders, he would stop the Emperor transporting his troops to the Hungarian front or moving ships to intercept the Turkish fleet. However, by

March 1541, it appeared that the Sultan was staying in his own territories and did not intend to attack the Empire.

Katheryn Howard was honoured as Queen Consort by Henry on 19 March 1541. Henry and Katheryn 'went from Westminster to Greenwich by water, accompanied by the mayor and crafts masters of London, with the solemnity and triumph [customary] at the first passage of new queens'. 'The first passage' refers to passing under the Bridge.

Trouble was brewing along England's border with Scotland in March 1541. Anna's former nephew through Henry, James V of Scotland, reportedly gathered upwards of 60,000 men. Henry calculated that James V would not do such a thing unless he anticipated support from Francis I. Another bad sign was that Francis sent men to Turin in Piedmont. It was under the pretence of making repairs and providing reinforcements to garrisons after the winter, but Henry was concerned that this meant Francis was making further preparations for war with the Emperor.

Emperor Charles V entered Nuremberg with his arms, prepared to meet with the Electors and Dukes for the Diet of Regensburg. Wilhelm represented that he intended to be present in person. Charles 'warned the Duke to bring titles and documents of his claim to Guelders in order that the dispute might be examined and decided by the Imperial Chamber. Whereupon the Duke dispatched certain lords of his court and representatives of his chief towns to go to the Diet and obtain that their master might not appear personally.'

Wilhelm was going to have a hard time attending the Diet in person, as he was preparing to leave for France by late March. Neither Wilhelm nor the Elector of Saxony appeared at the Diet. This frustrated the whole purpose, and showed the Emperor that a substantial number of the German princes were not willing to negotiate with him. They showed that they did not trust the Emperor and refused to put their persons in danger.

Before Wilhelm headed to France, reportedly over 4,000 *Landsknechte* were seen in the area around Cleves. Unsettled, Wilhelm sent his representatives to order the *Landsknechte* to disperse immediately. The number was exaggerated. They moved on, nonetheless. It was suspected in Cleves that the *Landsknechte* gathered in anticipation of the Diet of Regensburg leading to more disagreements. They wanted to be available for hire. Wilhelm sent almost five hundred horsemen in case the *Landsknechte* were that close for a more nefarious reason.

Anna's mother and brother were supposed to spend the Easter holiday together in the area around Düsseldorf. It was rumoured that Wilhelm intended to meet with their cousin, the Bishop of Munster. Instead, Wilhelm rode to Castle Hambach, not far from Düren, on Sunday 9 April. Anna's mother the Duchess Maria was staying there, a traditional hunting lodge for the Dukes of Jülich. She had fallen ill. (Wilhelm would later renovate this castle, between 1558 and 1565, in the Renaissance fashion. He hired the architect Alessandro Pasqualini to carry out the work. Upon completion, Wilhelm commonly used the castle as his hunting lodge.)

Wilhelm stayed with the Duchess Maria for two days. On 11 April he quietly left for Paris with a select few of his counselors. He made sure to bring along someone who spoke French, as he was not fluent in the language of his new bride.

Henry was left in the dark about these negotiations between Wilhelm and Francis I. It is possible that Anna did not know either, especially if she had somehow communicated to Wilhelm that all their letters were being read and reviewed by Henry's orders. Wilhelm reportedly left with about five people, and a further fifteen gentlemen from various parts of the United Duchies left to join him. They included the Marshal of Guelders, 'who, both in Duke [Karl]'s time and now, has chief authority in Guelders, and is the best man of war in these parts and very popular with everyone. He speaks good French and serves the Duke in affairs of Guelders.'

After meeting in Paris, Wilhelm and his company moved on toward Blois. He was to marry Jeanne d'Albret, then twelve years old, in France. Jeanne would then remain in Navarre until she came of age. The Scots had abandoned plans for the invasion of England by mid-May 1541.

The Diet of Regensburg ended in May 1541, and the Emperor departed for Italy. He had not obtained any concessions from Wilhelm concerning Guelders, or from Francis concerning Milan.

The deputies of Guelders, who were summoned to this Diet to hear the Emperor declare his title, are grieved at being kept so long there, but expect that in the end the Emperor will do somewhat in it, setting his matter forth as odiously against the duke of Cleves as can be devised. Others muse as much at t'other side, at his sudden departure from the Diet without leavetaking. The ambassadors of Cleves have no hope of agreement about religion, as the Emperor condescends to nothing till he have referred it to the bp. of Rome, and the Protestants till they have referred it to their apostle, Dr. Martyn [Luther].

Wilhelm, still in France, tried to maintain his relationship with Henry to some extent. He sent greetings to Henry from there, but nothing of note beyond simple cordiality. After Regensburg, a lord from the Low Countries was sent by the Emperor to raise a force of *Landsknechte*. By 25 May 1541 in Cleves, 'The Council here have therefore ordered the Duke's horsemen to lie on the borders, and proclaimed that if the lanceknights [*Landsknechte*] begin to run through the country, the people shall rise and slay them.'

Summer Progressions

In England, Henry began planning his progress to the North of England. He intended to have a large retinue of around 5,000 horses.

His object in going with so large a train seems to be to gain a reputation in parts of his kingdom that he has never yet visited, and that the money spent may remain in the country, as the people of the North complain that the King has seized the rentals, not only of the abbeys but of the principal lords like Northumberland; so that the money which formerly circulated in the North now comes up to London.

Henry was dealing with Katheryn's anxiety that he intended to discard her for Anna, in order to avoid war with France and Scotland. Henry surely did his best to assuage the young queen's fears.

Anna gained a youthful sister-in-law on 14 June 1541. The day before, Wilhelm first met with Marguerite, Queen of Navarre and spoke with her. The people of the United Duchies rejoiced at news of the wedding and fabulous match, which would ultimately expand the holdings of the United Duchies once the current King of Navarre passed away. The people of Cleves fretted over coming under the dominion and control of the Elector of Saxony, should Wilhelm die without issue. Cleves itself was a primarily Catholic territory, in stark contrast to Lutheran Saxony. There was a real fear that Wilhelm would be intercepted by the Emperor on his way back to Cleves. The longer Wilhelm dallied in France, the more anxious the counselors and citizens of Cleves became.

Henry was galled by his former brother-in-law's marriage. Marillac reported to Francis:

What weighs more upon [Parliament] is the alliance of Francis and the duke of Cleves, from which they doubt annoyance someday, because of the injury they did to Madame [Anna of Cleves], his sister, who is repudiated. As [the English] suspect all friendships of their neighbours and have no more trust in their intelligence with the Germans, it is probable that they will try to make their league closer with the Emperor, to make him forget the injury to him through his aunt queen Katherine [of Aragon], or else seek to make war between the Emperor and Francis, that they may be secure and sought by both sides.

Wilhelm finally departed for Cleves on 20 June 1541. The Emperor was coming suspiciously close to the United Duchies, though the Imperial troops were in reality on their way to reinforce troops in Hungary under attack from the Turks.

Henry and Katheryn departed on their progress on 30 June 1541, and planned not to return until late October. Henry was taking over 4,000 horse with him, compared to his usual 1,000. It was not the 5,000 horse originally desired, but impressive nonetheless:

[m]ore than 200 tents are carried, artillery is sent by sea and river to within 10 miles of York, and the great horses are

taken as if it were a question of war; all because the King, during his reign, has never visited these places, where, for his first entry and for the danger of the daily rebellions, he wishes to be well accompanied by men of these parts in whom he has more trust.

Marillac was the only ambassador who accompanied Henry and Katheryn. At some point, news of Wilhelm reached Henry's ears. Marillac reported around 29 July 1541 to Francis:

The Imperials ... have maliciously set forth that the duke of Cleves, on account of his alliance with Francis and his contumacy to the Emperor, in refusing to appear at the assemblies of Ratisbon [Regensburg], had been prevented from returning home by some of his chief towns, especially of Guelders, objecting to him that it became him to keep Guelders by decision of the Imperial Chamber, not by alliance with Francis. This bruit was so common here for some days that nothing else was talked of, yet, two days ago, Marillac received letters from Flanders, written by subjects of the Emperor, saying, simply, that the Duke had returned home well and safe, without mentioning that his subjects had attempted anything against him, which news he communicated to the English to efface their former impression.

In Scotland, Henry's nephew James V was making quiet preparations for war. James V moved with his council to Edinburgh. 'Command is given in Scotland for all to have harness and be ready to serve the King. Workmen in Edinburgh castle have long been making guns and other ordnance, and they have a mill there that has made six barrels of gunpowder within three weeks since Easter.'

A Scottish abbot was sent to France, though this could have been merely to inform the French court of the sad loss of James V's children by Marie of Guise. With the death of the Scottish princes, Scotland's claim to Guelders through their mother Marie ended, unless James and Marie had another son. Philippa of Guelders, who did not pass away until 1547, must have been crushed to learn of the death of her two great-grandsons within fourteen hours of each other.

On 10 July 1541, Anna's former betrothed, Francis of Lorraine, married Christina of Denmark. To show that he did not believe the marriage to be lawful, Henry instructed his ambassadors and dignitaries not to attend. If Henry acted as though the marriage between Francis and Christina were legal, then he would be admitting that his own marriage to Anna of Cleves was legal (or at least that one of the grounds for the annulment was false).

In Cleves, the people rejoiced over the marriage of Anna's brother. Wilhelm faced the tricky prospect of travelling through the Imperial Low Countries, and tried to receive a passport for his safe conduct from Maria of Austria, Regent of the Netherlands. She claimed that the matter was out of her hands. Wilhelm took a route crossing as little of the Low Countries as he could. Francis sent a 1,000-horse escort to bolster Wilhelm's own small force of 80 horse. Back in Cleves, the Duchess Maria placed 800 horse at the ready to assist Wilhelm.

The Emperor finally left the failed Diet around 26 July 1541. He headed toward Italy with a force upwards of 7,000 *Landsknechte*. In response to that, Francis arranged for about 10,000 Swiss Guard to be readied at his fortifications in Piedmont. The concern was that the Emperor intended to move on Milan. Francis was incensed at reports that the Emperor specifically requested assistance against Francis's new nephew, Duke Wilhelm.

Henry hoped for a rapprochement with the Scots. As early as August 1541, Henry hoped to meet with his Scottish nephew and enter a league with him. James V declined, stating that he could not act without Francis's blessing.

By the end of August 1541, Wilhelm began hiring a small force of *Landsknechte* to keep about Friesland. The rumour that war between Francis and the Emperor would soon be made grew even stronger. In October 1541, the Imperial Ambassador Chapuys reported that unless Francis 'thoroughly changes his opinion, there will be war next spring, for the King fully intends invading the Low Countries, now that he has the Duke of Cleves under his orders, the latter having promised to do wonders and obey his command implicitly.'

It is not known how much Anna knew about her brother's actions, and it seems she was not told anything of a secretive nature directly. On 18 October 1541, Henry's older sister Margaret, Queen Consort of James IV of Scotland, died. Anna of Cleves was now the only woman alive who could call herself the King's Beloved Sister.

In a final meeting between Henry and the Imperial Ambassador Chapuys during Christmastide, Chapuys claimed that Wilhelm could not have cared much for Anna judging by his actions, in particular, the Franco-Cleves alliance, which extinguished any remnants of amity between England and the United Duchies. Henry appeared to have very little patience for Marillac, the French ambassador, around this time. Henry believed that Francis would attack the Low Countries in spring 1542. Henry's belief was almost perfectly correct.

12

A SECOND BITE AT THE CHERRY

The pending marriages between the Pope Paul III's niece and Marie of Guise's nephew Francis of Guise,[51] and Wilhelm and Jeanne, heightened the anxieties of Henry's council: '...one, on account of religion, and the other, for the treatment of his sister, may allure [Francis] from their amity.'

Francis fortified the Spanish border with France. The small Kingdom of Navarre was in danger of Spanish aggression on behalf of Charles V. Francis was already reluctant to send his very young niece Jeanne out of French-allied territory. Jeanne's mother Marguerite by this time affectionately wrote to Wilhelm as her son, and remained pleasantly disposed to the Cleves match; though Marguerite's disposition may have been only to please her brother Francis.

On 10 February 1541, Marguerite, Queen of Navarre, and her husband confirmed the marriage agreement between Jeanne d'Albret and Duke Wilhelm. The King and Queen were leaving Paris in the middle of the month for Navarre to acquire the consent of Navarre's nobility to the marriage. Wilhelm was expected to arrive in Navarre by Easter of 1541, at which time the wedding ceremony would take place.

---

51 Francis of Guise would marry Pope Alexander VI's granddaughter Anna d'Este, daughter of Lucrezia Borgia.

By the middle of March 1541, Wilhelm was expected in Blois at any moment to marry Jeanne d'Albret. Some speculated that Wilhelm might marry one of Francis I's daughters, instead. Either way, Wilhelm was coming and Anna was about to have a new sister-in-law related to the Valois.

The Cleves-Navarre Wedding

Wilhelm received a grand reception in France. He arrived at Amboise on 6 May 1541, and on 8 May a triumph was held in his honour. The spectacle was an assault of a bastillion. Around fifty French lords defended the structure, while the Dauphin Henry of France and Duke Charles of Orleans led 200 footmen and 100 horsemen in the attack. Duke Charles and his men won the day.

> The King and Queen [of France] and duke of Cleves, and all the ladies stood upon scaffolds, and afterwards supped at Howard's lodging. The King spoke to him. The duke of Cleves embraced him and asked how Henry did, but asked no question of his sister [Anna].

On 9 May, Wilhelm accompanied Francis I and the rest of the French court on a barge to Tours. Wilhelm was left at Tours while Francis prepared the young Jeanne to meet her fiancé. Francis intended so to do, 'by greatly praising the Duke's virtues'. The sickly Jeanne entertained her Uncle Francis's words well enough, but the young girl was very much against the match with Wilhelm. Jeanne wished for a French husband and not a foreign prince. She reportedly told Francis that she 'would rather enter a convent than marry the Duke of Cleves'. Francis reminded his twelve-year-old niece that she must obey the commands of her parents. In a display of pre-teen dramatics recognisable to many down through the ages, Jeanne then informed her uncle the King of France that she would rather 'throw [herself] down a well than marry the Duke of Cleves'.

Wilhelm called on Jeanne later that day. The meeting between the future bride and groom lasted no more than fifteen minutes.

Jeanne was asked on 10 May if she had changed her disposition toward the marriage, to which she replied she would commit suicide rather than marry Wilhelm.

Wilhelm spent considerable time throughout the rest of May 1541 and early June with the future Henri II of France. It was rumoured that the pair were planning on travelling to Boulogne, not far down the coast from Calais. Wallop, then at Calais, sent one of his spies to Boulogne to keep an eye on things.

The pre-marriage festivities took place at around seven o'clock in the evening on 13 June at Châtellerault. A pavilion was set up outside the entrance to Châtellerault to a hold a ball. The arms of Duke Wilhelm and Jeanne d'Albret were displayed about the pavilion, which was lit with chandeliers and adorned with tapestries. During the ball all eyes were on Wilhelm, who was a couple weeks away from his twenty-fifth birthday.

[When] the ball was all over, the King and Queen of Navarre, the Princess their daughter, and a great number of princes, lords, and ladies arrived. The King [Francis] then took the hands of the Duke of Cleves and the Princess de Navarre, his niece, and, after having spoken to them for a few moments privately, he presented them to the Most Reverend Cardinal de Tournon, who performed the betrothal ceremony. The King gave them several light, affectionate pats on the shoulder, as is the custom.

Jeanne objected up to the very last moment.

The ceremony took place on 14 June. Foreign dignitaries were present, including the English ambassador. The Emperor's representative was noticeably absent. The wedding ceremony took place in the pavilion where the ball had been held the night before; 'a rich altar had been erected, draped with cloth of gold, bearing the arms of the Duke and the Princess.' A blue velvet canopy hung over the altar. Queen Marguerite of Navarre brought her daughter Jeanne at around eleven o'clock, and Duke Wilhelm was accompanied by the Dauphin. After greeting his new bride, Wilhelm slipped a diamond ring onto her finger.

Either in protest or owing to the incredible weight of the sickly twelve-year-old bride's garments, she did not move toward the altar. Jeanne's silver and gold skirt had gems on its trim, while her red satin cloak was trimmed with ermine. Jeanne wore a gold crown upon her head. Francis, no doubt fed up with Jeanne's recalcitrant behaviour, ordered that she be carried to the altar.

After the customary post-nuptial feasting, Wilhelm and Jeanne were escorted to their bedchamber. The new couple symbolically consummated their marriage, according to Olisleger, by being placed

> ...in their night clothes, side by side in bed. The King [Francis] made everyone leave the room except the King and Queen of Navarre [and a few other German and French dignitaries]. The King had pulled the curtains, and he withdrew into an alcove near the window with the others. There they chatted merrily until one in the morning. Then the King and Queen of Navarre conducted the Duke to his own room. The King took the Duke by the arm and called him 'my son'. After the King had gone to bed, the King and Queen of Navarre went to the Duke's bedside and talked to him for a long time in a friendly way.

Due to her young age and sickly disposition, it was agreed that Jeanne would remain in Navarre for at least another year, if not two.

Another Chance? Anna, Queen Redux

Rumours about Henry taking back Anna began in October 1540. Perhaps this was wishful thinking by the general population, who enjoyed having Anna as their queen. The rumours stemmed from Anna having a bout of illness, which was enough to indicate that Anna was pregnant. After several days, it became clear that her symptoms were not due to pregnancy.

Things took a dramatic turn for Anna in November 1541, serious enough to cause her young sister-in-law Jeanne d'Albret to commission what may have been a wedding gift for her. At some point, a book of hours or prayer book, now in possession of the Kantonsbibliothek at Trogen, Switzerland, was created for her. The book is personalised for Anna von Kleve or Anna von Cleve[52] with 'AC' monograms and coats of arms. There are several prayers to the Virgin Mary, and the scenes from the life of the Virgin. The book was intended for private devotional use. Anna's elder sister Sybylla, who married the Elector of Saxony in 1526, received a prayer book around the time she was engaged to Johann Friedrich. The richly decorated book still exists, with 214 folios intact. Sybylla's prayer book is held in Munich at the Bayerische Staatsbibliothek.

In a letter to Wilhelm dated 12 November 1541, Jeanne writes, 'I am also sending you two hour-books to Mademoiselle de Clèves, which I ask you to give her for me.'[53] Marillac tells Anne de Montmorency in 1540 that Anna had taken up the name 'Madame de Clèves' after her annulment. The use of 'Mademoiselle' in 1541 further reinforces the idea that Anna was never married.

In November of 1541, Henry started the painful process toward repudiating the successor in Anna's affections, the young Katheryn Howard. Katheryn's prior sexual history came to light in the autumn of 1541 and on 1 November 1541 a warrant for Katheryn's arrest was issued.

On 29 October 1541, a few days before the issuance of Katheryn's warrant, it is recorded that a few French gentlemen went to visit an Englishman stationed at Ardres under the pretence of fishing, and wound up discussing the proposed marriage between Henry's oldest daughter Mary and Francis I of France's son, the Duke of Orleans. Though not documented in an English source, it is not farfetched to think that information about Queen Katheryn's compromised position was either discussed or already known to the French on this date. Further, the Bishop of Winchester visited Germany around this time. The news of Katheryn's downfall would not have taken long to reach the ears of Jeanne or her husband Wilhelm, Duke of Cleves.

---

52 The spelling 'Kleve' was adopted in the 1930s. Prior to this time, 'Cleve' was a common Germanic spelling. Anna signed her documents as, 'Anna, gheborene herzogin von Cleve.'

53 'Ausy janvoye deux [livres] doeures a ma seur, madamoyselle de Cleves, que je vous prye luy bailer, atandant que moy-mesmes luy en porte.'

A letter dated 10 November 1541 to Maria of Austria states: 'three months hence the estates of the kingdom will be assembled – Chapuys suspects to cancel their former declaration on the nullity of the Cleves marriage... At least, such is the belief of the French ambassador.'

Chapuys was worried that Henry VIII's annulment would be cancelled by the estates of England, and Anna's marriage reinstated. The letter also mentions that the Bishop of Winchester had recently returned from Germany with evidence that would further support a lawful marriage between Henry and Anna.

There exists a second letter from November 1541 which refers to Mademoiselle de Clèves. Marguerite of Navarre, sister to King Francis I of France, Jeanne's mother and Wilhelm's mother-in-law, wrote a postscript to Wilhelm, stating, 'Please recommend me to my daughter, the Mademoiselle de Cleves,[54] and I want to pass along to you a letter from the ambassador of the king [Francis I] to England, and if you please, keep it secret.' ('Daughter-in-law,' 'mother-in-law' and so on, were not terms used at the time.)

Wilhelm attempted to marry off the youngest Cleves daughter, Amalia. Wilhelm may have begun conducting marriage negotiations in late 1541 to either Bernhard of Baden or Karl of Baden. However, it is highly unlikely that these negotiations took place before 1545 because, at the time, the house of Baden-Baden from whence Bernhard and Karl came was Catholic and loyal to the Holy Roman Emperor, both boys were yet to be legitimised by the Emperor, and Wilhelm was at war with the Emperor until then. Karl was twelve years younger than Amalia, who was born in 1517, which would have made Karl twelve years old at most in 1541 and Amalia 24. Thus, it is reasonable to assume that the 'Mademoiselle de Clèves' refers to Anna. There is no reason for Marguerite to refer to anyone other than Anna as the 'Mademoiselle de Cleves'; and this letter was sent

---

54 'Vous voudres bien que ma fille, Mademoiselle de Cleves, treuve icy mes recommendacions, et je vous envoie une lettre de lembasador du Roy en Engleterre que vous tiendres, sil vous plest, secrette.' This letter follows immediately after the letter from Jeanne d'Albret to Wilhelm of Cleves.

around the same time or shortly after the letter of November 1541 from Jeanne to Wilhelm mentioning the books of hours and 'Mademoiselle de Cleves'.

With Katheryn Howard's swift downfall, there was a chance for Henry to re-marry Anna. Because Katheryn and Henry's marriage was annulled, Anna's marriage to Henry was potentially technically no longer void; that is, until Henry took another wife.

The idea of again taking up the Cleves marriage gained momentum and Anna's brother's ambassador met with members of Henry VIII's council on 14 December to propose the idea. Hope had been reawakened for the renewal of an Anglo-Cleves alliance.

A book of hours, as mentioned above, was a common gift for new brides. Jeanne, as a dutiful sister-in-law may have been giving her books as a wedding gift in anticipation of Anna's remarriage. Anna had in 1540 taken up the moniker, 'Daughter of Cleves' after her annulment, which was based on non-consummation. Thus, in the eyes of the church, and the young Jeanne, Anna was indeed a mademoiselle. It is unknown whether the book of hours ever made it into Anna's possession. Unfortunately, there is a large gap in the history of who possessed the book between its creation and its introduction into the Kantonsbibliothek.

Francis I was in favour of Henry taking back Anna, which would bring England back into an alliance of some kind with Cleves. The Emperor would have to face France, England, the United Duchies, and possibly Saxony, should he start any wars. In England, Olisleger sent a letter to the Earl of Southampton, asking that he support Anna and stating that Wilhelm trusts him.

In early December 1541, Henry went hunting. A lady named Jane Rattsey mused, 'What if God worketh this work to make the lady Anne of Cleves queen again?' It was suspected that Henry was using the hunt as an excuse to come near to Anna, but no such thing happened. If Anna and her family hoped that Henry would reunite with her, he was not giving any obvious signs. The situation was serious enough that Horsey, Anna's German-speaking steward, was called to appear before the Privy Council on 11 December 1541.

A fresh rumour about Anna being pregnant by Henry was investigated. The rumour suggested that Henry impregnated Anna in August 1541 when he visited her at Richmond. The rumour had come to the court's attention possibly as early as October 1541, just before Katheryn's fall from grace. Such a situation would probably have put Anna in danger, depending in part on how Queen Katheryn would have responded. There was no guarantee that Henry would acknowledge any baby from Anna, legitimate or otherwise.

The rumour was unfounded, and completely illogical. Anna would have had to conceive the baby at a time when Henry was married and presumably in love with Katheryn Howard. Why would Anna risk becoming pregnant with a bastard, even a royal one? And at a time when all things pointed to Henry being quite content with the youthful Katheryn Howard? It would ruin the 26-year-old Anna's prospects of making a suitable match in the future.

In the end, it turned out that Anna was again experiencing illness in late 1541. One of her ladies had recently given birth. Anna, feeling better, was seen holding the little infant. After that, the rumour spread that it was Anna's baby with Henry. The rumour might have been a ploy by pro-Anna individuals to see her made queen once more.

On 12 December 1541, Southampton did as Olisleger requested: he sent a letter to Henry in support of Anna.

> This morning the ambassador of Cleves came to say he had letters of credence from the Duke, his master, and also letters from Olisleger to my lord of Canterbury and from the Duke to my lord Great Master, with one from Olisleger to the writer. He said his credence was to seek to reconcile the Duke's sister with the King, and that he would either wait upon the King or declare his charge to the Council. Encloses his own letters from Olisleger.

Emboldened by events surrounding Katheryn Howard, the Cleves ambassador approached Thomas Cranmer, Archbishop of

Canterbury, at Lambeth. Cranmer wrote a letter on 13 December to Henry about the meeting:

> Yesterday the ambassador of Cleves brought him letters (enclosed) from [Olisleger] ... commending the cause of the lady Anne of Cleves. The ambassador said the cause was the reconciliation of the King with lady Anne. Replied that it was strange that Oslynger should write to him to move the King to receive her in matrimony again, and so trouble the King's succession. The ambassador would have reasoned the matter, so as to grope Cranmer's mind, but he cut him short, saying the matter was too important for him to discuss without command from the King.

The Cleves ambassador presented himself before the Privy Council, and

> ...prayed them [to find] means to reconcile the marriage and restore her to the estate of queen. They answered, on the King's behalf, that the lady should be graciously entertained and her estate rather increased than diminished, but the separation had been made for such just cause that he prayed the Duke never to make such a request. The ambassador asking to have this repeated, Winchester, with every appearance of anger, said that the King would never take back the said lady and that what was done was founded upon great reason, whatever the world might allege.

Henry moved to Greenwich for Christmastide, unusually without a new bride in tow. Anna visited Henry on New Year's Day 1542, and presented him with gifts. In the collection of the Folger Shakespeare Library in Washington DC, there is a book of hours given to Henry by Anna, in which she wrote, 'I beseech Your Grace humbly when ye look on this, remember me. Your Grace's assured Anne, the Daughter of Cleves.' The date when Anna gave Henry this gift is not recorded. Henry gave Anna flagons and glass pots, while she gave Henry cramoisy (crimson) cloth. One must wonder if Henry was comforted by the presence of Anna, or if she was able to lift his spirits. Anna may have held onto the hope that she would again be Queen.

In January 1542, Katheryn's and Anna's fates were undecided. Katheryn removed to Syon house, and Anna stayed at Richmond as she had since the annulment. Marillac was corresponding with the Queen of Navarre about Anna, and the idea of her reuniting with Henry. Wilhelm sent an ambassador to England with the power to negotiate matters concerning Anna. The Queen of Navarre sent her best wishes to her via Marillac. Marillac wrote of Anna's behaviour during this time that she

> ...wants neither prudence nor patience. All [Anna's] affairs could never make her utter a word by which one might suppose that she was discontented; nay, she has always said she wished nothing but what pleased the King her lord; thus showing an example of rare patience in dissembling passions common to everyone, which could only come of singular grace of God and a heart resolved to accept what could not be remedied. She has behaved, with her household, so wisely that those who visit her marvel at such great virtue [*honnesteté*], others who hear of it are loud in her praise, and all regret her much more than they did the late Queen Katherine.

Marillac changed his tune about Anna's appearance from his initial dispatch in January 1540. Recall that neither he nor Chapuys were very physically close to Anna when they first caught sight of her. Marillac reported Anna as looking closer to thirty than twenty-four, and that she was not considered beautiful. In January 1542, Marillac reported that Anna was 'very well, and said to be half as beautiful again since she left Court'. This volt-face may have been because Anna was now related to the French royal family through Wilhelm's marriage to Jeanne. Criticising the Daughter of Cleves, if she would once more be Queen Consort of England and strengthen Francis I, was now imprudent.

The End of Katheryn Howard

Katheryn Howard was condemned by Parliament on the charge of
High Treason on 25 January 1542. Over in France, a declamation
was published aimed at Henry and the Privy Council about the
treatment of Anna. It was written by John of Luxembourg, whose
father was Count of Brienne and Ligny. John himself was the
Abbot of Ivry at the time. The title of the tract was, 'The Prayer
and Remonstrance of the High and Powerful Madame Marie of
Cleves, sister of the highest and most powerful Lord, the Duke
of Jülich, of Cleves, and of Guelders, to the King of England and
His Council'. John of Luxembourg seems to have been not very
familiar with the Von der Marks, given that he mistakenly called
Anna by her mother's name.

Charles V ordered Chapuys to do everything possible to stop
Anna from reuniting with Henry. In late January 1542, England
and the Empire were slowly coming to an official alliance.
Chapuys was given powers to give conditional consent to Henry's
requests, but nothing more.

Katheryn Howard was beheaded on 13 February 1542.
Between late January and late February, Anna's brother and
several other German princes drafted letters to Henry. The aim
was to encourage the English king to take Anna back. However,
Francis suggested to Wilhelm, via ambassadors, that the letters
not be given to Henry just yet.

The book by John of Luxembourg about Anna was vexing
Henry enough that in February his ambassador was instructed
to ask King Francis about the matter. Francis 'promised to stay
the printing, and recover the copies that were out, saying that,
surely, the Duke of Cleves knew not of it, for it were folly ...
especially now at this time; for men's affections do alter, and the
lady Anne is yet of age to bear children, and albeit the wind hath
been contrary it may fortune to turn.'

Charles V in a letter to Chapuys again urged him to do
whatever he could to prevent Anna becoming Queen Consort of
England once more. In mid-March 1542, Charles was actively

exchanging information with Henry about the activities of Wilhelm and Francis.

Anna was taken ill with tertian fever in March 1542. Tertian fever is related to malaria, with symptoms including spasms or seizures once every couple of days. Anna remained at Richmond during this time. Henry sent a physician to assist. Fortunately he probably did nothing, as she was well again after about a month.

The rest of 1542 saw Anna in a precarious position, one which endangered the safety of her family and the United Duchies.

13

THE VON DER MARKS
IN DECLINE, 1542–1557

On 12 July 1542, Francis I declared war against the Holy Roman
Empire, which of course included the Low Countries, bordering
Anna's home, the United Duchies in Germany. The Fourth
Hapsburg-Valois War started in Perpignan, in present-day France,
very close to the modern Spanish border. Francis once again
allied himself with Suleiman I of the Ottoman Empire. A second
front attacked Artois in Flanders. Another army led by the Duke
d'Orleans attacked Luxembourg, with a final army encroaching
from Cleves. Christian III of Denmark, who usurped the throne
from Emperor Charles V's brother-in-law, attacked from the north
and stopped Imperial trade going through the Baltic.

   The Fourth Hapsburg-Valois War included the Third War of the
Guelderian Succession. As a simplified background, the First War
of the Guelderian Succession took place from 1371 to 1379. Duke
Rainald III and his brother Edward both died in 1371. Neither
man had any children. Two of their sisters, Maria and Mathilde,
had sons whom they wished to see inherit the Duchy of Guelders.
Maria, who was married to William II, Duke of Jülich, was
ultimately successful. In 1377 Holy Roman Emperor Charles IV
eventually settled all of Guelders and the County of Zutphen on
the son of Maria of Guelders and William II of Jülich.

After more skirmishes with territories loyal to Mathilde, Maria's young son William finally gained complete control over Guelders in 1379, becoming William I of Jülich-Guelders and Berg. The duchies of Guelders and Jülich were only united by virtue of William I being the son of William II of Jülich and Maria of Guelders. It was not a true union like the one later established between the United Duchies of Jülich-Cleves-Berg.

The Second War of the Guelderian Succession took place from about 1423 to 1444. The following is a basic version of what happened. Duke Rainald of Jülich and Guelders died in 1423. He and his wife had no children during their roughly eighteen-year marriage. Over time, the minor branch of Jülich became the noble house of Jülich-Berg because of a marriage between the houses of Jülich-Heimbach and Ravensberg-Berg in the mid-14th century. The first Duke of Jülich-Berg came to power in 1423. Arnold von Egmond paid a substantial amount of money to obtain the Duchy of Guelders, along with the County of Zutphen.

During the Second War, Egmond had the support of Cleves, and Jülich-Berg was supported by the King of the Romans. Duke Arnold of Egmond, backed by Cleves, was defeated and captured in 1444. The duchies of Guelders and Jülich were divided, and remained so until Wilhelm became Duke of Guelders. The division effectively ended the Second War, though the Duchy of Guelders was passed around amongst several Egmond dukes throughout the rest of the 15th century.

In October 1528, Duke Karl of Egmond and Charles V drew up the Treaty of Gorkum to resolve any lingering rebellious intent by Duke Karl from his involvement with the Black Heap (discussed in Chapter 2). Part of the treaty settled that if Karl died without any direct male descendants, then Charles V would inherit Guelders. A second document, the Treaty of Grave (1528), reinforced Charles V's claim to Guelders.

When it was becoming clear in late 1538 that Duke Karl would not live much longer, the nobles of Guelders decided they wanted a German hereditary prince. The only options were the foreign Spanish-Burgundian Emperor Charles V or Anton of

Lorraine, Duke Karl's nephew through his twin sister Philippa of Guelders. The nobles turned to Anna's family for their next duke, as descendants of William II of Jülich and Maria of Guelders. On 27 January 1538, Duke Karl and Anna's father Johann III signed a contract establishing Anna's brother Wilhelm as the new hereditary Duke of Guelders.

Adding Guelders to the United Duchies massively increased the regional power of the Von der Mark dukes. The United Duchies began in what is now the Netherlands at the coast of the South Sea, or Suden See, southeast toward Cleves and then on to Jülich, and finally south toward Berg. To the east, the United Duchies extended as far as Lippstadt. Put another way, the United Duchies now covered most of modern Westphalia, the Rhineland, and a portion of the Netherlands. This made the Von der Mark dukes not only a territorial threat to the Holy Roman Empire, but also a religious one. The Von der Mark dukes were at the least not hostile to Protestantism, meaning that the reformed religion could gain a stronghold in the United Duchies.

The Cleves War

The Third War of the Guelderian Succession, also known as the Jülich Feud or Cleves War, was at its fiercest in 1543. The Cleves War itself was hot for only three months, but tension had been mounting since 1538 when the Duchy of Guelders was left to Wilhelm. Wilhelm's marriage to Jeanne d'Albret in June 1541 meant that Wilhelm would be a candidate for the crown of Navarre under Salic law. This made Wilhelm an ally of Francis I, and the two had a common enemy in the Holy Roman Emperor.

Wilhelm was ready to support his new ally, Francis I, as early as 26 February 1542. The Cleves force was numbered at about 20,000. Around 4,000 of those soldiers were horsemen. In April, the Turks were a very real threat on the eastern border of the Holy Roman Empire. The German princes were supposed to provide troops to fight off the invaders, but Wilhelm refused unless Charles V agreed not to attack Wilhelm before 1562.

Later that month yet another rumour circulated, this one at the French court, that the Emperor would give up his claim to

Guelders if Wilhelm and his bride Jeanne d'Albret would give up their claim to Navarre. That was not acceptable either to Wilhelm or Jeanne.

The Emperor Charles V urged Chapuys 'to induce Henry to aid in the recovery of Guelders and Zutphen, or, at least, promise not to aid the duke of Cleves'. The news of Wilhelm amassing an army in early 1542 must have added to the pressure on Anna to become Henry's queen once more. Anna's homeland was in considerable danger and needed her help. Anna was powerless.

By 28 June 1542, it was reported that Francis was preparing a sort of pincer move by augmenting his forces at Luxembourg with additional infantry assembled at Guelders and Cleves. When the Treaty of Nice was referenced Francis brushed it off, stating that the forces at Guelders and Cleves were for defence only. French troops were on the move toward Cleves, with them the future Grand Master of France. The purpose was to apologise for the delay in delivering Wilhelm his bride, Jeanne, and to request that Wilhelm send more troops to Guelders.

Henry seemed awfully close to making a formal alliance with the Emperor by the end of June 1542. However, perhaps due to the care and concern he had for his former wife Anna, Henry wanted to know the Emperor's intentions toward Guelders. Henry discussed the matter with Chapuys, expressing his thoughts on the possible conquest of the duchy. Following that conversation, Chapuys opined to Charles V that capturing Guelders

...would be difficult, owing to the hatred of the people to the inhabitants of Brabant, and, considering his relations with Germany and France, the Duke might be a dangerous enemy if the marriage so much talked of [between Anna and Henry] should take place; also while using his forces against Guelders the Emperor would be prevented from driving the French out of Piedmont.

Henry thought it more prudent for the Emperor to sue for peace with Wilhelm, as Francis continuously failed to bring Jeanne d'Albret,

Wilhelm's Duchess Consort of Cleves, out of Navarre. Henry suggested that he would give Wilhelm either the Lady Mary or the Lady Elizabeth as a wife. That way, Wilhelm would be aligned with Henry and thereby with the Emperor, and be allowed by the Emperor to keep title to Guelders. The Emperor would then have the support of the United Duchies, which could be used against Francis. Chapuys argued that it was best for the Emperor to have control over Guelders; but Henry would not agree to help the Emperor against Cleves, and would not agree to a treaty with the Emperor that involved Cleves.

On 1 July 1542, a defensive and offensive league was concluded between France and Sweden, with allies listed as the Duke of Guelders and Cleves, the Duke of Prussia, and the Kings of Scotland and Denmark. Around the same time, the husband of Anna's sister Sybylla, Johann Friedrich, was preparing to attack the pro-Imperial Duke of Brunswick. The Duke of Brunswick was helping defend the Hungarian front against the Turks.

All Hell Breaks Loose; the Fall of the United Duchies
As early as 7 July 1542, it was assumed by many that war was declared by France, Saxony, and Cleves against the Holy Roman Empire's holdings in the Low Countries. Francis's troops were apparently stationed at Lorraine. The Saxon and Cleves captains were at the ready.

It was reported on 9 July that the Dukes of Guise and Orleans would lead the attack on Imperial Luxembourg. Luxembourg was bordered by France to the west and Germany to the east. The French forces were bolstered by around 2,000 horse and 10,000 infantry sent by Wilhelm from Cleves. Wilhelm was seen visiting and staying with the Duchess Maria at one of his castles along the Rhine River, maybe Swan Castle in Cleves or Moyland Castle in nearby Bedburg-Hau. The Emperor's men kept a close eye on Anna's brother, causing him to remain within the castle.

Francis I declared war against Charles V on 12 July 1542. On 15 or 16 July 1542, Anna's brother sent a force led by Maarten van Rossum to invade the Low Countries. On 16 July Wilhelm's troops invaded the Imperial Low Countries. Wilhelm was a major threat to the Low Countries at this point. Maria of Austria reported to the Imperial ambassador Chapuys:

> On the side of Cleves, M. de Longueval and Martin van Rossen, who has taken the title of Marshal of Guelders, have penetrated into the district of ['s-Hertogenbosch], but have gained no place of importance. They have taken Hochstrate, the country seat of the La Laing family, but it is only a pleasure house. They threaten Antwerp, but will find it no easy place to besiege, with our forces in their rear, which can soon be concentrated.

Regent Maria of the Low Countries began an offensive campaign against the United Duchies on 1 October 1542. Her troops managed to gain control of Düren, where Hans Holbein the Younger painted Anna's portrait in 1539. Maria held onto the city until around 28 December 1542 when Wilhelm managed to seize Düren back after eight days of fighting. On Easter Sunday 1543, the Regent's troops were soundly defeated by Wilhelm's. Charles V was unable to help his sister the Regent because the French were keeping the Imperial troops busy in Italy.

A *Reichstag*, or Parliament, was called in Nuremberg in early 1543. Wilhelm and Charles V agreed to a two-month armistice, to take effect on 12 May 1543. Wilhelm hoped this would give the French time to send reinforcements to the United Duchies. If that did not happen, then it was hoped that Anna and Wilhelm's elder sister Sybylla and her husband the Elector of Saxony would send help. If Saxony failed, there was the final hope that members of the Schmalkaldic League would come to Wilhelm's aid. No help ever came.

The Imperial army arrived at Düren on 24 August 1543. The siege of Düren was devastating – and hardly a siege: after only two days of fighting, the allegedly impregnable Düren was taken. About 2,500 of the 3,000 defenders in Düren and about 15,000 of the more than 60,000 Imperial troops were slaughtered. The city was heavily bombarded by Imperial artillery. The ensuing incidental fires all but consumed the city. The day after the siege around 600 houses were ash or rubble, as were the St Anna Church, the town hall, and other important buildings.

The Emperor left the ruined city on 27 August 1543. Two days later, the strong-willed, capable and respected Duchess Maria of Jülich and Berg died. Anna was devastated by the news of the destruction of her homeland and the demise of her beloved mother, who died mad with grief over the ruination of Jülich-Berg. The town and castle of Nideggen, the ancestral home of the Dukes of Jülich, was similarly destroyed by the Emperor. The ancient castle with very thick walls sat atop a high hill, and was thought to be impregnable as well. The square shape of the castle with its flat walls could not withstand the Emperor's artillery. The castle was not designed for the modern threat, and easily succumbed to the mortars being fired at will by the Imperial forces from a neighbouring hill. The fortified cities of Heinsberg and Sittard were also destroyed. Jülich surrendered to the Emperor without a fight.

The City of Jülich became the centre for the Duchy of Jülich after the fall of Nideggen. In 1546 Wilhelm contracted with Alessandro Pasqualini of Bologna to build Jülich after the style of a *palazzo in fortezza*. The reconstruction suffered what looked like a major setback in May 1547 when a great fire burned down most of the remaining medieval buildings. A blessing in disguise, the fire allowed Wilhelm and Pasqualini to achieve their architectural aim. A square-shaped fortification was built within Jülich using the bastion system. The citadel exists today in the centre of modern Jülich.

Divorced, Beheaded, Survived; The United Duchies Capitulate

During the Third War of the Guelderian Succession, Henry VIII took his sixth and final wife. Catherine Parr was twice-widowed by the time she married Henry. She had experience soothing aging husbands and looking after stepchildren, though she had no children of her own. Catherine joined the Lady Mary's household in February of 1543, coming to Henry's attention around this time. Henry reportedly gave Catherine gifts in early 1543. Anna remained in England and there was still the occasional speculation that Henry might take her back. Before and during the Cleves War, Henry was unwilling to ally himself formally with the Emperor or, at least, was unwilling to become a declared enemy of Cleves. By marrying Catherine Parr on 12 July 1543, Henry accomplished three things outside of wanting a new queen and hopefully begetting more heirs. First, Henry was no longer available to marry Anna. Second, his marriage with Anna was once again made legally void. Third, Henry was passively allying himself with the Emperor by making it impossible for him to renew the Cleves match. By marrying Catherine, Henry did not, however, overtly turn his back on Wilhelm.

Once the marriage to Katheryn Howard was annulled, Elizabeth reverted to being fully illegitimate. By marrying once more, Elizabeth's illegitimacy became moot once again. The Third Succession Act of 1543 was passed by Parliament in spring 1544, outlining a place in the succession for the Lady Mary and the Lady Elizabeth should there be no children with Catherine, and should Prince Edward die without heirs. This is not to say that the taint of bastardy and the shadow of Anne Boylen's demise was fully, legally removed from Elizabeth; it was not. Henry's legal manoeuvrings occasionally left grey areas and ambiguity.

Henry visited Anna at Richmond to inform her that he had married Catherine Parr. Anna was devastated at the news. According to Chapuys, Anna had wanted very badly to return to Cleves and be with the Duchess Maria, her mother. Anna's life was crashing down on all sides: she was stuck in England, losing hope of ever being queen or even marrying again, and her brother was in the midst of a war he was losing.

Wilhelm could not contain his rage toward Francis I over the fall of the United Duchies. Tortured over his loss of power and by his grief for Maria, he lashed out at his counselors during the preparations for the funeral. Wilhelm later attacked Francis's ambassador, looking for someone to blame. He was out of his mind with grief and, probably, regret.

Wilhelm capitulated to Charles V through the Treaty of Venlo, signed on 7 September 1543. In it, he agreed to give Guelders to the Emperor, observe the Catholic faith, and hold the United Duchies as a fiefdom to the Holy Roman Empire. Francis was on his way to the United Duchies, ostensibly to deliver Jeanne and ask for aid, when he learned of Wilhelm's capitulation.

Wilhelm sent Francis a letter to explain his actions, but it was not enough for Francis. Wilhelm offered to send a delegation from Cleves to France to retrieve Jeanne, or alternatively, to renounce his marriage to her. Francis and his sister Marguerite, Queen of Navarre, wasted no time in beginning the annulment process.

Marguerite was a poetess and author, as well as a Queen. She wrote the *Heptaméron*, a collection of stories after the fashion of Boccaccio's *Decameron*. In it there is a tale about a Count Guillaume of Fürstenberg and his intention to assassinate Francis. Guillaume is French for Wilhelm, or William. It describes Guillaume as 'of the House of Saxe', and says that he was 'one of the finest men in Germany'. In the story Francis is warned that Guillaume plans to murder him. Francis confronts Guillaume when the two are out hunting, making it clear that Guillaume must leave or forfeit his life. Guillaume leaves in great haste. This is arguably an allusion to Wilhelm of Jülich-Cleves-Berg, who was tied to the Electorate-Duchy of Saxony through his sister Sybylla. The tale in effect accuses Wilhelm of attempting to stab Francis in the back.

Henry finally joined the Emperor against Francis on 31 December 1543, almost four years after his first meeting with Anna. An offensive by England against France no longer meant an offensive against Cleves, too, given that Wilhelm surrendered to the Emperor in September of that year. The plan was for Henry and Charles to attack Paris, but Charles was slow in reaching the city and Henry was restless. While waiting, Henry directed his troops to attack Boulogne. The English army began its attack on 19 July 1544. The siege lasted until September 1544, with Henry present for the whole of it.

The German princes were a continuing concern to the Emperor, who was short on resources from crossing this way and that on the Continent. Charles V did not wish to continue the campaign in France, and sent Henry a letter advising the same. Before Henry received the letter, Francis and Charles V agreed to the Treaty of Crépy on or about 18 September 1544, about a week after Boulogne surrendered. Francis and Charles would each abandon their various claims and return things to as they were in 1538; the Emperor would relinquish his claim to the Duchy of Burgundy and the Francis would do the same for the Kingdom of Naples, as well as renouncing his claims as suzerain of Flanders and Artois, and his claims to the duchy of Savoy.

Wilhelm's marriage to Jeanne was officially annulled on 22 October 1545 by Pope Paul III. Wilhelm then married Charles V's niece through his brother King Ferdinand of the Romans, who was also named Maria of Austria. Likely named after either her mother or the Regent of the Low Countries, Maria was fifteen years old on their wedding day of 18 July 1546. The much-celebrated union took place in Regensburg. Together they had seven children, five girls and two boys. The marriage to Maria further bound Wilhelm to the Holy Roman Empire.

Saxony and the Schmalkaldic Wars; The Siege of Wittenberg

In 1546, the Lutheran states in the Schmalkaldic League decided to take action against the Emperor. One of the primary founders of the Schmalkaldic League was Anna's brother-in-law, the Elector – and Duke – of Saxony. Sybylla of Cleves became a duchess of Saxony through her marriage to Johann Friedrich. In some portraits of Sybylla, the letters, 'SHS' are embroidered on her clothing: *Sybylla, Herzogin von Sachsen*, 'Sybylla, Duchess of Saxony'. There were two lines of Saxon dukes, the Albertine and Ernestine, after the two sons of Elector Frederick II of Saxony. Johann Friedrich was descended from the Ernestine branch. His cousin Maurice, also a Duke of Saxony, was an Imperialist descended from the Albertine branch.

By summer 1546, Charles V was moving toward Germany with a force of over 50,000 men. The Imperial army was assembling by the mouth of the Danube, the headwaters of which are in Donaueschingen in the very southwestern corner of Germany, roughly 300 miles or 500 kilometres south of Düsseldorf. ('Donaueschingen' can be roughly translated as 'where the Danube is made'.) It then heads east before breaking into three tributaries, one of which goes down toward Austria and the Imperial seat. Donaueschingen is located on the very western edge of the Swabian cultural region. In the 16th century, Swabia extended all the way into Bavaria, on the eastern side of Germany.

In Bavaria, a group of pro-Lutheran troops seized Füssen. They expelled the Imperial troops and planned to move toward the Tyrol to gain control over the land between Italy and Austria to the east of Bavaria. The Schmalkaldic League was not supportive of the plan. Johann Friedrich and the Landgrave of Hesse, as leaders of the Schmalkaldic League, were effectively outlawed by an Imperial ban on 20 July 1546. An Imperial ban had the effect of automatically excommunicating the subject, taking away his rights at law and to property.

With Johann Friedrich's holdings in Saxony – and arguably his title as Prince-Elector – up for grabs, Johann Friedrich's cousin Maurice joined with the Emperor in October 1546. He and the Emperor's brother Ferdinand invaded. Ferdinand, King of the Romans, came in from Bohemia and Maurice attacked from his own Saxon lands. Johann Friedrich was successful in repelling the attacks before the winter of 1546–47. No serious action occurred again until March 1547, when Charles and his Spanish troops headed to Bohemia to support Ferdinand. This time, the Imperial army was successful in breaching the League's defences.

Anna's feisty older sister Sybylla was in Wittenberg Castle with two of her surviving sons during the battle of Mühlberg on 24 April 1547.[55] The Emperor attacked Johann Friedrich at Mühlberg. Johann Friedrich was captured. The Emperor next turned his attention to Wittenberg, the seat of power for Elector Johann Friedrich and his beloved wife, Sybylla of Jülich-Cleves-Berg.

Wittenberg was a great walled city with a moat fed by the River Elbe. On the other side of Wittenberg was a swamp, making the

---

55 Johann Ernst, Sybylla's third son, was born and died in 1535.

city difficult to besiege. People from the area around Wittenberg gathered within the walls, fleeing from the plundering and burning going on outside. Wittenberg had a force of roughly 3,000 troops augmented by those who had flown from Mühlberg. Heavy artillery defended the city walls.

Sybylla and her two youngest sons, Johann Wilhelm and Johann Friedrich the Younger, aged seventeen and nine, were hiding with the court inside Wittenberg Castle. The castle had two large defensive towers, the roofs of which were removed so cannons could be emplaced on them.

The Emperor arrived at Wittenberg to find the city ready for him. The bridge was removed and all defences prepared, including the addition of myriad earthworks. Emperor Charles V set up his camp just outside the range of the cannons. Duke Maurice was heading up the Elbe.

The Emperor's siege of the city began on 4 May 1547. A man from Nuremberg described the Emperor's artillery as consisting of 60, 80, and 100-pound guns. The man described the weapons as being of a sort he had never before seen used by the Imperial army. News of Sybylla's and his sons' peril broke the imprisoned Johann Friedrich's spirit. He was condemned to death on 10 May. In an effort to save himself and his wife and sons, Johann Friedrich surrendered his control of Saxony.

Sybylla was continuing to hold Wittenberg when Johann Friedrich, still a prisoner of the Emperor, entered into the Capitulation of Wittenberg on 19 May 1547. After the Capitulation, the Emperor ceased the attack on Wittenberg. Despite the peace, the Spanish troops continued to pillage the area. An eyewitness account reported that none of the villages were spared, and that people's bodies were strewn about the surrounding fields. Finally, on 23 May, the gates of Wittenberg were opened to the victorious Holy Roman Emperor Charles V.

A day or so later, Sybylla went with her entourage to the Emperor's camp. The Emperor requested that other Imperial dignitaries be present with him to receive Sybylla. Sybylla did not know the fate of her husband Johann Friedrich or their eldest son, who was at Mühlberg. Dressed in mourning clothes, Sybylla sank to her knees in front of the Emperor, her face stained with tears. She offered to exchange a captured Imperial officer for her husband Johann Friedrich. The Emperor was touched by Sybylla's plea, and lifted her to her feet. The Emperor promised Sybylla that she could see Johann Friedrich, who was kept in the Imperial camp outside Wittenberg.

The Emperor went to Wittenberg Castle the next day to once more meet with Sybylla. He allowed Johann Friedrich to stay with Sybylla and all three of their sons from 28 May 1547 to 3 June. After that, Johann Friedrich submitted himself to his undetermined period of imprisonment.

There was no news of import to report to the Emperor about Anna in mid-June 1547, other than that she was making her way to London.

Anna in England; and a Plea to Edward VI

Any reports about Saxony that Anna heard in England must have been extraordinarily distressing. Her sister Sybylla and two of her nephews were facing almost certain imprisonment, or worse; and this was as Anna was adjusting to life under the reign of Edward VI. Henry VIII died not four months before the Battle of Wittenberg, on 28 January 1547.

In early April 1547, Anna had to petition Edward VI for an increase in her pension. She succeeded, but lost one of her favourite properties. Edward VI awarded Bletchingley to a member of Anna's household who had served Henry in his Privy Chamber. Anna was told she had access to similar resources and diversions at Penshurst anyway, which was near to Anna's property of Hever. High inflation – the result in part of Henry VIII's debasement of the coinage – had impoverished anyone on a fixed income, like Anna.

On 1 April 1547, Regent Maria of the Low Countries inquired 'in what reputation stands the widow of the late King, and the daughter of Cleves?' With Henry gone, no one knew how Edward VI would deal with the unmarried thirty-one-year-old Anna. The English appeared to be friendly with the French again, which carried the concern that a new alliance between the two countries could be established to the detriment of the Holy Roman Empire. Regent Maria received the reply: 'Not a word is said about Madam Cleves.'

In November 1547, Sybylla and her new sister-in-law Maria, Duchess Consort of Cleves, the Emperor's niece, wrote to Edward VI to ask him to intercede with the Emperor for the release of Johann Friedrich. The Duchess Consort of Cleves was distraught over the treatment of her husband Wilhelm's family.

Johann Friedrich, as a leader in the Lutheran Reformation, was important to the Protestant Edward VI. Edward was 'desirous of complying with the request of the Duchess, and also because he likewise desired the liberation of [Johann Friedrich]'. Edward sent his Imperial ambassador to meet with the Emperor. He hoped that 'out of consideration for the King of England, we would display clemency towards the person in question'.

The Emperor's reply was ambiguous. He praised Edward and also damned him for being easily persuaded: 'Being a young prince as he was, it was quite right and proper that he should incline to clemency, and should be easily persuaded to accede to the prayers and requisitions of other princes and princesses to gain and preserve their friendship.' Edward's request fell on deaf ears. The Emperor Charles V determined that 'the imprisonment of John Frederick of Saxony was of such grave importance and concern for the public welfare of the whole of Germany that at present we were unable to decide touching the disposal of the person...' Charles concluded that if it ever became safe to liberate Johann Friedrich, the Emperor 'would rather do it on the intercession of the King than of anyone else'.

Johann Friedrich was a prisoner of the Emperor for about five years before finally being released in 1553. The position of Elector was stripped from him and given to his cousin, Duke Maurice. Sybylla died in February 1554, quickly followed by Johann Friedrich in March. They were buried together in the City Church of Weimar.

Grief must have quickly followed Anna's joy over Johann Friedrich's release when news reached her of Sybylla's death.

Anna and Sybylla, despite their occasional sibling rivalry, maintained a good relationship. They must have bonded for a time over their husbands, who were both men of extraordinary power. Both young women went to courts quite foreign to them, though Anna made the longest journey, geographically and culturally.

One can imagine what a horrible year 1547 must have been for Anna. First, Henry VIII died on 28 January 1547. Anna was not much more than an historical footnote to her stepson Edward VI and the Lord Protector, Edward Seymour, 1st Duke of Somerset. Next, there was the news of her sister Sybylla and nephews under attack from the Emperor, quickly followed by the imprisonment of Johann Friedrich. One must wonder how Anna and her little sister Amalia, both of whom were close to Sybylla, felt about Wilhelm being unable or unwilling to give aid to Sybylla against the Emperor.

In reality, Wilhelm could not defeat the Imperial army; and he was now allied with the Emperor because of the 1543 Treaty of Venlo and marriage to the Emperor's niece. Amalia, a headstrong Daughter of Cleves like Sybylla, must have felt a helpless fury when she learned of the Imperial troops heading into Saxony.

Anna continued to live quietly away from court throughout Edward VI's reign. Remittance of her funds was slow in coming, and Anna occasionally had to beg for money or assistance from the King. The outlook seemed grim. It is not specifically known how Anna passed her time during Edward's reign, nor how much contact she had with the Lady Mary, who was the same age as Anna, or the Lady Elizabeth, who turned fourteen in September 1547. Edward VI took Richmond Palace away from Anna in early 1548 for his own use. She went to London in May of that year

> ...to speak to the Protector on certain complaints as to her treatment in money matters, and especially as regards the recompense for the house at Richmond, which has been taken away from her and prepared for the King. I understand that a favourable reply has been given to her.

She was now without two of the properties given to her by Henry, splitting her time between Hever and her other remaining properties.

Anna's financial situation had become so severe by December 1549 that Wilhelm 'sent to the King of England [representatives] … to obtain the payment of arrears of the pension that has here been accorded and granted to his sister'. Wilhelm also petitioned Van der Delft, the Imperial ambassador to the English court, for help on Anna's behalf, 'The Duke has also sent [Van der Delft] a letter asking me to favour them in their mission. It is thought there will be no difficulty.'

Wilhelm wanted his thirty-five-year-old sister home; but Anna was quite content to remain in England, so long as her pension was paid. It was rumoured around this time that the English were 'anxious to be rid of' Anna. Several petitions were made by the Cleves ambassadors on Anna's behalf. Between the actions of the ambassadors and the sponsorship of Thomas Cranmer, Archbishop of Canterbury, some financial relief was granted to Anna.

Would it have been possible for Anna – even if she had wanted to, and there is no evidence she did – to re-marry while still in England? A fascinating conversation is reported between one of Edward VI's attendants, John Fowler and the King in the spring of 1547. Thomas Seymour, brother of Jane, wished to marry Catherine Parr, now one of the wealthiest women in England, and asked Fowler to broach with Edward VI the subject of marriage for the 1st Baron Seymour of Sudeley in general terms. Edward said he was quite content that Seymour marry.

> Then I asked his majesty whom his Grace would he should marry? His Highness said, 'My Lady Anne of Cleves,' and so, pausing a while, said after, 'Nay, nay, wot you what? I would he marry my sister Mary, to turn her opinions.'

Seymour had no intention of marrying Anna, he had a far bigger fish to land and did so; though it is of interest that the king's first thought was of Anna. Did the young king see such a union (if only for a moment) as a way of offloading an expensive responsibility? Or as an alliance useful to his Protestant cause?

Mary I

Edward VI died on 6 July 1553, roughly three months before his sixteenth birthday. Anna watched on as the Lady Jane Grey was briefly enthroned. The Third Act of Succession from 1543 barred any changes to the succession without parliamentary approval, so despite Lady Jane Grey being a legitimate child of the Tudor bloodline and named heir to the throne through Edward's Device for the Succession, she could not lawfully be queen because Parliament had not approved it.

Anna surely had some knowledge of what this meant to the future Mary I during those days in the middle of July 1553. Anna may have even felt a sense of injustice on behalf of Mary, relating to her as a queen discarded for someone younger. This is speculation, but worth considering when looking at Anna's later years and obvious closeness to Mary I and the Lady Elizabeth.

On 19 July 1553, Mary and her forces descended upon London. Lady Jane Grey was captured and imprisoned without difficulty. A couple weeks later, on 3 August, Mary I officially entered London. On 27 September Queen Mary went to the Tower of London 'by water, accompanied with the Lady Elizabeth ... and other ladies, before whose arrival there was shot a great peal of guns'. The 'other ladies' could have included Anna.

By late August 1553, the singing of Mass was restored in England. It was reported that Anna and Elizabeth, the latter now almost twenty years old, had yet to show themselves in church. This was not well received by the new Queen. On 30 September 1553, Anna and Elizabeth rode together behind Mary on her procession from the Tower of London to Westminster Palace:

> The Queen of England was led from the Tower of London to Westminster with the wonted ceremonies, in an adorned open litter, with the small crown on her head. She was followed by two coaches in one of which rode the Lady Elizabeth and [Anna], and several ladies of the Court in the other. [Anna stood behind Elizabeth in] a chariot having canopy all of one covering, with cloth of silver all white, and six horses

betrapped with the same ... and therein sat at the end, with her face forward, the Lady Elizabeth, and at the other end, the Lady Anne of Cleves.

Elizabeth and Anna wore red velvet dresses for the occasion. Anna and Elizabeth attended Mary I's coronation banquet, too. Once Mary arrived at Westminster on 1 October 1553 for her coronation,

> There her Grace heard mass, and was crowned upon a high stage, and after she was anointed Queen, the first day of October. When all was done, her Grace came to Westminster hall ... and there the duke of Norfolk rode up and down the hall ... and there was [great melody]; ...and at the end of the table dined my Lady Elizabeth and my Lady Anne of Cleves; and so it was candlelight or her Grace or she had dined, and so [anon] her Grace took barge.

This is a telling glimpse into Anna's cordial relationships with Mary and Elizabeth.

After the death of Henry's widow Catherine Parr on 7 September 1548 due to complications from childbirth, the position of Queen Dowager of England was vacant. Almost immediately after Mary I's coronation in October 1553, Anna took steps toward undoing her annulment from Henry VIII. If successful, then Anna would be the only woman living who could claim status as the Queen Dowager of England. This would ensure Anna's financial stability, something which was never established during the reign of Edward VI. This is another example of Anna's good relationship with Mary, in that it shows Anna trusted Mary to concern herself with Anna's well-being.

Being the Queen Dowager of England would give Anna the means to return to Cleves as well, if she wished. In England, Anna was a wealthy landowner, but in the United Duchies, custom dictated that she would be entirely reliant on her brother or any subsequent husband. Though as a queen dowager, Anna would have more control over her future, even if she did return to the United Duchies. Anna was never recognised as Queen Dowager, so her ultimate intentions in seeking such an elevation remain a mystery.

Anna even felt comfortable enough with Mary to put forward an option for a groom. Anna recommended Ferdinand, Archduke of Austria. Ferdinand was born in 1529, thirteen years Mary's junior. He was also the brother of the current Duchess Consort of Cleves. Anna suggested this match to Mary in mid-October 1553. It would indirectly strengthen Anna's relationship with Mary and more firmly ally Cleves with England through Imperial marriages. Following up on Anna's suggestion, Ferdinand, King of the Romans, sent ambassadors in November 1553 to discuss the match with Mary. In the end, Mary wed Philip II of Spain, son of Emperor Charles V. Philip was slightly older than the Archduke Ferdinand, being only eleven years younger than Mary.

Trouble for Anna

In January 1554, Wyatt's Rebellion took place. It was led by the son of Sir Thomas Wyatt, the poet and former ambassador. The rebellion was an attempt to place the Protestant Elizabeth on the throne. Mary was suspicious of Elizabeth's involvement, and imprisoned her, though nothing was ever proved against her.

February 1554 brought serious trouble for Anna with Mary. It was reported to the Emperor that Anna's brother Wilhelm, at Elizabeth's behest, promised the French King Henri II to attack Mary. Wilhelm and Henri established their relationship when Wilhelm visited France before his marriage to Jeanne d'Albret. Mary was under the impression that an attack by Henri II would in part be for Wilhelm to 'revenge himself for Henry VIII's repudiation of his sister' and to position the Germans to rebel once more against Mary's cousin, Charles V.

Anna played a curious role while Elizabeth was imprisoned at Woodstocke in 1554. Following Wyatt's Rebellion in January, Elizabeth was taken to Woodstocke after spending time in the Tower of London. A man named John Gaier passed along intelligence to Elizabeth, 'under a colorable pretense of a letter written unto Mistress Cleve from her father'. Though it is not completely clear in Holinshed's *Chronicle* whether 'Mistress Cleve' is Anna, and 'her father' is Henry VIII, it is worth briefly considering. If 'Mistress Cleve' is indeed Anna, allowing Elizabeth to receive a letter that was between Anna and Henry may show the regard in which Anna was held by Mary. And hearing from her former stepmother would bring some comfort to Elizabeth. Mary I may have been comfortable with the communication because Anna was a Catholic, unlike Elizabeth.

In March 1554, it was heard in England that the citizens of Guelders were agitating for Wilhelm to become their duke once more. If Mary thought there was any truth in it, no matter the love she bore for Anna, she could no longer publicly show Anna any affection or respect. Mary was set to wed Philip II of Spain, allying herself even more firmly with the Holy Roman Empire. If the United Duchies were entering into another period of unrest and rebellion against Mary's cousin Charles V, she could not take the political risk of seeming too friendly to Anna.

Wilhelm sent a servant to England in late March or early April 1554 to inform both Mary and, with Mary's leave, Anna, of the deaths of Johann Friedrich and Sybylla. The servant offered the felicitations of Wilhelm and his wife the Duchess Consort Maria to Mary on account of her marriage to Philip II. Wilhelm

> ...thanked the Queen for her favourable treatment of the Duke's sister, and asked leave to go and console her for the loss she has sustained by the death of her brother-in-law and sister ... He obtained leave, and said he would not be away more than six or eight days.

Despite the sad news the servant was charged with delivering, the Imperial ambassador was concerned that it was a cover for discussing rebellious activities with Anna. This again made it important for Mary to keep her distance from Anna.

After Wyatt's Rebellion and the renewed concern about another Cleves War against the Holy Roman Empire, Anna all but disappeared from the English court. There was a small upheaval for Anna in 1556 when Wilhelm demanded that three of her servants be returned to Cleves for a reckoning. Wilhelm petitioned both Mary I and her husband Philip, which surely angered the ever more isolated Anna.

Anna's Personal Relationships

Anna maintained a close bond with Catherine Willoughby, Duchess of Suffolk, who was roughly four years Anna's junior. Catherine was one of the people appointed to receive Anna when she first set foot in England. Catherine was the wife of Charles Brandon, Duke of Suffolk, at the time. After Charles's death in 1545, Catherine married Richard Bertie, probably in 1553. In 1555, the Protestant Duchess of Suffolk, her new husband, and their infant daughter fled to the Continent with a small group of servants to escape the Marian persecutions. The Duchess of Suffolk and her family passed into the United Duchies, still governed by Anna's brother Wilhelm. They went by the city of Xanten, and stayed in Wesel before heading farther east. The Duchess of Suffolk returned to England in about 1559, after Mary's death in November 1558. Though further research is needed, it is possible that Anna's relationship with Catherine Willoughby assisted her in her flight out of England by allowing Catherine and her family to stay safely in the United Duchies.

The relationship between Anna and her brother Wilhelm was soured somewhat by his behaviour surrounding the annulment. This could also be attributed to communication becoming increasingly difficult, with all of Anna's correspondence being read before it was sent or received by her. Even if she logically understood why Wilhelm did not help Sybylla during the Schmalkaldic War, she may not have been emotionally willing to accept his abandonment of Sybylla in her time of need. Anna may also have resented the lack of effort on the part of Wilhelm to bring her back to the United Duchies. Again, Anna may have understood on a logical level why that was not possible; but it must have hurt her to be trapped on English soil with few friends.

Nevertheless, Anna had adapted extraordinarily well to life in England. She struggled under the reign of Edward VI, who reduced her properties and income, but enjoyed a brief return to favour under Mary I. After Wyatt's Rebellion in early 1554, Anna quietly slipped away from court and remained out of the public eye until 1557.

Anna maintained her dignity, prudence, and gentle disposition throughout her time on foreign soil.

14

THE KING'S BELOVED SISTER

Anna's health began to decline in early 1557, with her illness becoming obvious by April. Her ailment was abdominal, and could have been a form of cancer, though it was never discovered from what illness she suffered. Anna moved to her manor at Chelsea that spring, where she showed no signs of recovery. Anna's illness was terminal.

Anna's last will and testament was prepared in mid-July 1557. She is identified as the daughter of Johann, lately the Duke of Cleves, and sister of the distinguished current prince, Duke Wilhelm of Cleves, Jülich, and Berg. Anna is described as having a sickly body, but with all her mental faculties at the time her testament was written. It was Anna's hope that her creditors would be satisfied, and she asked for her eldest stepdaughter, Queen Mary I, to intercede on her behalf. Anna hoped that the executors and Mary could effect the settlement of Anna's debts by the Feast of St Michael, or 29 September 1557. Anna further hoped for the proper payment of her servants and household.

Anna left money to several of her servants explicitly, and asked Mary to distribute alms in the amount of four pounds to each village in the areas of Hever, Bletchingley, Dartford, and Richmond. Anna requested that the money be given to the churches in those areas for distribution. Anna left her best jewels to those whom she loved in both England and Cleves.

To her younger brother Wilhelm, Duke of the United Duchies of Jülich-Cleves-Berg, Anna left a ring that had several diamonds in the shape of a heart, and engraved wings. To Anna's sister-in-law, Duchess Consort Maria, Anna left a golden ring with a large, dark ruby. Anna gave Amalia a golden ring with a triangular-shaped diamond. To Catherine Willoughby, Duchess of Suffolk and a woman with whom Anna maintained a relationship from her very first days in England, she gave another gold ring with a square-shaped diamond. To her cousin Waldeck Anna gave a necklace adorned with a ruby. Anna left her best jewel to Mary I, and her second-best jewel to Anna's younger stepdaughter, the future Elizabeth I.

Anna requested that her servants be paid to Lady Day 1558, Lady Day being the legal start to the Tudor year, much like modern fiscal years. Specifically, she 'did most earnestly pray' for her faithful servants to receive the extra monies. Anna's gifts to specific servants showed her kind and generous nature. She wished to be buried, 'according to the Queen's will and pleasure and that we may have the suffrages of the Holy Church according to the Catholic faith wherein we end our life in this transitory world'.

Anna Von der Mark, Born Duchess of Jülich-Cleves-Berg, Beloved Sister to Henry VIII of England, briefly Queen Consort of England and later the Daughter of Cleves, died quietly on 16 July 1557, surrounded by her household. Her body was quickly cered, or wrapped in a wax cloth to preserve it, and placed in a lead casket.

Anna asked that Mary I choose where her body was to be interred and requested that her burial be performed according to the rites of Rome. At Richmond on 27 July 1557, the Privy Council learned that Mary sent a letter to the Lord Treasurer,

> ...that where it hath pleased Almighty God to call to His mercy the Lady Anne of Cleves, the Queen's Majesty, being careful that she should be honorably buried according to the degree of such an estate, have referred the consideration of the order thereof to [the Lord Treasurer], praying him ... to draw a plat [plot] of the same as he shall think convenient, and send the same hither.

Mary chose to bury Anna in Westminster Abbey on 4 August 1557. Anna was buried on the south side of the High Altar. Anna's testament was submitted to probate on 2 September 1557 in front of William Cook, a Doctor of Laws. Cardinal Reginald Pole notarised the soundness of her testament.

Funeral and Burial

Anna's funeral was a grand affair. The diarist Henry Manchyn provides a full description of the solemnities for Anna. Manchyn noted that Anna died on 16 July and was a queen of Henry's, but had never been crowned. On 29 July, 'began the hearse at Westminster for my Lady Anne of Cleves, with carpenters work of 15 principals, as goodly a hearse as...' The diary trails off here, having been damaged over time. Manchyn continues that on 3 August,

> My Lady Anne of Cleves, sometime wife unto King Henry the VIII came from Chelsea to be [buried] unto Westminster, with all the children of Westminster and [many] priests and clerks, [including] ... the monks of Westminster, and my Lord Bishop of London and my Lord Abbott of Westminster [who] rode together next the monks, and then the 2 secretaries Sir Edmond Peckham and Sir (Robert) Freston, Cofferer to the Queen of England; and then my Lord Admiral, my Lord Darcy of Essex, and many knights and gentlemen. ... afore her servants, and after her banner of arms; and then her gentlemen and her head officers; and then her chariot with 8 banners of arms of diverse arms, and 4 banners of images of white taffeta, wrought with fine gold and her arms.

This lengthy train of mourners went by Saint James[56] 'and so to Charring Cross, with a hundred torches burning, and her

---

56 St James's Palace may have originally been intended as a residence for Anna when she was Queen Consort. Cromwell employed an artist, most likely Holbein the Younger, to decorate or design the decoration of the ceiling of the Chapel Royal with Anna's and Henry's coats of arms, with references to the United Duchies.

servants bearing them, and the 12 bed-men of Westminster had new black gowns; and they had 12 torches burning, and IV white branches with arms'.

After this large retinue of men came 'ladies and gentlewomen all in black, and horses, and 8 heralds of arms in black, and their horses, and arms said about the hearse behind and before; and 4 heralds bearing the 4 white banners'. Once at Westminster Abbey,

> All did alight and there did receive the good Lady my Lord of London and my Lord Abbott in their miters and copes, censing her [with incense], and there men did bear her with a canopy of black velvet, with IV black staffs, and so brought into the hearse and there tarried ... and so there all night with light burning.

Banners referencing various saints were held aloft around Anna's coffin as it was brought into Westminster. All the men took off their hoods before entering the church.

> The IV day of August was the mass of requiem for my Lady Princess of Cleves, and daughter to [Johann III of Cleves and sister to Wilhelm] Duke of Cleves; and there my Lord Abbott of Westminster made a godly sermon as ever was made, and [then]... the Bishop of London sang mass in his miter; [and after] mass my Lord Bishop and my Lord Abbott mitered did cense the corpse; and afterward she was carried to her tomb, [where] she lies with a hearse-cloth of gold, the which lies [over her]; and there all her head officers broke their staffs, [and all] her ushers broke their rods, and all they cast them into her tomb; the which was covered her corpse with black, and all the lords and ladies and knights and gentlemen and gentlewomen did offer, and after mass a great [dinner] at my Lord Abbott's; and my Lady of Winchester was the chief mourner, and my Lord Admiral and my Lord Darcy of either side of my Lady of Winchester, and so they went in order to dinner.

A Role Model to Gloriana?

Though specifics are not and may never be known, it appears that Anna had a good relationship with Mary and Elizabeth. Mary was only a few months younger than Anna, and Anna was the first stepmother to genuinely show interest in little Elizabeth. Jane Seymour did not have much time to acquaint herself with the princess, and may not have wished to because Elizabeth was the illegitimate daughter of Jane's predecessor.

It has been repeatedly asserted that Elizabeth I chose never to marry because of what happened to her mother Anne Boleyn, what she saw happen to her stepmothers Jane Seymour, Anna of Cleves, and Katheryn Howard, not to mention the ill-treatment of Katherine of Aragon, and Mary I's diminished position in the realm after her marriage to Philip II of Spain. But what if there was more to it than fear of what had gone before? What if Elizabeth had a role model? A woman who was independent, prudent, intelligent, bold, tolerant, and managed her own affairs?

Anna is just such a figure for Elizabeth I. Despite the annulment, Anna was frequently at court during the rest of Henry VIII's reign. Little Elizabeth was six years old when Henry married and cast off Anna, but thirteen by the time Henry died. Elizabeth had ample time to become close to her former stepmother and watch Anna's example of how a husbandless noblewoman could survive in England.

While there is very little in the way of records showing Anna's relationship with the child Elizabeth, some things can be deduced from their interactions in later years. Anna received Anne Boleyn's childhood home of Hever Castle as part of her separation from Henry. It is not farfetched to think that Anna, who remained on good terms with her 'beloved brother' Henry, could have invited Elizabeth to visit her during her time at Hever.

Elizabeth was far more religiously tolerant than either her brother Edward VI or sister Mary I. Anna's father and brother were both religiously tolerant, even though Anna's mother was devoutly Catholic. As mentioned before, Anna was, according to the evidence we have, a Catholic. But Anna did not flee England for the safety of Cleves once the Marian persecution began.

Anna and Elizabeth were guests of honour at Mary's coronation, showing that the women maintained a benign relationship for years after Anna's annulment and following Henry's death. Anna even made provisions in her will for both Elizabeth and Mary.

Most important but often overlooked, is the location of Anna's tomb, on the south side of the altar in Westminster Abbey. Mary I had certainly not 'done but greenly, in hugger-mugger to inter her'. It is an exalted location, even if Anna's tomb is plain and understated when compared to some of the other magnificent tombs of the nobility. It is made of stone, with her stylised 'AC' initials, crowned by a ducal coronet inscribed on the side, along with the escarbuncle of Cleves and a lion's head, possibly meant to be a lion of Jülich or any of the other territories bearing a lion on its heraldic achievement. Anna's personal heraldic lozenge featured her mother's lion of Jülich on the right and her father's escarbuncle of Cleves on the left. Anna, from her tomb, has witnessed all coronations of monarchs that have taken place at Westminster Abbey, beginning with that of Elizabeth I, who became queen sixteen months after Anna passed away. One must wonder if Elizabeth I was saddened that Anna was not present.

Anna held her head high throughout her troublesome times in England. A loyal woman, Anna never went against Henry VIII's wishes, even if her initial faith in him was misplaced. Anna was unable ever to marry again. This was in part because of Wilhelm's and Sybylla's conflict with the Emperor, and the subsequent lack of suitors willing to press for Anna's hand. Amalia of Cleves, Anna's younger sister, never married for the same reasons.

Anna's life serves as an example of just how politically entwined the burgeoning powerhouse of Tudor England was with Continental politics. It shows how powerful Parliament became, and brings into focus the extent of Henry's power according to Cromwell's concept of the King in Parliament. Her life illustrates what a noble woman might have to endure on the international marriage market.

Most startlingly, the depositions from Anna's annulment show just how long slander and rumour can last. The depositions show that gossip was just as appealing to 16th-century society as it is to 21st-century society. All reports of Anna being unattractive were from individuals who did not look upon her from a close distance, or were pulled from the depositions. The idea of Henry being repulsed by her physically of course supported the non-consummation argument.

Anna's life shows a side of Henry in his later years that is arguably – and it certainly is a constestable position to take up – overlooked: that of a caring man, doing what was necessary to keep his country out of harm's way while providing for an innocent victim of international politics. Henry refrained from fully allying with the Emperor until after Anna's brother was defeated. Henry perhaps married Catherine Parr in the midst of the Guelders War in part as a way to show the Emperor that England would not support Cleves. Henry visited Anna and invited her to court for the rest of his life, and treated her with respect. One must wonder if Henry ever regretted annulling his marriage to Anna, even if it seemed safest for England at the time.

Anna, Born Duchess of Jülich-Cleves-Berg, lived an extraordinary life. Anna proved herself to be an intelligent, capable woman. Her actions in a foreign land during very dangerous times show how astute and politically aware she was, even as a young woman. Anna earned the affection of the English people through her words and deeds, leaving a mark on the history of her adopted country.

EPILOGUE

After the early death of Anna von der Mark in 1557, the United Duchies continued to face change both for the better and for the worse. Her brother Wilhelm and sister-in-law Maria of Hapsburg had already provided Anna with four nieces – Marie Eleanore, Anne, Magdalene, and Elisabeth – and one nephew, Karl Friedrich. After her death, Wilhelm and Maria had another daughter, Sybille, and son, Johann Wilhelm. Anna's eldest niece Marie Eleanore, born in 1550, went on to marry Albrecht of Prussia and died in 1608. Magdalene, born in 1553, married the Pfalzgraf of Zweibrücken, John I; she died in 1633. Karl Friedrich, just over two years old when Anna died, died himself in 1575. Anna's niece Elisabeth died only four years after Anna, in 1561, at the age of about five.

Anna would have known that her sister-in-law was pregnant. Sybille, presumably named after Anna and Wilhelm's sister Sybylla, Duchess of Saxony, was born on 26 August 1557, a month and a half after Anna passed away. Wilhelm and Maria welcomed Anna's final nephew, Johann Wilhelm, in May 1562. Johann Wilhelm would be the undoing of the United Duchies of Julich-Cleves-Berg. Descendants of Anna's brother Wilhelm and sister Sybylla would see the duchies torn apart along religious lines.

Karl Friedrich, likely named after the Emperor Charles V and Saxon Elector Johann Friedrich, was a very intelligent youngster. Wilhelm and Maria saw to it that Karl Friedrich was educated as a Catholic. Karl Friedrich was declared a Defender of the Faith by the pope, just like Henry VIII of England. After a bout of illness, Karl Friedrich died in Rome at the age of just twenty.

Johann Wilhelm, a second son never intended to rule, was as immature when he took over the United Duchies as Henry VIII was when he took over England. Possibly named after the Saxon Elector Johann Friedrich, and his father Duke Wilhelm of Cleves, Johann Wilhelm was originally intended to enter the Church. Anna's brother had no desire to divide the United Duchies between his two sons. Anna's parents and Wilhelm had worked too hard to create and maintain the region. The boy was sent to St Viktor's in Xanten, a religious school, at the age of nine. Johann Wilhelm became Bishop of Münster in 1574 at the age of eleven, only about a year before his older brother Karl Friedrich died. Upon the death of Karl Friedrich, plans changed dramatically. Johann Wilhelm was sent to Bavaria for safekeeping and to be better raised by the bishopric there for ruling.

On 14 September 1584, Johann Wilhelm was engaged to Jakobe von Baden. They wed on 16 June 1585 in the chapel of the rebuilt Düsseldorf castle. Their marriage was an utter disaster. At some point before the marriage, Johann Wilhelm began a long-term affair with a woman of low social rank named Anna op den Graeff. This relationship produced one illegitimate son, Herman op den Graeff, born in 1585. Herman became a merchant as he was unable to inherit. From approximately March 1589, it became more and more clear that Johann Wilhelm was afflicted with mental illness. Throughout the marriage, Jakobe openly carried on affairs, which threatened the legitimacy of any children Jakobe and Johann Wilhelm might have. Early in the New Year, Johann Wilhelm descended into complete madness. Anna's brother Wilhelm, still alive, must have felt a great sense of despair knowing that he was approaching the end of his life and that the only person left to assume the United Duchies was now utterly incapable.

Wilhelm, not unlike Elizabeth I of England at the end of her reign, was elderly and alone on 1 January 1590. He was seventy-two years old and a widower. Maria of Hapsburg died in 1581. Anna's sister

Amalia died in March 1586 at the age of sixty-eight. Wilhelm's parents, sisters, second wife, and even his first wife, Jeanne d'Albret, who died in 1572, were all gone. The only people Wilhelm had left to care for the United Duchies were four daughters who could not inherit, an illegitimate grandson, and a severely ill son.

Wilhelm suffered a stroke in 1566 at the age of roughly fifty, and never fully recovered. The impact of the stroke can be gleaned from a portrait painted in 1591. Wilhelm died on 5 January 1592, leaving the United Duchies of Jülich-Cleves-Berg to Johann Wilhelm. The United Duchies were partially Protestant and partially Catholic, leaving a rough path ahead for Johann Wilhelm.

Events under Johann Wilhelm's rule were dramatic from the start. One of the more astounding was the murder by strangulation of Jakobe von Baden in 1597. It was rumoured that Anna's nieces and Wilhelm's daughters, Anne and Sybille, were behind the woman's death.

Johann Wilhelm next married Antonia of Lorraine, a descendant of Christina of Denmark. The marriage, like the first to Jakobe von Baden, remained childless. By 1605 Johann Wilhelm had fallen into a catatonic state, and an exorcism was performed to try and revive him. The last Duke of Jülich-Cleves-Berg died on 25 March 1609, with no legitimate heirs from the Von der Mark family to maintain the United Duchies. So began the Jülich-Cleves succession crisis.

The struggle to gain control of the United Duchies involved several parties: Wilhelm's grandson by his daughter Magdalene, John II of Zweibrücken, plus a descendant of Sybilla's, the Elector of Saxony; also Wilhelm's daughter Anne's husband, Philip Ludwig of Pfalz-Neuburg; and John Sigismund of Brandenburg. To settle the matter, the Treaty of Xanten was agreed on 12 November 1614. Xanten is not far from Cleves. Philip Ludwig was deceased by this time, so his Catholic son Wolfgang Wilhelm was installed as Duke of Jülich and Berg. John Sigismund received Cleves, Mark, and Ravensberg, which became Calvinist.

The conflict over the United Duchies served as a run-up to the Thirty Years War, which took place from 1618 to 1648. Put quite simply, the Thirty Years War was absolutely devastating, with direct violence and the indirect famine, disease, and devastation brought along with the violence, massacring upwards of 8 million people. The Treaty of Xanten did not fully settle the matter. The sheer size and power of the United Duchies, plus the ongoing disputes over religious divisions, made control of the area very desirable. War breaking out in the previously united duchies was a serious threat to the stability of Europe. Eventually, the Treaty of Cleves was signed on 9 September 1666, followed by the Treaty of Cologne on 6 May 1672, firmly establishing the division of Jülich-Cleves-Berg as set out in the Treaty of Xanten. The United Duchies of Jülich-Cleves-Berg were no more.

BIBLIOGRAPHY

Primary Sources

Acts of Parliament

31 Hen. 8 c. 14

32 Hen. 8 c. 10

32 Hen. 8 c. 15

32 Hen. 8 c. 25

Archaelogia: or, Miscellaneous Tracts Relating to Antiquity. Vol. 47. London: Nichols and Sons (1883).

Barnes, Robert and Douglas H. Parker. 2008. *A Critical Edition of Robert Barnes's 'A Supplication Unto the Most Gracyous Prince Kynge Henry The. VIIJ. 1534'*. Toronto: University of Toronto Press Incorporated.

Bouterwerk, Karl Wilhelm and William Crecelius. 1867. 'Anna von Cleve, Gehmahlin Heinrichs VIII. Von Demselben.' Vol. 4. *Zeitschrift des Bergischen Geschichtsvereins*. Elderfeld: Sam Lucas.

Bouterwerk, Karl Wilhelm and William Crecelius. 1869. 'Anna von Cleve, Gemahlin Heinrichs VIII., Königs von England. Zweiter Theil.' Vol. 6. *Zeitschrift des Bergischen Geschichtsvereins*. Elderfeld: Sam Lucas.

Bouterwerk, Karl Wilhelm and William Crecelius. 1871. 'Sibylla, Kurfürstin von Sachsen.' Vol. 7. *Zeitschrift des Bergischen Geschichtsvereins*. Elderfeld: Sam Lucas.

Brewer, J. S., J. Gairdner, and R. H Brodie, editors. 1876-1932. *Letters and Papers, Foreign and Domestic, of the Reign of Henry VIII*. Vols. X—XXI. London: Eyre and Spottiswoode.

Byrne, Muriel Saint Clare. 1989. *The Lisle Letters: An Abridgement*. Chicago: The University of Chicago Press.

Crecelius, Wilhelm. 1887. 'Der Gelderische Erbfolgestreit Zwischen Kaiser Karl V. und Herzog Wilhelm von Jülich, Berg, und Cleve (1538–1543).' Vol. 23. *Zeitschrift des Bergischen Geschichtsverein*. Elderfeld: Sam Lucas.

d'Angoulême, Marguerite. n.d. *Heptameron*. Translated by Walter K. Kelly. London: Published for the Trade.

Ellis, Henry. 1824. *Original Letters, Illustrative of English History; Including Numerous Royal Letters: From Autographs in the British Museum, and One or Two Other Collections*. Vol. II. London: Harding, Triphook, and Lepard.

Erasmus, Desiderius, Charles Fantazzi, and James M. Estes. 2016. *The Correspondence of Erasmus. August 1530, March 1531*. Toronto: University of Toronto.

Erasmus, Desiderius, James K. McConica, Alexander Dalzell, and James Martin. Estes. 2012. *Correspondence of Erasmus: Letters 2082 to 2203*. University of Toronto Press.

Gayangos, Pascual de. 1888–1890. *Calendar of State Papers, Spain*. Vol. 5, Pt. II and Vol. 6, Pt. I. London: Her Majesty's Stationery Office.

Holinshed, Raphael. 1808. *Holinshed's Chronicles of England, Scotland, and Ireland*. Vols. III and IV. London: Brooke, Paternoster-Row.

Howard, Henry, Earl of Surrey; Sir Thomas Wyatt the Elder; and George Frederick Nott, D. D., F. S. A. 1816. *The Works of Henry Howard Earl of Surrey and of Sir Thomas Wyatt the Elder*. Vol. II. London: T. Bensley, Bolt Court, Fleet Street, for Longamn, Hurst, Rees, Orme, and Brown, Paternoster-Row.

Jansen, Jan. 1610. *Des Fürstlichen Geschlechts Und Hauses Gülich/Clef/Berg Und Marck/ u. Stamm Register*. Arnheim.

Kastner, Ruth and Thomas A. Brady, Jr. 1994. *Quellen zur Reformation 1517-1555*. Darmstadt: Wissenschaftliche Buchgesellschaft.

Kunde, Anne-Katrin. 2017. *Das Stammbuch Der Grafen Und Herzöge Von Kleve*. Kleve: Museum Kurhaus Kleve - Ewald Mataré Sammlung.

Luther, Martin and C. A. H. Burkhardt. 1866. *Dr. Martin Luther's Briefwechsel*. Leipzig: Verlag von F. C. W. Vogel.

Manchyn, Henry and John Gough Nichols, F.S.A. 1848. *The Diary of Henry Manchyn, Citizen and Merchant-Taylor of London, from A. D. 1550 to A. D. 1563*. New York and London: AMS Press.

Melanchton, Philipp, Christine Mundhenk, Heidi Hein, and Judith Steiniger. 2006. *1648-1979: (1536-1537)*. Stuttgart-Bad Cannstatt: Frommann-Holzboog.

Nichols, John Gough. 1850. *The Chronicle of Queen Jane and of Two Years of Queen Mary*. London: J. B. Nichols and Son, Printers, Parliament Street.

Bibliography

Pizan, Christine de, and Rosalind Brown-Grant. 1999. *The Book of the City of Ladies*. London: Penguin Books.

Pizan, Christine de. 2004. *The Treasure of the City of Ladies*. Penguin Classics.

Policeysambt anderen Ordnungen unnd Edicten/des Durchleuchtigen hochgebornen Fürsten unnd Herren/ Herren Wilhelms Herzogen zu Gülich/ Cleue und Berge/Grauen zu der Marck und Rauensperg/ Herren zu Rauenstein etc. Im Jar Tausent/ Fünffhundert unnd Acht unnd Fünffzig aus gegangen. Cologne: Jacob Soter (1558).

Rechts Ordnung des durchleuchtigen hochgebornen Fursten und Herrn Wilhelms Herzogen zu Gulich, Cleve und Berg/Graven zu der Marck und Ravenßberg/Herrn zu Ravenstein/etc. Neben anderen Constitutionen/ Edicten und erklerungen etzlicher selle/wie es derenthalben in beiden irer F. G. Furstenthumben Gulich und Berg gehalten/geurtheilt und erkandt werden soll. Etzo aus gnedigem beuelch/des auch Durchleuchtigen hochgeborenen Fursten und Herrn/Herrn Johans Wilhelm Herzogen zu Gulich/Cleue und Berg Grauen zu der Marck/Rauenßberg und Mörtz/Herrn zu Rauenstein/ etc. auffs new reuidirt/und mit etzlichen zugesetzten Edicten in truck bracht. Düsseldorf: Bernhardt Buntz (1606).

Strype, John. 1822. *Ecclesiastical Memorials Relating Chiefly to Religion, and the Reformation of it, and the Emergencies of the Church of England.* Vol. 1, Part II. Oxford: Clarendon Press.

The Statutes of the Realm. Printed by Command of His Majesty George the Third. In Pursuance of an Address of the House of Commons of Great Britain. From Original Records and Authentic Manuscripts. Vol. III. London: Dawsons of Pall Mall (1817. Reprinted 1965).

Tanner, J. R. 1922. *Tudor Constitutional Documents A. D. 1485–1603 with an Historical Commentary by J. R. Tanner, Litt. D.* Cambridge University Press.

Urkundliche Widerlegung Der Von Dem Ehmaligen Adel Der Lande Jülich, Kleve, Berg Und Mark Dem Fürsten Staatskanzler Berreichten Denkschrift. 1819. Rhenanien: Rheinpreussen.

von Below, Georg. 1895. *Landtagsakten Von Jülich-Berg: 1400-1610.* Vol. 1. Düsseldorf: Druck und Verlag von L. Voss & Cie., Kgl. Hofbuchdruckern.

von Kleve, Sibylla, and Karl August Müller. 1838. *Briefe Der Herzogin Sibylla von Jülich-Cleve-Berg an Ihren Gemahl Johann Friedrich Den Grossmüthigen, Churfürsten Von Sachsen – Primary Source Edition.* Dresden and Leipzig: Gerhard Fleischer.

Wassenberch, Johann, and Arend Mihm. 1981. *Die Chronik Des Johann Wassenberch: Aufzeichnungen Eines Duisburger Geistlichen über Lokale Und Weltweite Ereignisse Vor 500 Jahren ; Nach d. Orig.-Hs. Hrsg., Ins Neuhochdt. übertr. u. Kommentiert.* Duisburg: Mercator-Verl.

Wriothesley, Charles; Lieut.-General Lord Henry H. M. Percy K.C.B., V.C., F.R.G.S.; and William Douglas Hamilton, F.S.A. 1876. *A Chronicle of England During the Reigns of the Tudors, from A.D. 1485 to 1559*. Vol. II. Westminster: J. B. Nichols and Sons, 25, Parliament Street.

Secondary Sources

Anderson D. D., James. 1732. *Royal Geneaologies, or, the Geneaological Tables of Emperors, Kings, and Princes, from Adam to these Times; in Two Parts*. London: James Bettenham.

Bautz, Friedrich Wilhelm, and Traugott Bautz. 2011. *Biographisch-Bibliographisches Kirchenlexikon*.

Bax, E. Belfort. 1894. *German Society at the End of the Middle Ages*. London: W. Swan Sonnenschein & Co. Reprinted in New York: Augustus M. Kelley Publishing (1967).

Blickle, Peter, Thomas Allan Brady, and H. C. Erik Midelfort. 1991. *The Revolution of 1525: the German Peasants War from a New Perspective*. Baltimore: The Johns Hopkins University Press.

Brüll, Wilhelm. *c.* 1895. *Chronik der Stadt Düren*. Düren: L. Vetter & Co.

Burnet, Gilbert. 1820. *Bishop Burnet's History of the Reformation of the Church of England: A New Edition, Embellished with Twenty-Two Portraits and Frontispiece*. Vol. I, Part 1. London: J. F. Dove, for Richard Priestley.

Cooke, Joseph. 1679. *The First Part of the History of the Reformation*. London: Richard Chiswell.

De Ruble, Alphonse. 1877. *Le Mariage de Jeanne d'Albret*. Paris: Adolphe Labitte.

Fimpeler-Philippen, Annette and Sonja Schürmann. 1999. *Das Schloss in Düsseldorf*. Düsseldorf: Droste Verlag.

Gehrt, Daniel and Vera von der Osten-Sacken. 2015. *Fürstinnen und Konfession: Beträge hochadliger Frauen zur Religionspolitik und Bekenntnisbildung*. Göttingen: Vandenhoeck & Ruprecht.

Gillet, Myrtle Mann. 1918. 'Woman in German Literature before and after the Reformation.' *The Journal of English and Germanic Philology* 17, no. 3.

Heidrich, Paul. 1896. *Beiträge zur deutschen Territorial- u. Stadtgeschichte*. Series I, Book 1: 'Der geldrische Erbfolgestreit 1537–1543.' Kassel: Max Brunneman.

Heidrich, Dr. Paul. *Der Geldrische Erbfolgestreit (1537–1543)*. Kassel: Max Brunneman.

Hirzel, Hans Caspar. 1784. *Lese-Buch für das Frauenzimmer über die Hebammenkunst*. Zurich: Johann Caspar Fueßli.

Bibliography

Jackman, Donald C. 2009. *Hochstaden: Public Succession in Ripuaria of the High Middle Ages.* No. 7. Archive for Medieval Prosopography. State College, PA: Editions EnLaPlage.

Jahn, Johann Gottlieb. 1837. *Geschichte des Schmalkaldischen Krieges: eine reformationsgeschichtliche Denkschrift zur Errinerung an das, für die ganze damalige protestantische Kirche verhängnissvolle Jahrzehend von 1537 bis 1547.* Leipzig: Mintzel in Hof.

Kühn Norbert, and Stefanie Schild. 2015. *Schloss Burg an Der Wupper.* Köln: Rheinischer Verein für Denkmalpflege und Landschaftsschutz.

L'Art de Vérifier les Dates des Faites Historiques, des Chartes, des Chroniques, et autres Anciens Monuments, depuis le Naissance de Notre-Seigneur. Book III. 3d Edition. Paris: Alexandre Jombert Jeune, rue Pavée S. André-des-Arcs, no. 28. 1787.

Leppin, Volker, Georg Schmidt, and Sabine Wefers. 2006. *Johann Friedrich I. – Der Lutherische Kurfürst.* Gütersloh: Gütersloher Verlagshaus.

Lockhart, Paul Douglas. 2004. *Frederik II and the Protestant Cause: Denmark's Role in the Wars of Religion, 1559–1596.* Leiden, Boston: Brill.

MacCulloch, Diarmaid. 2018. *Thomas Cromwell: A Revolutionary Life.* New York: Viking.

Matusiak, John. 2013. *Henry VIII: The Life and Rule of England's Nero.* Stroud: The History Press.

Müller, Albert. 1907. *Die Beziehungen zwischen Heinrichs VIII zu Anna von Cleve.* Calw: A. Oelschläger'schen Buchdruckerei.

Norton, Elizabeth. 2010. *Anne of Cleves: Henry VIII's Discarded Bride.* Stroud: Amberley Publishing.

Ollman-Kösling, Heinz. 1996. *Der Erbfolgstreit um Jülich-Kleve (1609–1610); ein Vorspiel zum Dreißigjährigen Krieg.* Regensburg: Roderer.

Paravicini, Werner, Jan Hirschbiegel, and Jörg Wettlaufer. 2003. 'Höfe Und Residenzen Im spätmittelalterlichen Reich. Ein Dynastisch-Topographisches Handbuch.' *Residenzenforschung.* Ostfildern: Jan Thorbecke Verlag.

Paravinci, Werner, Jan Hirschbiegel, and Jörg Wettlaufer. 2005. 'Höfe und Residenzen im spätmittelalterlichen Reich. Bilder und Begriffe.' *Residenzforschung 15 II.* Vols. 1 and 2. Ostfildern: Jan Thorbecke Verlag.

Potter, Philip J. 2012. *Monarchs of the Renaissance: The Lives and Reigns of 4 European Kings and Queens.* Jefferson, North Carolina: McFarland & Company, Inc.

Réthelyi, Orsolya. 2010. *Mary of Hungary in Court Context (1521–1531).* Budapest: Central European University.

Rex, Richard. 2017. *The Making of Martin Luther.* Princeton: Princeton University Press.

Richartz, Hermann J. 2004. *Basilika St. Lambertus Düsseldorf-Altstadt*. Lindenberg: Kunstverl. Fink.

Ritsema, Alex. *Pirates and Privateers from the Low Countries, c. 1500–1810*. Deventer: Alex Ritsema.

Roelker, Nancy Lyman. 1968. *Queen of Navarre, Jeanne DAlbret: 1528–1572*. Cambridge, Massachusetts: The Belknap Press of Harvard University Press.

Scheible, Heinz. 1997. *Melanchthon: Eine Biographie*. München: C.H. Beck.

Schnütgen Wiltrud. 1990. *Literatur Am Klevischen Hof Vom Hohen Mittelalter Bis Zur frühen Neuzeit*. Kleve: Boss-Verlag.

Sicking, Louis. 2004. *Neptune and the Netherlands State, Economy, and War at Sea in the Renaissance*. Leiden: Brill.

Starkey, David. 2003. *Six Wives: The Queens of Henry VIII*. New York: HarperCollins.

Stollberg-Rilinger, Barbara. 2013. *Das Heilige Römische Reich Deutscher Nation: Vom Ende Des Mittelalters Bis 1806*. München: C.H. Beck.

Strickland, Agnes. 1852. *Lives of the Queens of England, from the Norman Conquest; with Anecdotes of their Courts, Now First Published from Official Records and other Authentic Documents, Private as well as Public. New Edition, with Corrections and Additions*. Vol. IV. Philadelphia: Blanchard and Lea.

Tracy, James D. 1990. *Holland under Habsburg Rule, 1506–1566: The Formation of a Body Politic*. Berkeley: University of California Press.

Von Schaumburg, E. 1879. 'Der Jülich-Clevische Erbfolgestreit Vom 28. Juli Bis 2. September 1610.' No. 1. *Zeitschrift Des Aachener Geschichtsverein*, 1879.

Warnicke, Retha M. 2000. *The Marrying of Anne of Cleves: Royal Protocol in Tudor England*. Cambridge: Cambridge University Press.

Weir, Alison. 1989. *Britain's Royal Families: The Complete Genealogy*. London: Bodley Head.

Weir, Alison. 1991. *The Six Wives of Henry VIII*. New York: Grove Press.

Weir, Alison. 1997. *The Children of Henry VIII*. New York: Ballantine Books.

Weir, Alison. 2002. *Henry VIII: The King and His Court*. New York: Ballantine Books.

INDEX

Erasmus, Desiderius 29, 36, 44, 46, 48, 49

Farnese, Cardinal Alessandro 121, 128
Field of Cloth of Gold 56
France, Francis I of 36, 44, 51, 53, 54-57, 59, 60, 62, 71, 72, 78, 79, 82, 83, 84, 88, 92, 99, 102, 103, 118, 121, 127-129, 132, 134-136, 138-140, 143, 144, 146, 151, 163, 175, 187, 190, 191, 192, 195, 203-205, 211-215, 217, 218, 222-224, 226-236, 239-242, 244-246, 249-251
France, Louis XII of 23, 30
Franco-Cleves Alliance 146, 188, 229
Frauenzimmer 28-30, 108, 111, 210, 211, 213
Friesland 37, 38, 87, 228
Frisian Revolt 37, 38

Gardiner, Stephen, Bishop of Winchester 88, 124, 170, 188, 189, 195, 234, 235, 238
Genoa 55, 70
German Reformation 22, 33, 35
Ghent 52, 78, 82, 83, 96, 97, 127, 137, 142, 159-163, 165, 187, 214
Gral, Elias 13
Great Peter 37, 38
Greenwich 103, 109, 111-113, 116, 117, 119, 121, 149, 171, 175, 179, 183, 184, 223, 238
Grenville, Honor, Lady Lisle 101, 116
Grey, Lady Jane 258
Groff, Heinrich de, Ambassador of Guelders 169, 183
Guelderian Succession, First War of 242

Guelderian Succession, Second War of 243
Guelderian Succession, Third War of 142, 166, 242, 244, 248
Guelders 13, 23, 32, 38, 40, 51, 52, 57, 58, 60, 66-70, 72, 75-79, 82, 83, 87-91, 96, 98, 103, 126-129, 131-134, 136-138, 140-142, 144-146, 154, 155, 156-160, 163-166, 169, 173, 191, 205, 206, 212, 214, 215, 219, 222-225, 227, 242-247, 249, 261, 270
Guelders, Karl of 23, 38, 40, 51-53, 57, 58, 75, 166, 169, 223, 243, 244
Guelders, Maria of 242-244
Guelders, Philippa of 40, 57, 77, 156, 166, 212, 219, 220, 227, 244

Hagenau 206
Hagenau, Diet of 206, 207, 215, 218
Hall, Edward 106, 111, 112
Hambach Castle 22, 30, 132, 218, 224
Hamm 14, 130
Hampton Court Palace 60, 93, 101, 103, 123, 202, 220, 221, 222
Hapsburg, Charles V, Holy Roman Emperor 17, 23, 25, 36, 41, 42, 44, 45, 51-63, 65, 67, 69-72, 77-80, 82-84, 87, 88, 90-92, 97, 102-104, 126-129, 131-143, 151, 154-160, 162, 163, 165, 166, 175, 184, 187, 188, 190, 195, 199, 201, 203, 205, 206, 213-217, 220, 222, 223, 230, 240, 242-247, 249-251, 253, 255, 260, 261, 271, 274
Hapsburg, Eleanor, Queen Consort of France 52, 53, 56, 57, 103, 138, 219